SEEING IS BELIEVING

An Introduction
to Visual
Communication

SEEING IS BELIEVING

An Introduction to Visual Communication

Fourth Edition

Arthur Asa Berger

SAN FRANCISCO STATE UNIVERSITY

Mc Graw Hill

Connect
Learn
Succeed™

SEEING IS BELIEVING: AN INTRODUCTION TO VISUAL COMMUNICATION, FOURTH EDITION

ISBN 978-0-07-351202-0
MHID 0-07-351202-8

Vice President & Editor-in-Chief: *Michael Ryan*
Vice President EDP/Central Publishing Services: *Kimberly Meriwether David*
Publisher: *William Glass*
Sponsoring Editor: *Susan Gouijnstook*
Executive Marketing Manager: *Pamela S. Cooper*
Development Editor: *Nikki Weissman*
Senior Project Manager: *Lisa A. Bruflodt*
Design Coordinator: *Brenda A. Rolwes*
Cover Designer: *Studio Montage, St. Louis, Missouri*
Cover Image: *This photo of a detail from a mosaic was taken by Arthur Asa Berger at the Bardo Museum in Tunisia.*
Buyer: *Kara Kudronowicz*
Media Project Manager: *Sridevi Palani*
Compositor: *Glyph International*
Typeface: *10.5/12 Berkeley*
Printer: *Quad/Graphics*

Library of Congress Cataloging-in-Publication Data
Berger, Arthur Asa, 1933-
    Seeing is believing : an introduction to visual communication / Arthur Asa Berger.—4th ed.
        p. cm.
    Includes bibliographical references and index.
    ISBN 978-0-07-351202-0 (alk. paper)
    1. Visual communication. I. Title.
P93.5.B445 2011
302.23—dc22   2010048331

www.mhhe.com

CONTENTS

v

4 TYPOGRAPHY AND GRAPHIC DESIGN: TOOLS OF VISUAL COMMUNICATION   103

5 PHOTOGRAPHY: THE CAPTURED MOMENT   125

FILM: THE MOVING IMAGE   153

PREFACE TO THE FOURTH EDITION

The first edition of *Seeing is Believing* was published in 1989, so in one edition or another, this book been around for a long time. The book has found an audience because it is written in an accessible style and discusses concepts and ideas that students find interesting and useful. When I wrote the previous editions, Google wasn't a verb; Twitter, YouTube, and smart cell phones didn't exist; and students weren't texting or sexting. There weren't as many free photo editing programs, and software programs that can be used to edit films and videos on computers hadn't been developed.

There are many interesting new developments to deal with relative to visual communication, which explains why I have written a fourth edition of this book. There are more than two dozen new and interesting images in the book along with new drawings I've made. I have added new material, and in some cases new images, on topics such as:

visual culture	iconic buildings
tattoos	images and advertising
Aristotle's theory of imitation	photography and narcissism
Baudrillard on advertising	photography and oil painting
facial expression	Eisenstein on montage
culture codes	postmodernism
geometrical illusions	Freud on dreams
typographic theory	the power of landscape
McLuhan on print	

PREFACE

In 1989, when I published the first edition of *Seeing Is Believing,* I felt it was important to help students learn some of the most fundamental things about visual communication. That is, I wanted to help my readers develop their "visual literacy"—their ability to interpret and create visual communication. Now, in an era when visual images are playing an increasingly important role in our politics, our entertainments, and our everyday lives, I think developing visual literacy is even more crucial than ever. We must learn how to examine and to interpret images and other kinds of visual communication to determine better what impact these phenomena may be having upon our lives.

In this second edition, I have added new material on a number of topics such as **communication models, ethics, postmodernism, animation,** and how the eyes process visual information. I have also expanded my checklists for studying advertisements and television commercials, enhanced my discussion of **semiotics,** color, and MTV, and added many new and interesting images.

I hope that this revised edition of *Seeing Is Believing* will help students learn how to analyze and interpret visual communication better and to understand the role it plays in their lives, the lives of their friends and families, and in society.

THE AUDIENCE

In recent years there has been a rapidly developing movement in our colleges and universities, especially in schools of communication and journalism, to do something about what can be described as the "visual illiteracy" of many of our students. It is possible, and quite likely often the case, that our students graduate without knowing very much (if anything at all) about how images communicate and people find meaning in them, about typefaces and graphic design, or about the difference between the film image and the television image.

Ironically, a significant number of our students hope to work in fields such as advertising, public relations, television, or journalism—fields where they will be involved, either directly or indirectly, with visual communication. Visual communication plays an important role in everyone's life; we all watch television, we read newspapers and magazines and books, and we go to the movies. And we all live in an "information" society where much of the information we consider has a visual nature. It is important that everyone know something about how images function and how people learn to "read" or interpret images and various forms of visual communication. But it is particularly important that students in communication (and related areas) do so since those who create and use images have a responsibility to those who will be affected by them.

MASS MEDIA FOCUS

One of the distinctive features of this book is that it focuses upon the mass media and deals with material of interest to students, material with which they are familiar. In this respect it differs from a number of books that deal primarily with visual communication as it relates to the fine arts.

USE OF SEMIOLOGICAL AND PSYCHOLOGICAL CONCEPTS

Seeing Is Believing uses semiotic and psychological concepts to help readers gain an understanding of how we find meaning in visual phenomena and how our minds process images. These concepts are presented in a readable manner, and numerous illustrations are offered to show how the principles discussed have been applied. These theoretical discussions are supplemented by a number of quotations from authorities that students will find useful and that will help them better understand the principles of semiotics and psychology.

SETTING A GOOD EXAMPLE

A great deal of attention was paid to the design of *Seeing Is Believing;* a book on visual communication should be attractive and show what good design is instead of merely talking about it. The book uses the power of graphic design and the visual image to facilitate learning. In addition, the images are quite remarkable and were chosen to illustrate, in a very direct and forceful manner, the topics discussed in the book.

TEACHABILITY

Seeing Is Believing was written to be a teachable book:

- It is written in an accessible style.
- It deals with topics that are of interest to students and that are part of their experience.
- It has arresting and remarkable images and visual materials to illustrate these topics.
- It is designed to be functional; that is, the book explains a number of concepts that readers can then use to interpret the images all around them. In addition, they are asked to use these concepts and ideas in interesting and creative ways.

Thus, at the end of each chapter, a section of "Applications" requires readers to think about the textual material and then apply what they have learned in doing various projects—projects that they will frequently find entertaining.

A manual for teachers is available from the publisher; it contains a number of additional activities and exercises—to be used in the classroom or as assignments—as well as discussion questions and test questions.

THE STYLE OF THE BOOK

Although the book deals with matters that are often complicated, the style of writing is, as has been suggested, readable. It might also be described as informal and perhaps even "breezy," though the latter term might be a bit extreme.

This style of writing was adopted consciously as a means of attracting the attention and maintaining the interest of the reader. The writing "sugar coats the didactic pill" as a means of enticing students to deal with material that is occasionally technical and that they might otherwise try to avoid.

In other words, this book might not strike some as reading like a textbook; it also, to my way of thinking, is so attractively designed that it doesn't look like a textbook.

There is also a good deal of humor in *Seeing Is Believing,* another means of making it more attractive and less anxiety-provoking for its intended readers. (This may be a rationalization. The author is a humorist who, like many professors, sees himself as "really" being in training to be a stand-up comedian.)

If readers find this book entertaining, half the battle will have been won. And if there are a number of ideas as well as illustrations and images (by the author and others) that amuse readers and help humanize this text and make it more attractive to its readers, so much the better. The most important thing is to get students to read the book and learn something about visual communication.

ACKNOWLEDGMENTS

I would like to express my appreciation to the following people who have contributed images to this edition of my book: Gerald Hill, Roland Greenberg, David Yurkovich, Irfan Essa, Joanna Ebenstein and Denis McNicoll. The other photographs in this edition of the book were taken by myself. I also appreciate the efforts, in my behalf, of my editor Nicole Bridge and my development editor Craig Leonard.

IMAGE AND IMAGINATION

The fovea is a small circular pit in the center of the retina containing roughly 25,000 closely packed color-sensitive cones, each with its own nerve fiber. The fovea contains cells at the unbelievable concentration of 160,000 cells per square millimeter (an area the size of the head of a pin). The fovea enables the average person to see most sharply a small circle ranging in size from ⅙₆ of an inch to ¼ of an inch (estimates differ) at the distance of twelve inches from the eye . . . In man, needle-threading, removal of splinters, and engraving are some of the many activities made possible by foveal vision . . .

Surrounding the fovea is the macula, an oval yellow body of color-sensitive cells. It covers a visual angle of three degrees in the vertical plane and 12 to 15 degrees in the horizontal

Images are something of a mystery to us, even though they pervade our lives. How do we make sense of them? How is it they have the power to generate emotional responses in us? These are some of the questions we must deal with when we think about images.

IMAGE

We live in a world of things seen, a world that is visual, and we expend much of our physical and emotional energy on the act of seeing. Like fish, we "swim" in a sea of images, and these images help shape our perceptions of the world and of ourselves. It is estimated, for example, that most of us receive more than 80 percent of our information through our eyes.

Images pervade our societies; we find them on billboards; in newspapers and magazines; on film screens and television screens; in our snapshots of children, friends, and relatives; in the paintings on our walls. These paintings, for example, both enrich our lives and convey to others something about our aesthetic sensibilities, socioeconomic class, and taste. As Kenneth Clark explains in *Looking at Pictures:*

> I believe that one can learn to interrogate a picture in such a way as to intensify and prolong the pleasure it gives one; and if . . . art must do something more than give pleasure, then "knowing what one likes" will not get one very far. Art is not a lollipop, or even a glass of kümmel. The meaning of a great work of art, or the little of it that we can understand, must be related

plane. Macular vision is quite clear, but not as clear or sharp as foveal vision because the cells are not as closely packed as they are in the fovea. Among other things man uses the macular for reading.

The man who detects movement out of the corner of his eye is seeing peripherally. Moving away from the central portion of the retina, the character and quality of vision change radically. The ability to see color diminishes as the color sensitive cones become more scattered.

–Edward Hall,
The Hidden
Dimension

to our own life in such a way as to increase our energy of spirit. Looking at pictures requires active participation, and, in the early stages, a certain amount of discipline.

We communicate through images. Visual communication is a central aspect of our lives, and much of this communication is done indirectly, through symbolic means: by words and signs and symbols of all kinds. Our emotional states and our creative impulses need some kind of visual and symbolic expression to develop and maintain themselves, which explains why many organizations pay so much attention to visual phenomena such as costumes and uniforms, symbolic objects, signs, flags, and portraits and statues of important figures.

These images are needed to make philosophical abstractions or important figures from the past more real or concrete and to channel or focus our emotions more directly. It is very difficult to get emotionally involved with an abstraction, and so religious and political groups focus much attention on heroes and heroines, on great figures—who can be portrayed visually, with whom people can identify, and whose beliefs people can internalize.

In his classic *Guide to the Perplexed,* the great medieval Jewish philosopher and sage Maimonides (A.D. 1135–1204) deals with images. He compares the concept of image (*tzelem* in Hebrew) with that of likeness (*demut* in Hebrew) and of form (*taoro* in Hebrew) in order to understand the meaning of the phrase in Genesis, "Let us make man in our image." As he writes:

> Image (tzelem) and likeness (demut). People have thought that in the Hebrew language image denotes the shape and configuration of a thing. This supposition led them to the pure doctrine of the corporeality of God, on account of His saying, "Let us make man in our image, after our likeness" (Gen. 1:26). For they thought that God has a man's form, I mean his shape and configuration. The pure doctrine of the corporeality of God was a necessary consequence to be accepted by them.

But, as Maimonides explains a few paragraphs later (and I am greatly simplifying his argument), the statement "Let us make man in our image" refers to God's form, not his (or her) visual image, and form involves intellectual apprehension, not shape and configuration, as Maimonides defines them.

IMAGINATION

Imagination refers to the remarkable power our minds have to form a mental image of something unreal or not present and to use this power creatively—to invent new images and ideas. We can see a strong link between the terms *image* and *imagination*. Imagination exists in the mind, while the image—for our purposes—is tangible and visual. But the image is

❙ FIGURE 0.1
A rendering by Arthur Asa Berger of a famous image—a snake with its tail in its mouth—found originally in a third-century B.C. Greek manuscript. The nineteenth-century chemist Kekule had a dream about a snake with its tail in its mouth, and this dream image led him to discover the molecular structure of benzene.

often a product of imagination, which means that the visible image is strongly connected to the mental one.

Creativity is defined in many different ways, and numerous theories try to explain what it is and why some people are creative and others are not (or don't seem to be). There seems to be a link between creativity and imagination—our ability to generate images in our minds, images *not* always representational or connected to anything in our experience.

Visual images help us discover things. In *Man and His Symbols,* the psychologist Carl G. Jung recounts the role dream images played in the discovery of benzene. Jung writes (1964:26):

> The 19th-century German chemist Kekule, researching into the molecular structure of benzene, dreamed of a snake with its tail in its mouth. [A representation of this from a third-century B.C. Greek manuscript is shown in Figure 0.1.] He interpreted the dream to mean that the structure was a closed carbon ring . . . [Figure 0.2].

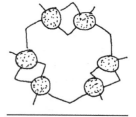

❙ FIGURE 0.2
A rendering by Arthur Asa Berger of the closed carbon ring that Kekule drew in his *Textbook of Organic Chemistry* (1861).

This anecdote suggests that there is a strong link between visual images and what we call creativity. The images we see, whether in our dreams or daydreams, in drawings and doodles in our notebooks, or images we find in printed matter or films or the broadcast media—all are connected to our ability to focus our attention on something, to deal with it in other than abstract and intellectual ways, and ultimately to "break set" (escape from conventional ideas and beliefs) and come up with something new. If necessity is the mother of invention, the visual image is its father.

THE VISUAL AND THE PSYCHE

Images have the power to reveal our mental states. The neurologist and founder of psychoanalysis Sigmund Freud, in an early formulation, describes the **psyche** as being divided into two parts: one accessible to our consciousness and one buried beneath our consciousness, an "unconscious." (There is actually a third part of the psyche, the preconscious, just

I Figure 0.3
Freud's ideas about the human psyche can be represented as an iceberg. By Arthur Asa Berger.

below consciousness, which is accessible to our consciousness.) We can represent the psyche by an iceberg. The conscious element is the small part of the iceberg that is above the waves. Just underneath the waves, there is an area we can see into, which is the preconscious. Underneath the preconscious is a huge mass, which we cannot see and which is not accessible to consciousness, that represents the unconscious (Figure 0.3).

Freud also explains, in a later refinement of his theories, that the psyche comprises three elements: the *id*, the *ego*, and the *superego*. The id represents drives, impulses, and sexual desire. The superego embodies moral beliefs (conscience) and ideal aspirations. The ego mediates between the two forces and involves the way individuals relate to their environment. The ego employs various defense mechanisms to achieve a balance between the forces of the id and superego. One of the most important of these defense mechanisms is sublimation, which involves the redirection of id energy from sexual matters to other areas, such as artistic expression. (Freud's theory is one explanation of artistic creativity.)

We can see the relationship between these elements of the psyche in the chart that follows:

Id	*Ego*	*Superego*
Drives	Balances id/superego	Conscience
Impulses	Uses defense mechanisms	Guilt
Sexual desire	Knowledge of reality	Aspirations
Energy		Focus and direction

If the id is too dominant in people, they have a great deal of energy but lack direction and they flit from one thing to another, always satisfying their momentary impulses. If the superego is too dominant in people, they have focus but they lack energy and are consumed by guilt. If the ego is able to balance the id and superego, the two opposing forces in our psyches, then we can lead productive lives and are not dominated by either our drives and impulses or by our sense of guilt.

Jung, another great psychologist, has a different set of concepts. He believes there are archetypes, "universal images" that are found in myths, dreams, religions, and works of art. These archetypes are reflections of what Jung calls the "collective unconscious," a concept that is extremely controversial. (We can see how a person has an unconscious, but it is difficult to explain the existence of a *collective* unconscious.) The hero, according to Jungians, is the most important archetype.

The psyche, according to Jung, is divided into the shadow (the dark side that is kept hidden from consciousness) and the ego (the light side). But the shadow contains some positive elements, such as creativity, and the ego contains some negative elements, such as destructive attitudes. Jungians also believe that men have a feminine side, the anima, and women have a masculine side, the animus, which play an important role in human development. In his book, *Man and His Symbols,* Jung explains his ideas about the unconscious. He writes (1968:5):

> There are certain events of which we have not consciously taken note; they have remained, so to speak, below the threshold of consciousness. They have happened, but they have been absorbed subliminally, without our conscious knowledge . . . What we call the "psyche" is by no means identified with our consciousness and its contents.

We can see a similarity here with Freud's thinking. Jung also adds that the unconscious is the repository of things that we have seen, things that have happened to us, and ideas we have had that we have forgotten about. These phenomena are important because, as Jung explains (1968:20), "Without realizing it, they influence the way in which we react both to events and people."

In this respect he discusses mass hysteria, which used to be called "possession," and mentions that some dancers in Bali, in a frenzy (1968:21), "fall into trances and turn their weapons against themselves." In the Balinese dance with the Barong and the witch Rangda, there is a scene in which dancers, hypnotized by Rangda, turn their knives upon themselves, and some dancers have been known to actually stab themselves.

I FIGURE 0.4
Photograph by Arthur Asa Berger.

Jung offers an important insight relative to willpower and the unconscious. We may think that if we have enough willpower we can "filter" everything that happens to us and that we will be aware of these phenomena. But this is wrong. As Jung explains (1968:22):

> Many people mistakenly overestimate the role of will power and think that nothing can happen to their minds that they do not decide and intend. But one must learn to discriminate carefully between intentional and unintentional contents of the mind.

The intentional contents of our minds are connected to our egos; the unintentional contents are derived from id elements in our psyches.

In sum, Jungians offer a considerably different understanding of the human psyche and of dreams and images than Freudians do, though both believe in the importance of the unconscious.

In 1977, a German therapist, Anneliese Ude-Pestel, wrote *Betty: History and Art of a Child in Therapy,* a book about one of her patients—a little girl who was significantly disturbed (if not almost psychotic). Betty loved to make drawings and had done hundreds of them, which her father had saved. The paintings were all ghastly—full of monsters and horrifying images, reflecting her psychological state. As the treatment progressed, Betty's drawings changed—and by the end of the therapy, when Betty had been restored to mental health, her drawings were those of a typical little girl (Figures 0.5, 0.6, and 0.7).

The visual image, we see, has the capacity to show the anguish of a tormented soul just as it has the power to stimulate sexual desire, to generate intense feelings, to lead people to perform selfless acts of bravery or cruel acts of barbarism. It is not the image or symbol itself that is responsible, but rather the ability of the image to evoke responses in people that are connected to their beliefs and values.

❙ Figure 0.5
Betty's drawing, *Strangled Deadman,* drawn when she was six years old, before she started therapy. Courtesy of Annaliese Ude-Pestel, author of *Betty: History and Art of a Child in Therapy.*

❙ Figure 0.6
Indian Girl on the Cross, drawn by Betty in the middle of her therapy. Courtesy of Annaliese Ude-Pestel, author of *Betty: History and Art of a Child in Therapy.*

| FIGURE 0.7
Dancing Girl, by Betty. This picture was drawn by Betty near the end of her therapy and reflects her progress in overcoming her problems and becoming a normal little girl. Courtesy of Annaliese Ude-Pestel, author of *Betty: History and Art of a Child in Therapy.*

This power means, of course, that those who create images and symbols must think about the moral implications of what they do. Those individuals who, in some almost magical way (which they may not completely understand themselves), have the ability to harness the power of the image must take responsibility for what they do. To the extent that seeing is believing, we must make sure that the images we create do not generate beliefs that are individually or socially destructive.

IMAGES AND VISUAL RECALL

If we look at something and then close our eyes and try to create the image we've just seen in our minds, scientists have discovered that we use the same nerve cells for both processes. As Brenda Patoine writes in "The Mind's Eye: Imagery and Visual Perception Share Common Brain Mechanism":

> Scientists have known for some time, based primarily on animal studies, that individual neurons in the brain are specialized for categories of images; for example, some are activated only when images of famous people are presented, some respond only to animals, some to food, etc. This helps ensure that the brain—and the organism—can respond to visual stimuli in the most efficient manner possible, firing up only those neurons essential to the recognition of the specific object. The strategy makes sense from an evolutionary perspective: to survive, animals would need to respond instantly to stimuli that represented, for example, food or danger; having neurons dedicated to those stimuli would ensure swift response. (2005:1)

This article, in the March/April 2001 issue of *Brainwork,* teaches us that seeing is a much more selective process than we might have imagined.

The neurons that become activated when we see an object or attempt to recall it are in the medial temporal lobe of the brain, which is the area involved in memory. So our ability to recall images suggests that our attention to images is much more tied to our interests and our memory than we believed to be the case before this research was done.

THE FUNCTIONS OF ART

In his book *The Unchanging Arts: New Forms for the Traditional Functions of Art in Society*, the art historian Alan Gowans suggests that the arts have always performed one (or more) of the following functions:

1. Substitute imagery
2. Illustration
3. Persuasion/conviction
4. Beautification

Gowans (1971:12, 13) explains his theory as follows:

> Instead of asking "What is Art?" we need to ask "What kinds of things have been done by that activity traditionally called Art?" And then we will find that activity historically performed four functions: substitute imagery; illustration; conviction and persuasion; and beautification. (1) In cases where the appearance of something needed to be preserved for one reason or another, art made pictures that could be substituted for the actual thing. (2) Art made images or shapes (including pictographs) that could be used in whole or part to tell stories or record events vividly ("illustrate," "illuminate," "elucidate" all come from the same root "lux" = "light"). (3) Art made images which by association of shapes with ideas set forth the fundamental convictions or realized ideals of societies (usually in more ephemeral media). (4) Art beautified the world by pleasing the eye or gratifying the mind; what particular combination of forms, arrangements, colors, proportions or ornament accomplished this end in any given society depended, of course, on what kinds of illustration or conviction or persuasion a given society required its arts to provide.

Whenever we look at any work of art or any image (or visual field in general), we might consider what the "function" of the work is—as far as the viewer, the creator, society in general, and anyone else is concerned— and which of these four functions is dominant. We might also think about how an image is affected by the medium in which it is found and how a given work relates to other works. (Many works consciously or unconsciously borrow from other works—a phenomenon known as *intertextuality*.)

IMAGES AND INTERTEXTUALITY

Intertextuality, as I mentioned above, involves the "borrowing" by the creators of texts from previous texts. In some cases, this borrowing is done consciously, but in many cases it is an unconscious process that takes place below the awareness of those doing the borrowing. The Russian media theorist M. M. Bakhtin describes this process of intertextual borrowing as follows (1981:53):

> Every extra-artistic prose discourse—in any of its forms, quotidian, rhetorical, scholarly—cannot fail to be oriented toward the "already uttered," the "already known," "the common opinion," and so on.

Creative artists, in all media, are influenced in subtle and different ways, by the works of earlier creative artists, who, in turn, were influenced, in turn, by those who preceded them.

The semiotician Marcel Danesi offers us an example of intertextuality in his book *Understanding Media Semiotics*. The example focuses on the film *Blade Runner*. He writes (2002:63):

> The main text of the movie *Blade Runner* . . . unfolds as a science fiction detective story, but its subtext is, arguably, a religious one—the search for a Creator. This interpretation is bolstered by the many intertextual allusions to Biblical themes and symbols in the movie.
>
> The search for replicants in the film also ties it into postmodern thought, which is concerned with simulations of all kinds and their relation to reality.

It may be that one of the reasons that *Blade Runner* is so powerful is that it deals, in subtle ways, with religious themes, though these themes are only implicit in the film.

The existence of these replicants raises a difficult question: how can we know reality? For replicants look exactly like human beings, which makes it difficult for Rick Deckard, the hero of the story (played by Harrison Ford), to find them and destroy them. A further complication comes from the fact that Deckard's love interest Rachael (played by Sean Young) is, most likely, a replicant who has been programmed to think that she is a human being. So we have a human in love with a replicant who thinks she's a human being.

Many films have been stylistically influenced by great filmmakers such as Sergei Eisenstein, Orson Welles, and Ingmar Bergman, and some films actually "remake" other films. In addition, many films adapt novels and comic strips. So intertextuality plays an important role in the creative process in many different media. Intertextuality is obvious in parodies, in which we ridicule famous texts or images in order to make fun of them. For example, there is a hilarious parody of Bergman in a short film called *Der Dove*. It spoofs Bergman's great films, *The Seventh Seal* and *Wild Strawberries*. In like manner, Grant Wood's famous painting, *American Gothic*, has been the subject of numerous parodies.

Intertextuality also plays an important role in giving images psychological resonance and impact. In the famous 1984 Apple Macintosh commercial, for example, when we see the blonde woman throwing her sledgehammer at the giant head on the screen in the auditorium, where the skinheads are sitting and being brainwashed, it calls to mind the story of David and Goliath.

We can read and understand this image on four different levels:

Literal:	What we see in the image
Textual:	Where the image fits in the text
Intertextual:	Similar images called to mind from other texts
Mythic:	Relation to myths and legends

Images work in many ways. One way they work is by connecting to information we already know and striking responsive chords in our minds. There is a theory of communication, the **responsive chord** theory, that argues that the communication process relies, to a great degree, on information people already know. Thus, what communication does, in effect, is to strike responsive chords using the material stored in our minds.

As Tony Schwartz explains in his book *The Responsive Chord* (1974:24–25):

> Many of our experiences with electronic media are coded and stored in the same way they are perceived. Since they do not undergo a symbolic transformation, the original experience is more directly available to us when it is recalled. Also, since the experience is not stored in a symbolic form, it cannot be retrieved by symbolic cues. It must be evoked by a stimulus that is coded the same way as the stored information.
>
> The critical task is to design our package of stimuli so that it resonates with information already stored within an individual and thereby induces the desired learning or behavioral effect. Resonance takes place when the stimuli put into our communication evoke *meaning* in a listener or viewer.

According to Schwartz, what communication does is not transfer information from a sender to a receiver but strike a responsive chord in people using information already stored in the mind of the receiver—that is, the listener or viewer. This theory begs the question of how people get the information that they store in their minds but it does suggest that information in our minds plays an important role in giving communication power and resonance. What theories about intertextuality add to this equation is the notion that much of this stored material is of a textual nature and thus is stirred when related texts are brought to our attention.

AN EXPERIMENT

In the pages that follow, you will find a number of images to examine (Figures 0.8–0.17). Instead of glancing at these images for the two or three seconds we ordinarily devote to such things (when flipping through a

▮ FIGURE 0.8
Ridley Scott, "1984"
Macintosh commercial
still, taken from television
screen. Courtesy of Apple
Computer, Inc. and
Chiat/Day Advertising.
1984 commercial.

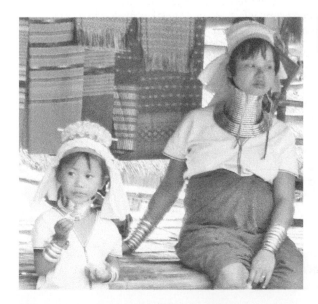

▮ FIGURE 0.9
Photograph by Arthur
Asa Berger.

❙ FIGURE 0.10
Note the incredible
amount of detail in this
painting by the Balinese
artist I Wayan Santica. It is
a painting of a Balinese
religious figure Barong—a
lion—and shows him
with a monkey, who
helps him. Collection of
Arthur Asa Berger. *Barong
and his Monkey Helper,*
by I. Wayan
Santica.

❙ FIGURE 0.11
Photograph by Arthur Asa
Berger of Barong in a
dance in Bali.

▌FIGURE 0.12
Examine this painting carefully. What can you tell about the artist from this work? For information about this artist, turn to page 43. Photograph by Arthur Asa Berger of a painting, *Elephant*.

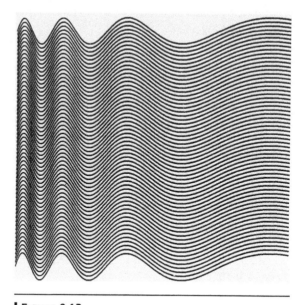

▌FIGURE 0.13
An image created by a computer, similar to oil paintings by op artists. Courtesy of Michael Noll. *Untitled*.

▌FIGURE 0.14
"1984" by Thomas Porter, based on research by Robert Cook. This is a computer simulation of moving billiard balls. © Pixar. All Rights Reserved.

▌FIGURE 0.15
(Left) Jason Berger, *Sketch of View from Graca,* 1978. (Right) Jason Berger, *View from Graca,* 1978. Oil on canvas.

▌FIGURE 0.16
Detail from Roman mosaic in Tunisia. Photograph by Arthur Asa Berger.

▌Figure 0.18
A different perspective on
an astronaut. It makes use
of cropping to create an
unusual image. © 1995.

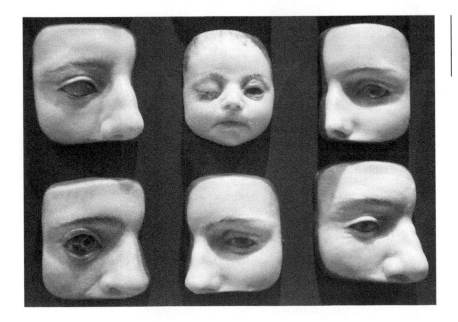

▌Figure 0.19
Wax models showing
disease and injuries of the
eye. Photograph by
Joanna Ebenstein.

I FIGURE 0.20
Adam by Marilyn Powers.

magazine, for instance), please study these works carefully. Then answer the following questions:

1. *What kinds of feelings did each of the works generate in you?* If you felt nothing, why not? If you felt strong emotions, how do you explain this? Did you, for example, experience envy, desire, anxiety, fear, repulsion, sadness, or joy? If so, why?

2. *To which element in your psyche* (id, ego, superego) *did each of the works primarily relate?* Why?

3. *Which of the four functions of art* (as explained by Alan Gowans) *dominated each image or work?* If you had trouble deciding the answer to this question, how do you explain that? Are there other functions that Gowans missed? If so, what are they?

4. *If you were asked to select some of these works to appear at the beginning of a book on visual communication, which ones would you choose?* How would you explain your choice of each work?

5. *Do you find any unifying element in the works selected?* If so, what is it?

6. *If you were asked to make an exhibition of a number of works of art, images, or visual phenomena that expressed your personality, what would you choose?*

7. *If you had to choose ten images to represent America, which images would you choose?*

8. *When was the last time you made a drawing or painting?* If you have not done one for a long time, how come? Why is it that when we are young children we love to draw, but when we get older we generally give it up?

KEY TERMS FOR THE INTRODUCTION

images

psyche

id

ego

superego

intertextuality

responsive chord

1

SEEING IS BELIEVING

Seeing is a complicated phenomenon. When we see an image, our brain breaks the image down into various components and processes them separately, before reconstituting these parts as an image. For example, the brain processes properties such as colors, textures, the edges of objects, light and shadow, and motion separately and then brings them together into an image (*how* it does this still is something of a mystery).

SEEING

The actual act of seeing is determined by the physical structure of the eye. What we perceive, of course, is affected by other factors. In *The Hidden Dimension,* Edward T. Hall describes the physical structure of the eye. He explains that the retina (the part of the eye that is sensitive to light) is composed of three main parts or areas: the fovea, the macula, and the section of the eye where peripheral vision occurs. Each of these areas performs different visual functions, enabling people to see in three somewhat different ways. Because the three types of vision occur at the same time and blend into one another, normally they aren't differentiated.

In his book *An Introduction to Visual Culture,* Nicholas Mirzoeff offers a description of the process of seeing (1999:5):

When we see, we are doing many things at once. We are seeing an enormous field peripherally. We are seeing in an up-to-down, left-to-right movement. We are imposing on what we are isolating in our field of vision not only implied axes to adjust balance but also a structural map to chart and measure the action of the compositional forces that are so vital to content and, therefore, to message input and output. All of this is happening while at the same time we are decoding all manner of symbols.

—Donis A. Dondis,
A Primer of
Visual Literacy

> According to one recent estimate, the retina contains 100 million nerve cells capable of about 10 billion processing operations per second. The hyperstimulus of modern visual culture from the nineteenth century to the present day has been dedicated to trying to saturate the visual field, a process that continually fails as we learn to see and connect ever faster.

His discussion of the power of the human retina suggests that in terms of our abilities to process visual data, human beings operate at speeds similar to those found in supercomputers.

We need this ability to process images rapidly since it has been estimated that people in America typically spend a great deal of time looking at screens. An article by Brian Stillter in *The New York Times* (March 26, 2009) titled "8 Hours a Day Spent on Screens, Study Finds" points out that adults typically spend 8.5 hours a day looking at screens of one kind or another such as television screens, computer monitors, GPS devices, and screens of cell phones. The study that produced this information was made by the Council for Research Excellence. It found that on a typical day Americans are exposed to 61 minutes of television commercials and other promotions.

The eye, then, is an incredibly complex organ, and the mechanism of seeing, though effortless for most people, involves extremely complicated relationships between our eyes and our brains—a subject that will be discussed in a later chapter.

The very structure of the eye, Hall points out, has an effect on the way we design and use space. As he notes, in Western countries, we tend to focus our attention on objects, not on the spaces that separate them. By contrast, in Japan, for example (1971:75), "spaces are perceived, named, and revered as the ma, or intervening interval." We all have the same eyes, but what we see, or perhaps what we focus our attention on, differs from culture to culture.

Rudolf Arnheim suggests in *Visual Thinking* (1969:37) that

> visual perception is not a passive recording of stimulus material but an active concern of the mind. The sense of sight operates selectively. The perception of shape consists in the application of form categories, which can be called visual concepts because of their simplicity and generality. Perception involves problem solving.

The same point is made by E. H. Gombrich in *Art and Illusion* (1960: 172), where he argues that perception "is always an active process, conditioned by our expectations and adapted to situations. Instead of talking about seeing and knowing, we might do a little better to talk about seeing and noticing. We notice only when we look for something." Perception is not automatic, then. It may be a bit of an exaggeration, but in many cases, we have to look for something in order to see it.

BELIEVING

What we believe depends on a number of factors, including our age, education, socioeconomic status, country, family background, and personality. Generally, when we talk about believing, it means we think that something is true. Philosophers talk about the correspondence theory of truth—the notion that there is a correspondence between what we believe and what is true about the "real world."

Our belief that things exist in the real world often is tied to what we have seen; our belief in the truth about propositions usually is tied to reasoning and inference. The title of this book, *Seeing Is Believing,* reflects people's sense, first, that if they see something, they can be confident it exists, and second, that seeing enables them to ascertain, with "their own eyes," the truth about events.

However, as this book will show, seeing isn't always a good guide to knowing what is happening. Seeing may give us a certain amount of truth, but it may not reveal the whole truth, especially because much of what we see is mediated—determined by someone else. And new computer technology enables artists, filmmakers, and the like to generate all kinds of remarkable images. We can now modify photographs, create special effects, integrate scenes from old films, incorporate dead actors and actresses into commercials, and do many other things that force us to question the relationship between seeing and believing. Much of what we see—in the media, that is—we can no longer believe.

THE SOCIAL ASPECTS OF THE VISUAL

Research suggests that many people are "obsessed" with their looks—with their hair, their faces, their complexions, their bodies, their arms and legs; and huge industries exist to help people lose weight, conquer acne, get rid of "saddles" on their hips or droopy eyelids—you name it. Surveys indicate that though people claim they choose their mates on the basis of personality, religion, occupation, and other traits, in fact, they are initially attracted to them on the basis of looks.

We gain a great deal of information about others (and provide a great deal of information about ourselves) on the basis of visual perceptions. For example, think how important our cars are to us and how important styling is for people when it comes to choosing a car. For most of us, cars are not simply a means of transportation; they are also, perhaps more importantly, statements about ourselves, our status, and our taste or style (Figure 1.1).

The same applies to our houses. People often judge us on the basis of where we live, how big our house is, what our house looks like, and whether

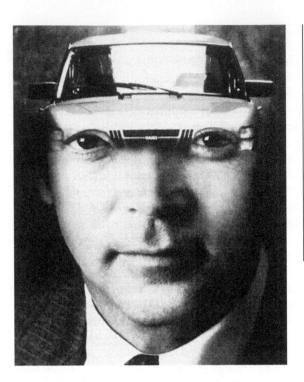

❙ FIGURE 1.1
An extremely controversial Saab advertisement. The fusion of a face and a car creates a remarkably compelling image. In making this image, it was necessary to widen the distance between the eyes of the man so that they would appear in place of the headlights, giving him a curious (and, some suggest, idiotic) look. Ally and Gargano Advertising. Art Director, Ron Arnold. Copyright Tom Messner.

we have a view. The way a house is decorated—the color of the walls, the kind of furniture, the spatiality—all of these things might seem trivial and insignificant, but we know that they are connected to powerful and very deep aspects of our psyches.

People also evaluate us, perhaps unconsciously, on the basis of how attractive we are and how attractive our mates are. Numerous surveys demonstrate that people judged "attractive" are generally better liked and higher rated on surveys than are people judged "unattractive." We learn whether we are attractive by the responses of others. Our identities, then, are to a great degree fashioned by what have been called "significant others" via the feedback they give us about ourselves.

This fact helps explain the anxiety people feel about "blind" dates. The term is important, for it directs our attention to the importance of the visual in our scheme of things. We might even have talked on the telephone to a so-called blind date, but because we have not seen this person, we generally feel uneasy. Numerous models and famous actresses tell tales of not having dates in high school or of having their mothers arrange for someone to take them to the prom. The same applies for many famous men—statesmen, actors, and businessmen who were not exactly social lions when young. Not having a date on a given day means absolutely nothing.

THE VISUAL AND PERSONAL IDENTITY

We've already suggested that visual perceptions confer status on people—that others evaluate us on the basis of our cars and clothes and houses and mates. The calculations these other people make generate ideas in their heads about who and what we are—about our identities.

And people often refer to us in terms of our physical attributes. Blondes supposedly "have more fun," and redheads are supposed to have tempers. Think also about baldness and the trauma it causes in men who often adopt bizarre hairstyles in a futile attempt to hide their baldness. People are also described in terms of whether they are short or tall, thin or fat (or skinny or husky), light or dark, and so on. Consider the role skin color has played in our history and in the history of many other nations.

Our physiques and other visible aspects can lead to nicknames that, it is likely, often play an important part in the way we develop our personalities. Undesirable identities probably lead to various kinds of compensating behaviors so that, to a certain degree, it might be argued that what we are or become is affected to a considerable extent by what we look like.

Consider the following markers of identity whose meanings are conventionally understood but can be misleading in certain circumstances. We must keep in mind the point made by Ferdinand de Saussure, that the relation between a **signifier,** or marker (what he called a sound or object), and its **signified,** or meaning, is arbitrary and based on convention:

Signifier (Marker)	*Signified (Meaning)*
Beret	Arty
Crew cut	Military, backward person
Purple hair	Punk
Shaved head (male)	Cool customer
Shoulder-length hair	Antiestablishment
K-Mart jeans	Working class
Briefcase	Old-fashioned
Attaché case	Conventional
Birkenstock sandals	Liberal egghead
Wingtips	Business
Aviator glasses	Middle-class square
Bow tie	Individualist
String tie	Hick, westerner

In addition to these more-or-less conventionally understood signs of identity, there are some people who try to mislead others about who they are and what they are like by the signs they use. Consider the following ways in which people play with their identities:

Transvestite	Wears clothes of different sex
Dyed hair	Different colors tied to different personalities
Impersonator	Pretends to be a different person
Impostor	Appropriates a different profession
Fake accents	Pretends to have a different nationality
Passing	Assumes a different race

My point is that there are many different ways in which to take on certain identities or play with signifiers in creating identities. **Semiotics** tells us that we are always sending messages to others about ourselves based on matters such as our hairstyles, our body decorations, our clothes, our shoes, our use of language, our body language, and our props. And others are sending messages about themselves the same way. Sometimes the messages we send others about ourselves are not correct in that they are not the messages we think we are sending. That's why people reading is an art, not a science.

One of the most important ways of our establishing our identities involves our hair. As Rose Weitz, a professor of women's studies and sociology at Arizona State University explains, "Our hair is one of the first things people notice about us and one of the primary ways we declare our identity to them." Her work is described in an article "It's All About Hair" in the Fall 2004 *Arizona Research* journal by Diane Boudreau. She writes:

> The ASU sociologist shows how hair is tangled up with all aspects of life, including sexuality, age, race, social class, health, power, and religion. The reasons for hair's leading role can be attributed to three things, according to Weitz: "It is personal, growing directly out of our bodies. It is public, on view for all to see. And it is malleable, allowing us to change it more or less at whim. As a result it's not surprising that we use our hair to project our identity and others see our hair as a reflection of our identity."

I Figure 1.2
Medusa was a mythical monster with snakes for hair. When men gazed at her, they turned to stone. By Arthur Asa Berger.

I have often wondered whether some women have what I call "The Medusa Complex." Medusa was a mythical creature with snakes for hair who killed people by turning them to stone when they looked at her. It seems possible to me that this ancient myth is now alive in some women in a highly diluted or diffused form. These women think their hair is an all-important means of looking attractive and being sexually alluring and that the right hair color and style can "knock 'em dead," so to speak.

In his book *The Collective Search for Identity*, sociologist Orrin Klapp suggests that identity is primarily connected to a number of different symbolic

---

THE SEASHELL

In a graduate seminar in semiotics and the media, I taught an exercise that was very revealing. I asked each of my students to bring in a simple object (in brown bags so nobody knew who brought which item) that they felt reflected their personalities and identities. I also asked them to include a slip of paper in the bag listing the qualities that the object reflected about themselves.

One student brought a light gray seashell, about six inches long. When I asked my class what the seashell suggested about the person who brought it they gave answers like "dead," "sterile," and "empty." The person who brought the shell, a vivacious and attractive woman, wrote "natural," "elegant," and "beautiful" (Figure 1.3).

The moral of this story is that we may think we are sending certain messages about ourselves through our hairstyles, clothes, body ornaments, and body language to others, but they may be misinterpreting these messages we send in the same way that we may misinterpret messages others send to us about themselves.

I FIGURE 1.3
A seashell—natural beauty or emptiness and sterility? By Arthur Asa Berger.

---

phenomena and is not just a matter of one's possessions. As he explains (1969:5):

> Strictly it includes all things a person may legitimately and reliably say about himself—his status, his name, his personality, his past life. But if his social context is unreliable, it follows that he cannot say anything legitimately and reliably about himself. His statements of identity have no more reliability than a currency which depends upon the willingness of people to recognize it and accept it.

So our identities are a combination of our personalities, our characters (including national character), our occupations, our genders, our races, our ages, our religions, and any number of other phenomena—many of which are communicated visually to others by our hairstyles, our clothes, our facial expressions, our accents, our possessions, and various other means.

From a semiotic perspective, then, we project our identities by such matters as (in alphabetical order):

Age	Hairstyle
Body language	Hair color
Body shape	Hats
Clothes	Race
Eye-glass styles	Shoes
Gender	Speaking voice
Gizmos	Use of language

To a considerable degree, our identities can be seen as sign systems that we put together to form an identity, hoping that others will "read" us the way we want to be read. This doesn't happen all the time, for people often misread the signs we send.

TATTOOS

People have been tattooing themselves for thousands of years, for a variety of reasons. Tattoos can be described as permanent forms of body modification using pigments to make designs and other images. At one time tattoos signified deviancy or criminality, but in the last 30 years, tattoos have become very popular with young men and women, who seem to regard them as little more than fashion accessories. In postmodern societies, where "anything goes," people no longer feel any stigma connected to getting tattooed. At the gym where I work out, around 10 percent or so of the men and women have tattoos, from those that cover much of their bodies to little tattoos, on various parts of their bodies.

There is a lack of agreement among mental health professionals about the significance of tattooing. Some psychologists and psychiatrists see tattoos in adolescents as tied to their desire to establish their own identities

I FIGURE 1.4
Woman with Tattoos.
Photograph by Gerald Hill.

and as a step toward separation and individuation. Many young men and women get tattooed to suggest that they are "arty" or to signify their rebelliousness or attachment to countercultural movements. Other psychologists and psychiatrists and people involved with mental health see getting tattooed is an indicator of personality problems and the possibility of risky behavior. There may also be an element of narcissism in those who have many tattoos on their bodies, since people with tattoos tend to be looked at more than people without them. What is most disturbing to many writers who discuss tattoos is the fact that tattooing is a permanent form of body modification. It is very expensive and painful to remove tattoos on a person's body and there are also medical risks from infections and other diseases in getting tattooed.

If we look at the photograph of the woman with tattoos over a large part of her body, we have to ask ourselves whether the tattoos enhance or detract from her attractiveness. We are drawn to look at the tattoos but do we do this instead of looking at her as a person? What kind of a message is the woman sending when she turns her body into a work of art?

SOCIAL IDENTITY AND THE IMAGE

Herbert Gans, a sociologist who has done work on popular culture, argues that there are five "**taste cultures**" in America, based on people's income, occupation and education, including not only what people learn in academic institutions but also what they learn from their exposure to the mass media as well as other sources. In his book *Popular Culture and High Culture: An Evaluation of Taste,* he writes (1974:x):

> I suggest that America is actually made up of a number of taste cultures, each with its own art, literature, music, and so forth, which differ mainly in that they express different aesthetic standards . . . The underlying assumption of this analysis is that all taste cultures are of equal worth . . . Because taste cultures reflect the class and particularly education attributes of their publics, low culture is as valid for poorly educated Americans as high culture is for well-educated ones, even if the higher cultures are, in the abstract, better or more comprehensive than the lower cultures.

His classification of these taste cultures is as follows: high culture, upper-middle culture, lower-middle culture, low culture, and quasi-folk culture. According to Gans, then, there are five major groupings in American society—and we can infer that similar groupings can be found in other societies—which have considerably different tastes as far as aesthetics and their reactions to images are concerned. His focus on income, occupation, and education means that he doesn't have to deal with ethnicity, religions, regional variations, and other variables.

In the chart that follows, I take material from Gans's second chapter, "A Comparative Analysis of High and Popular Culture," and elicit from it his suggestions about what each taste culture likes.

Level of Culture	*Visual Preferences*
High	Primitive art, abstract expressionism
Upper-middle	Bergman films, public television, documentaries
Lower-middle	Representational art, Norman Rockwell paintings
Low culture	Religious art, paintings with vivid colors
Quasi-folk	Comic books, graffiti

This chart only takes the topics that Gans discusses which have a visual dimension to them, but it is important to remember that for Gans, the preferences of people in each of these taste cultures are valid for them and these works serve their needs. The dominant taste level in America, Gans adds, is the lower-middle one.

What the Gans classification suggests is that our education, occupation, and income level (which roughly means our socioeconomic class) shape our notions of what is beautiful, and affect the way we respond to images and other visual phenomena.

SEEING ISN'T BELIEVING

If visual matters are so important, it makes sense for us to understand how visual communication works—the rules, principles, and codes that people use to interpret (or misinterpret) visual phenomena. *The principles discussed in this book can be applied anywhere—in magazine design, in newspaper layout, in advertising, in photography, in film and television making, or in something as humble as writing a résumé—because these principles apply wherever visual matters are important, and they are important everywhere.*

We know, from watching magicians, that we can be misled by a visual phenomenon. Magicians don't saw people in half; they only seem to. We also know that people often have delusions, see "apparitions" that really aren't there, have dreams that are "unreal," and can be fooled or misled by visual phenomena (Figures 1.4 and 1.5).

This book will help you learn how to interpret and understand visual phenomena more correctly and use them in a more reasoned manner. It will deal with principles of design and other matters involved in visual communication; with photography, film, television, typography, comics, and cartoons; and with the relationship that exists between visual matters and the imagination.

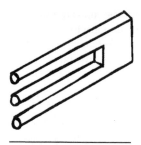

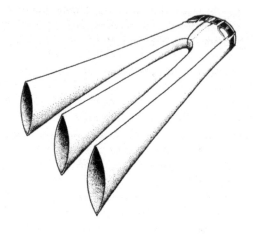

I **FIGURE 1.5**
Optical illusion, "Devil's Tuning Fork." Why is it so difficult to look at this image? That is, how does this optical illusion work? By Arthur Asa Berger.

DREAMS

Interpreting why we dream has been the subject of a considerable amount of controversy. We know that dreams play an important part in our psychological well-being, for in dreams we often work through problems that we face in our waking lives. Freud considers dreams to be the "royal road" to the **unconscious** and his book *The Interpretation of Dreams,* published in 1900, is generally considered to be his masterwork.

An important textbook on psychoanalytic theory, psychiatrist Charles Brenner's *An Elementary Textbook of Psychoanalysis,* describes dreams as follows (1974:150):

The subjective experience which appears in consciousness during sleep and which, after waking, is referred to by the sleeper as a dream is only the end result of unconscious mental activity during sleep which, by its nature or its intensity, threatens to interfere with sleep itself. Instead of waking, the sleeper dreams. We call the conscious experience during sleep, which the sleeper may or may not recall after waking, the *manifest dream.* Its various elements are referred to as the *manifest dream content.* The unconscious thoughts which threaten to waken the sleeper we call the *latent dream content.* The unconscious mental operations by which the latent dream is transformed into the manifest dream we call the *dream work.*

This latent dream content is based on nocturnal sensory experiences (such as noises we hear at night), ideas and thoughts we had when we were awake, and various id impulses that our egos and superegos prevented us from acting upon and which we repress.

Understanding and interpreting dreams is difficult because in our latent dreams, an image can stand for its opposite, and the manifest dream—what we remember from our dreams—is a set of disconnected images that we stitch together. There is a good deal of disagreement in the academic community about Freud's notion that dreams primarily involve wish fulfillment but, whatever the case, dreams play an important role in our lives.

Freud explains that there is a considerable difference between our dreams and our thoughts related to our dreams, which he calls "dream thoughts." As he writes in *The Interpretation of Dreams* (1900/1965:312–313)

> The first thing that becomes clear to anyone who compares the dream content with the dream thought is that a work of *condensation* on a large scale has been carried out. Dreams are brief, meagre and laconic in comparison with the range and wealth of dream thoughts. If a dream is written out, it may perhaps fill half a page. The analysis setting out the dream thoughts underlying it may occupy six, eight or a dozen times as much space.

Films often have dreamlike sequences and some films make use of dreams. Akira Kurosawa, one of the greatest film directors, did a remarkable film in 1990, *Dreams,* based on a number of his dreams. And many plays, films, television shows, music videos, and similar texts make use of dreams and dreamlike scenarios. One of the greatest works using dreamlike scenarios is Shakespeare's *Hamlet.*

COGNITION AND VISUAL IMAGES

We actually expend a great deal of energy in the process of seeing things. In *Understanding Video,* Jarice Hanson (1987:39) cites some fascinating statistics on this matter:

> It is estimated that 75 percent of the information entering the brain is from the eyes, and that 38 percent of the fibers entering or leaving the central nervous system are in the optic nerve. Current research indicates that the eyes have 100 million sensors in the retina, but only five million channels to the brain from the retina. This means that more information processing is

actually done in the eye than in the brain, and even the eye filters out information . . .

Thus, we allocate much of our energy to processing visual information. We do this in the service of our cognitive faculties, or the means by which we acquire knowledge. This is generally done through either perception, intuition, or reasoning. For our purposes, the term *perception* will be used to deal with visual phenomena. We might, then, distinguish between *sight,* or the ability to see; *seeing,* or the actual process of using sight; and *perception,* or the ability to apprehend and know the world by means of sight.

Robert E. Ornstein explains, in *The Psychology of Consciousness* (1972:27), that our eyes are always active: "Our eyes are also constantly in motion, in large eye movements (**saccades**) as well as in eye tremors (nystagmus). We blink our eyes every second, move our eyes around, move our heads and bodies, and follow moving objects." The term *saccades* is French and means "the flick of a sail." Each saccade takes about one-twentieth of a second— the same amount of time needed to make possible *persistence of vision,* the process that enables us to connect the frames of a film and "see" the film as continuous.

When we scan a fixed image, our vision fades after a few seconds, and we sweep it again and again to signal our brains to keep the image in our minds; when we follow a moving object, our eyes follow it and keep it fixed on our retinas (Figure 1.7). What we describe as vision is a physiological process that involves light striking our retinas and becoming registered by photo receptors located at the back of the retinas behind blood vessels and nerve fibers. This information is then processed by the brain. In the following excerpt, Ornstein suggests that we have to fashion an awareness out of the different inputs we get (1972:27):

> If we "saw" an "image" on our retina, the visual world would be different
> each second, sometimes one object, then another, sometimes a blur due to
> the eyes moving, sometimes darkness due to blinks. We must then construct
> a personal consciousness from the selected input, and in this way achieve
> some stability of awareness out of the rich and continuously changing flow
> of information reaching our receptors.

That is, we must learn to select from all the information that is available to us and, in a sense, *construct* the world we see.

The Disney Corporation and a number of other media companies are conducting research that follows the eye movements of people when they watch advertisements on the Internet. According to Brooks Barnes, in an article in *The New York Times* titled "Watching You Watching Ads" (July 27, 2009, pages B1 and B6) Disney's scientists not only track eye movements, but also heart rates, skin temperatures, and facial expressions—the last by

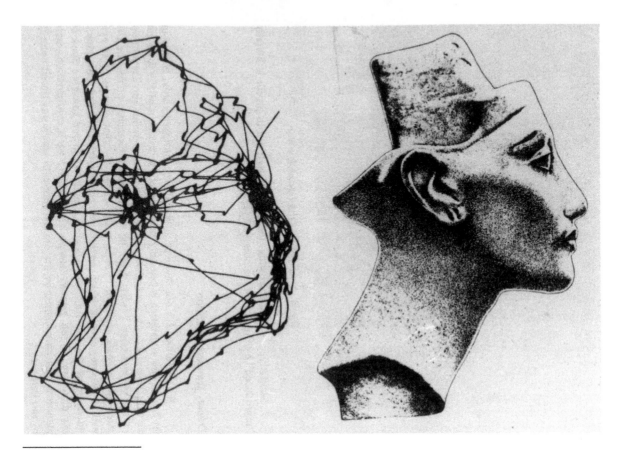

❙ Figure 1.7
Scanning a "Nefertiti" postcard. The image on the left shows the saccades we make as we scan the sculpture of Nefertiti. Seeing involves a great deal of activity by our eyes, even though we are not aware of *doing all this work.* Illustration by Lorelle Raboni in *Eye Movements and Visual Perception* by David Norton and Lawrence Stark. Reproduced courtesy of Lorelle Taboni.

attaching probes to facial muscles. CBS has a research facility in Las Vegas and tested 70,000 people in 2008 by monitoring their brain activity while they watched television and advertising.

In addition, many marketing companies are investigating neuromarketing techniques, which study brain waves in an attempt to find out which parts of our brains are activated when we are exposed to advertising for various products and services. Neuromarketing involves obtaining information by subjecting individuals to functional Magnetic Resonance Imaging (fMRI) to see how their brains respond to brands of products. The origins of neuromarketing are unclear, but it seems to have started when a marketing professor at Harvard University, Gerry Zaltman, began scanning people's brains to gain information about their preferences as consumers. Neuromarketing practitioners argue that asking people to talk about their feelings about brands of products isn't useful, because of the unreliability of their responses.

HEMISPHERES OF THE BRAIN

Our ability to process visual images seems to be related to our bicameral (two-hemisphered) brains. Research indicates that in normal people, even though both sides are involved in most activities, each hemisphere tends to specialize. Ornstein describes this phenomenon as follows (1972:51):

> The left hemisphere (connected to the right side of the body) is predominantly involved with analytic, logical thinking, especially in verbal and mathematical functions. Its mode of operation is primarily linear. This hemisphere seems to process information sequentially . . . If the left hemisphere is specialized for analysis, the right hemisphere (again, remember, connected to the left side of the body) seems specialized for holistic mentation. This hemisphere is primarily responsible for our orientation in space, artistic endeavor, crafts, body image, recognition of faces.

As far as vision is concerned, both hemispheres of the brain play an important role.

Hanson (1987:41) tells us that while the left hemisphere is "more accurate in its ability to focus attention on something than is the right," the left side also tires more rapidly "and often gives way to the right." The right side maintains a general vigil in the surveillance of the environment, but it must call on the left hemisphere when it is necessary to pay attention to some detail.

When the right side does not call on the left side, a process that might be described as image *narcotization* takes place—a sense of monotony and boredom. On the other hand, using the left side of the brain is tiring, and so it must be reserved for occasions when focus and detail are important. Thus, both the left and right sides of the brain are needed, working in tandem, for people to process visual information in an optimal manner.

We can see the relationships that have been discussed in the chart that follows:

Left Hemisphere	*Right Hemisphere*
Right side of body	Left side of body
Analytical	Holistic
Logical	Artistic
Linear	Orientation in space
Sequential processing	Combinatory processing
Visual focus, detail	Surveillance, generalized vigil

With this in mind, we are prepared to consider our next topic, aesthetics.

AESTHETICS

Aesthetics means different things to different people. Courses in aesthetics, as it is conventionally understood, generally are offered by philosophy departments and tend to be theoretical in nature. Philosophers typically deal with aesthetics in terms of the following abstract questions:

1. What is the nature of the beautiful?
2. What is the relationship between form and content?
3. Is beauty objective or subjective? Does it exist independent of our opinions, or is it mainly in the eye of the beholder, as some have suggested?
4. What is the relationship between truth and beauty?
5. What is the significance of ethical content? Need a work of art have moral value? If so, how do we define moral?
6. Should we consider the artist's intention in evaluating a work?

These questions are important, and we might bear them in mind as we proceed.

This book, however, is about *applied* aesthetics and focuses on the literal meaning of the term *aesthetics,* "space perception." The questions this book deals with are practical ones:

1. How do we obtain certain desired effects using the basic visual elements at our command?
2. How do we best exploit the powers (and deal with the limitations) of whatever medium we are working with?

In the world of applied aesthetics, we start with the *effect* we want and work backward, using whatever we can to obtain that desired effect.

Taste is an important factor, of course, but it is very subjective. Taste is idiosyncratic; it is affected by factors such as sex, education, socioeconomic class, values, time, and culture. (Think, for example, how old-fashioned cars from the 1960s or fashions from just a few years back look today.) As mentioned, sociologists have suggested that there are "taste cultures" that shape the way people perceive things. From our perspective, that of applied aesthetics, taste reminds us that we must always know our audience and keep it in mind.

A PRIMER ON COMMUNICATION THEORY

Many theories and *models* have been developed that deal with communication theory—how people communicate with one another. One of the most famous models, created by the political scientist Harold Lasswell, asks:

Who?

Says what?

In which channel?

To whom?

With what effect?

Let me offer my own model which focuses on the relationships that exist among a work of art, the audience for whom it is intended, the medium used, the artist, and society. These are what I call the focal points, which can be used in the communication process.

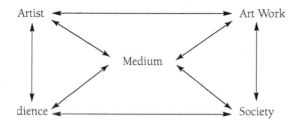

Focal Points in the Communication Process

The arrows in this model show that every focal point in the communication process is (or can be) connected to every other focal point.

This model with five focal points is a modification of one used by literary scholar M. H. Abrams in his book *The Mirror and the Lamp.* Abrams's model, shown below, deals with literary works, so it doesn't address the role of media.

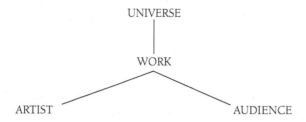

The addition of media into my model and the change from universe to society enabled me to cover the most important elements, or "focal points," that one might consider in dealing with communication of all kinds. Most scholarly studies of the mass-mediated communication process and of the effects of communication focus on the relationship that exists between media and one or more of the focal points.

Abrams discusses another matter of interest in his book. He points out that there are four opposing major theories that deal with the relationship between works of art and the audiences of these works. These four theories are:

Pragmatic	Art is functional, has a purpose.
Objective	Art creates a world.
Emotive	Art generates sensations, emotional reactions.
Mimetic	Art mirrors or reflects reality.

According to pragmatic theorists, art is always functional and has a purpose. Objective theorists argue that what artists do is to create their own worlds. The purpose of art for emotive theorists is to create sensations for audiences. Aristotle, who is the father of mimetic (from *mimesis,* Greek for "imitation") theories of art, argues that what art does is mirror reality.

ARISTOTLE ON IMITATION

Aristotle was born in 384 B.C. and died in 322 B.C. Richard McKeon, the editor of *The Basic Works of Aristotle,* writes in his introduction that Aristotle (1941:xv) "was reputed to have been bald, thin-legged, to have had small eyes, and to have spoken with a lisp" and that in his student days he was supposed to have been (1941:xv) "foppish in dress and to have affected gaudy jewelry." He is, unquestionably, one of the most important philosophers who ever lived.

In Aristotle's *Poetics,* his book on the arts, he argues that all art is based on imitation (mimesis). The reason imitation is so important, Aristotle adds, is that it based on something natural in all human beings (1941:1457):

> Imitation is natural to man from childhood, one of his advantages over the lower animals being this, that he is the most imitative creature in the world, and learns at first by imitation. And it is also natural for all to delight in works of imitation.

This assertion, that imitation is natural to human beings, forms the basis, then, of his theory of art and of his psychology.

A French literary theorist, René Girard, takes Aristotle's theory and uses it to explain the plays of Shakespeare and human behavior, in general. In his book, *A Theatre of Envy: William Shakespeare,* Girard argues that we desire what others desire and writes about what he calls "mimetic desire" (1991:3):

> When we think of those phenomena in which mimicry is likely to play a role, we enumerate such things as dress, mannerisms, facial expressions, speech, stage acting, artistic creation, and so forth, but we never think of desire.

▌FIGURE 1.8
*Aristotle. Drawing by
Arthur Asa Berger.*

Consequently, we see imitation in social life as a force for gregariousness and
bland conformity through the mass reproduction of a few social models.

This theory suggests that advertising is a major force in generating "mimetic
desire," and when we purchase products we are imitating not the behavior
but the desire of those sports heroes, actors and actresses, celebrities and so
on, who are used to sell things. Thus "mimetic desire," which is implicitly
based on visual images, can be seen as an important factor in consumer
behavior and in generating "consumer lust."

These theories operate at a very high level of abstraction and those
who support a specific theory claim that their theory best explains what
all art does. It is possible, I would suggest, to find works of art that combine a number of these functions. For example, a television commercial
has a pragmatic function. It is meant to sell products. But it also creates
its own little world, one which may or may not "mirror" the real world,
and it aims to generate emotions and desire in its audience. It's useful to
keep these theories in mind when you examine a work of art to determine which of them might be most important and how the theories
might help explain the appeal different works of art have to different
people.

Lasswell's and my model actually are very similar—except for the terminology— as the following chart shows:

Lasswell	Berger
Who?	Artist or sender
Says what?	Artwork
In which channel?	Medium used
To whom?	Audience or receiver
With what effect?	Social impact

Using Lasswell's model, we can understand that communication takes place when someone says something (interpreted broadly), using some medium, to someone (including groups of people), with some effect.

For our purposes, let us consider the "effects" Lasswell mentions as being linked to the ability to understand (or, in technical terms, "decode") what has been said and have it generate some kind of impact—personal as well as social. For example, if I say something to you in Italian and you don't know Italian, it will simply be gibberish as far as you are concerned. Italian, here, is a code, and knowing Italian will enable you to decode my message. That is why icons are used in airports and other public places. They transmit messages by images, which most everyone can decode, and not by words—though iconic signs may use words as well.

Another important model of the communication process comes from the linguist Roman Jakobson. He suggested that there are six elements in the process:

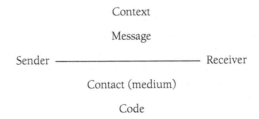

Context

Message

Sender ———————————— Receiver

Contact (medium)

Code

Jakobson's Six Elements of the Communication Process

These elements may be described as follows:

1. A *Sender* sends a message.
2. A *Message* is the content of what is sent.
3. A *Receiver* is the object or objects of the message (audiences).
4. A *Code* is the form of the message: language, images, sound.
5. A *Contact* is the medium used (television, film, radio, conversation) to send the message.

6. A *Context* is background which helps us understand the message.

Jakobson's model of communication offers us an insight into the people and complexities involved in the communication process. It also compares significantly with the Lasswell model:

Lasswell	*Jakobson*
Who?	Sender
Says what?	Message and code
In which channel?	Contact (medium)
To whom?	Receiver
With what effect?	Context

Jakobson's model doesn't deal directly with effects, but his inclusion of context in the communication process implies a social dimension to communication. Think how important context is. The statement "pass the hypodermic needle" means one thing in a hospital and another thing in a dark alley.

There are many other communication models, some of which are extremely complex. Some models incorporate elements such as feedback or context or "two-step flows" between opinion leaders and the general public into their formulations. But the models discussed here offer us an overview of the most important elements in the communication process, a perspective that can easily be applied to visual communication.

THEORIES OF MORALITY

What is morality? Is an action right or wrong only in relation to certain conditions, or is it right or wrong independently of any conditions? Are the grounds for judging human conduct always the same, or should they vary with social and individual needs, customs, and historical evolution? Theories of morality may be classified as relativist or absolutist depending upon the answers they offer to these questions. But either relativism or absolutism may involve different general assumptions and may support different moral principles. An absolutist may argue for the invariant character of particular rules of conduct on the ground that they are divine commands, or that they are laws of nature, or that they are deducible from the concept of reason, or that they are intuitively self-evident. A relativist may hold that the rules of right conduct vary with human conventions, or with social traditions, or with political, psychological, economic, or biological needs. The history of ethical philosophy is a continuous dialogue between progressively more refined forms of absolutism and relativism.

Source: Raziel Abelson and Marie-Louise Friquegnon, *Ethics for Modern Life*, 4th ed. (New York: St. Martin's Press, 1991), 7.

ETHICS AND THE IMAGE

The power to create images, videos, films, commercials, television programs, and the like—all of which profoundly affect viewers' emotions and beliefs, and have social and cultural implications as well—should not be taken lightly. We must be ever mindful of our responsibilities toward those who will see what we create and, in many cases, believe what they see.

Even if people don't always believe what they see, or believe everything they see, they are often affected emotionally by the media to which they are exposed. For example, we know that professional wrestling is "fake," but

---

CHECKLIST ON ETHICS AND THE MEDIA

Rather than dealing with ethics in terms of abstruse philosophical matters, let us operationalize our discussion and deal with some of the problems we face when we try to act in an ethical manner. Here are some key questions relating to ethical behavior for individuals who work with visual communication and other aspects of the media:

1. Will the works you create—videos, programs, commercials, print advertisements, and so on—give people distorted views of reality (to the extent that we can know reality, that is)?

2. Do your works use the power of images to exploit or manipulate people? Do your works attempt to get people to do things that are, or might be, self-destructive (like smoking cigarettes or drinking too much) or harmful to others?

3. Do your works stereotype people—members of racial or ethnic minorities or religious groups, for instance—and lead, as is often the case, to feelings of hatred toward and self-hatred by members of the stereotyped group?

4. Do your works have the power to disturb young viewers, who may not be

emotionally able to deal with what they see?

5. Do your works contain gratuitous violence? Do they sexually exploit women's bodies? Are they sensationalistic?

6. Are your works something that you are not proud of? Do you have to rationalize your behavior by saying, "If I don't do it, someone else will . . . and I have responsibilities to my family as well"?

7. Do you create works you wouldn't want your children to see? If so, is it acceptable to create something that other people's children might see?

8. Do your works suggest some actions or values that you would be willing to universalize?

This last question reflects the ideas of the philosopher Immanuel Kant, who believed that ethical behavior should be based on what he called the "categorical imperative." Kant wrote in 1785: "Act as if the maxim of your action were to become through your will a universal law of nature." That is, I would suggest, a very good principle to keep in mind when considering the ethical responsibilities of individuals who work in the media.

people who watch it are still *viscerally* affected by seeing performers who are (or who seem to be) violently battering one another. Theater is "fake," too—actors and actresses pretend to have certain emotions and feelings. Audiences know this, but they still can be brought to tears in some cases or made to laugh hysterically in others.

Therefore, those who work in the media must consider their ethical responsibilities toward others. **Ethics** is, for our purposes, that branch of philosophy generally defined as dealing with "correct behavior," with what is "right" and what is "wrong." But what is "correct behavior"? What does it mean to act "morally" and avoid acting "immorally"? How do we know we're doing "the right thing" and avoiding doing "something wrong"?

Philosophers have debated ethics for thousands of years. Some philosophers have suggested that ethical behavior involves utilitarian considerations—"the greatest good for the greatest number." But how do we determine what the greatest good for the greatest number is?

Some philosophers argue that there are absolute standards of right and wrong. But others—the ethical relativists—argue that it is impossible to say, with any finality, that anything is *always* right or wrong. For example, in some societies, men have many wives, while in other societies, men have only one wife. Therefore, we cannot say conclusively that having more than one wife—or, by implication, doing anything else—is always right or always wrong.

Finally, many people believe we should obey the golden rule—"Do unto others as you would have them do unto you." But others have disagreed with that notion, saying, "Do not do unto others as you would have them do unto you—their tastes may not be the same as yours."

Deciding what's the right thing to do in any given situation is not easy, which explains why ethics is, and always has been, a very contentious branch of philosophy. But it is important for us to think, at all times, about ethics and the impact of what we do, not only for the good of society, but also for our own peace of mind.

VISUAL PERSUASION

Scholarly research on the way people react to images indicates that there are certain hardwired responses that people make to certain kinds of images. As Paul Messaris writes in his book *Visual Persuasion: The Role of Images in Advertising* (1997:4)

> Real-world vision is intimately connected with emotion, which, in turn, is tied to our functional needs as biological and social creatures. When we look at the world, we are strongly predisposed to attend to certain kinds of objects or situations and to react in certain kinds of ways. These predispositions reflect the influence of culture, but . . . they have also been shaped to a certain degree by

biological evolution. In short, real-world vision comes with a set of built-in response tendencies. Consequently, to the extent that a picture can reproduce the significant visual features of real-world experiences, it may also be able to exploit the response tendencies that are associated with those features.

This explains why advertising uses certain techniques in an attempt to attract our attention and shape our behavior. Our responses in these situations are involuntary because they are, to a great degree, biological or natural.

The following is a list of a number of responses to certain techniques used in advertising:

1. We pay attention, as Messaris writes, "to unfamiliar objects when they are only slightly different from our expectations." (1997:7)

2. We are affected by visual **metaphors** (communication based on analogies) and visual **metonymies** (communication based on association).

3. When someone gazes into our eyes, we return the gaze, what Messaris calls **direct eye gaze.**

4. We are affected by displays of emotion in others, whether real or pretended (as in the case of print advertisements and television commercials).

5. We are pleased by humor that amuses us and most likely transfer our sense of pleasure from the advertisement to the product or service being advertised.

6. We identify with others and often imitate them. French scholar René Girard has argued in his book *A Theater of Envy: William Shakespeare* that imitation is a powerful social force and that we often imitate the desire of others, an activity he describes as **mimetic desire.**

7. We respond directly to sexual display and to beauty of all kinds. Thus, we are unconsciously affected by images in which a woman has dilated or enlarged pupils, which are signs of sexual arousal (Figure 1.9).

8. We can be "conditioned," to varying degrees, by continual repetition and by the use of cues that affect us much the same way that Pavlov was able to make dogs salivate by ringing a bell when he fed them.

9. We seek closure and want to know how narratives that attract our attention will be resolved—whether it is a long narrative, as in a television show or film, or a micronarrative, as in a television commercial.

This list suggests that advertising can do any number of things to automatically "push our buttons," and advertisers utilize these hardwired responses to the extent they can—whether they are selling soap or presidential candidates.

Advertisers use every one of these devices they can because they know that, generally speaking, people don't want to be subjected to print

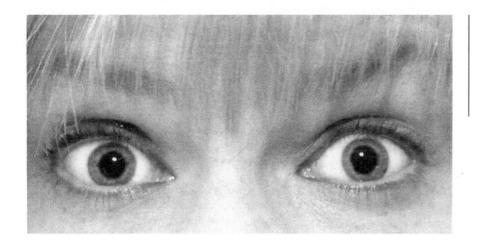

I FIGURE 1.9
Dilated pupils are indicators of sexual arousal and are used to excite people exposed to them in advertisements. They work below our level of consciousness.

advertisements and television commercials. Advertisers also have to face the problem of "clutter," the endless numbers of advertisements to which people are subjected and that generate information overload. It's an interesting exercise to watch commercials without the sound on. When you do this you notice in many commercials the extreme degree to which actors and actresses use facial expressions and body language to attract our attention and move us emotionally. They flirt with us, they plead with us and do everything they can to sell us whatever it is they are pitching.

What advertisers want us to do, generally speaking, is appeal to the id elements in our psyches, to our desire for pleasure and self-gratification and to phenomena buried in the unconscious part of our psyches. Advertisers wish to sidetrack or avoid ego and superego functions, which would ask us to decide, rationally, whether or not we needed that product or service being advertised.

From the list I gave of natural or hardwired responses we give to certain images, it would seem that the deck is stacked against the average consumer. That is why Ernest Dichter, one of the founding fathers of motivational research, suggests the following in his book *The Strategy of Desire* (1960:12):

> Whatever your attitude toward modern psychology or psychoanalysis, it has been proved beyond any doubt that many of our daily decisions are governed by motivations over which we have no control and of which we are quite unaware.

The illusion we have that we are in full control ourselves only helps advertisers pull our strings. Advertisers don't always succeed and people do have the ability to resist them to a certain degree, but advertising is a $150 billion a year industry in America (for 2010) for a good reason: companies that advertise are getting the results they want. Not all advertising campaigns are successful, but over the long term, advertising is a very effective and powerful tool of persuasion.

JEAN BAUDRILLARD ON ADVERTISING AND PERSUASION

The French social scientist Jean Baudrillard offers an insight from psychoanalytic theory into why advertising is successful "in the long run." He writes in his book *The System of Objects* (1968/1996:167) about advertising:

> Neither its rhetoric nor even the informational aspect of its discourse has a decisive effect on the buyer. What the individual does respond to, on the other hand, is advertising's underlying leitmotiv of protection and gratification, the intimation that its solicitations and attempts to persuade are the sign, indecipherable at the conscious level, that somewhere there is an agency (a social agency in the event, but one that refers directly to the image of the mother) which has taken it upon itself to inform him of his own desires, and to foresee and rationalize these desires to his own satisfaction. He thus no more "believes" in advertising than the child believes in Father Christmas, but this in no way impedes his capacity to embrace an internalized infantile situation, and to act accordingly.

Thus, in Baudrillard's view, advertising facilitates a kind of collective psychological regression—a state in which we are very susceptible to persuasion. It is not any particular print advertisements or television commercials that shape our behavior as consumers. It is, instead, the continual impact of all of these kinds of persuasion that leads us to regress and succumb to our desires to buy things—and, in some cases, to buy things we didn't even know we wanted.

I FIGURE 1.10
Jean Baudrillard. Drawing by Arthur Asa Berger.

I FIGURE 1.11
I saw this elephant paint
the image of the elephant
shown in Figure 0.19. It
took the elephant
10 minutes to paint the
picture. Photograph by
Arthur Asa Berger.

CONCLUSIONS

Seeing Is Believing aims to entertain you (in the best sense of the term—namely, giving you ideas to "entertain"), as well as to teach you about visual communication, with the goal of helping you learn to see the world (and yourself) with more clarity and understanding.

APPLICATIONS

1. In order of importance, what visual phenomena are most important in shaping your identity? Consider such things as height, body shape, hair color, hairstyle, complexion, teeth, eye color, clothes, and so on.

2. List the most important status symbols in our culture. How do these symbols confer status on people? How have status symbols changed in recent years? Is price the most important factor or are there things to consider when evaluating status symbols?

3. What makes a person "attractive"? Is beauty something that exists independent of people's opinions, or is it merely "in the eye of the beholder"?

4. It has been suggested that seeing isn't always believing—namely, that sometimes we are led astray by things we see. Give some examples of this. How can we use visual phenomena to deceive people?

5. In this discussion on aesthetics, a number of notions of what is most important in a work of art were mentioned: form, content, truthfulness, ethical qualities. Which of these concepts do you think is the critical one? What reasons can you offer to support your contention?

6. Aestheticians have suggested four theories of the purpose of art: (1) to generate emotional experiences in people, (2) to achieve certain consequences for individuals and society, (3) to mirror reality, and (4) to generate the artist's own reality. (These are known as the emotive, pragmatic, mimetic, and objective theories of art, respectively.) Which of them strikes you as best? Why?

7. What is taste? Is taste a valid and useful means of evaluating works of art and other phenomena? If so, why? If not, why not?

8. Select some advertisements from fashionable and upscale magazines such as *Vogue* and *Architectural Digest* and middle-scale magazines such as *Better Homes and Gardens*. What differences do you notice in terms of such matters as the physical features of the models (male and female) in the advertisements? In the way men are shown relating to women? In the way women are portrayed?

9. Select some photographs or advertisements (with people in them) that reflect "beauty" in women and "handsomeness" in men. What do you find in common with selections made by your classmates? Have our definitions of beauty and handsomeness changed in recent years? If so, how do your photographs and advertisements reflect this? Are our definitions destructive? If so, how?

10. If you had to bring a simple object to class that reflected your personality, what would it be? What attributes about you does it reflect? How might your classmates misinterpret what the object reflects about you?

11. Record a dream and examine the symbolism reflected in it. You might want to read some of Freud's book on dreams for help in this matter.

12. Which model of the communication process do you think best explains the various aspects of communication? Explain your answer.

13. Using the information on visual persuasion you've read in this book, make a tape of an interesting television commercial and analyze the way it uses images to persuade its viewers to purchase something.

14. The painting of an elephant, made by an elephant (Figure 1.12), raises an interesting question—can animals be artists? If you don't think they can, what do you say about the elephant painting done by an elephant?

15. Have you ever purchased something or wanted to buy something because a sports star, movie star, or celebrity pitched it on a television commercial? If so, were you experiencing "mimetic desire"?

KEY TERMS FOR CHAPTER 1

signifier	taste cultures
signified	unconscious
semiotics	saccades
aesthetics	metonymy
ethics	direct eye gaze
metaphor	mimetic desire

2

HOW WE SEE

Studies indicate that vision is about one-tenth physical and nine-tenths mental. In visual perception, sensory input in the form of light patterns received by the eye is transformed by the brain into meaningful images. The interpretation depends on preconditioning, intelligence, and the physical and emotional state of the viewer.

The variety of our responses to visual stimuli is demonstrated by artists. Twelve people depicting the same subject—even from the same vantage point—will create twelve different images because of their different experiences, attitudes, interests and eyesight.
　　　　–DUANE AND
　　　　SARAH PREBLE,
　　　　ARTFORMS

This chapter deals with how we make sense of what we see. It introduces some basic principles of semiotics, or the science of signs, and some material from psychoanalytic theory, which can be used to help us understand how we find meaning in images and, by extension, in life, in general.

LEARNING TO SEE

The first thing we must recognize is that we don't just "see" but have to learn *how* to see and *what* to see. We cannot focus our attention on everything around us; somehow, we select certain things to look at. And what we decide to see is determined by what we know and what we believe and what we want. Consider our behavior in a supermarket, where we are surrounded by thousands of products, each clamoring for our attention. We "see" an estimated eight products every second that we're in the supermarket. We may try to neglect the products we feel we do not need or want—but it is very difficult for most people to avoid purchasing some products on the basis of "impulse." (More than 60 percent of all supermarket purchases are not planned in advance, which means that impulse buying is a major factor in our trips to the supermarket.) And it is primarily as a result of packaging— that is, the way products look—that we are attracted to them. We are also affected by the design of supermarkets and the placement of products on the shelves. If we have to stoop down or reach up to get a product, we are less likely to purchase it than if it is at eye level and easy to reach.

I FIGURE 2.1

Three renderings of fire. Our attitudes about fire are connected with everything from the myth of Prometheus (who stole fire from the gods and gave it to humans) to our beliefs about the existence of hell. What other images of fire can you think of? By Arthur Asa Berger.

The way we think about visual phenomena is affected by our knowledge. In *Ways of Seeing,* John Berger points out that in the Middle Ages, when people believed in the existence of hell, fire had a meaning much different from and more powerful than its current meaning (Figure 2.1).

We all have to be taught what different objects are (a plane, a ship, a dog, and so on, ad infinitum), but we learn so quickly and with so little effort that we generally don't recognize that a learning experience has taken place. We simply seem to pick up much of this information by osmosis. But the fact is, we do have to learn, and much of this learning involves visual phenomena.

There is a vast literature on visual matters—everything from highly abstract theoretical and philosophical treatises to experimental research studies. And in between are countless reports on applied research, on such topics as the way we perceive spaces or relate to colors, the responses generated by various kinds of film shots, the impact of editing, and the relationship between a medium and its message, to cite just a few.

We can't cover everything in this brief book, but by dealing with some of the most important aspects of visual communication, we can take that important first step on the "royal road" to visual understanding.

SIGNS, SYMBOLS, AND SEMIOTICS

How do we make sense of the visual world? Many of us never bother to think about this question because we do a pretty good job of interpreting the world around us and rarely reflect on *how* we know *what* we know.

Consider the following:

1. A drawing of a person (Figure 2.2)
2. A picture of a house with smoke coming out of a window (Figure 2.3)
3. An image of a cross (Figure 2.4)

▌FIGURE 2.2
A very simple drawing of
a man. By Arthur Asa
Berger.

▌FIGURE 2.3
A house on fire. "Where
there's smoke, there's fire."
By Arthur Asa Berger.

▌FIGURE 2.4
A cross. By Arthur Asa
Berger.

The list might go on endlessly: a photograph of a friend, a Rolls Royce, a flag, the Mona Lisa, the Eiffel Tower, the White House, the Pentagon, a Russian tank, a Big Mac, a computer, a great white shark, the Washington Monument, the Leaning Tower of Pisa, a football, and so on.

But how do we "make sense" of these three items?

In Figure 2.2, the matter is quite simple: the drawing looks like a person; and so we can say that drawings (as well as photographs, paintings, sculptures, and the like) communicate by *resemblance*. In Figure 2.3, we know from our experiences with fires—in fireplaces, at ceremonial events, in television news shows or films—that "where there's smoke, there's fire." Thus, we have good reason to believe that the smoke is *caused* by fire and that the building is on fire. In Figure 2.4, the cross is an object that we have *learned* is associated with Christianity and is an artifact having great resonance and emotional power for many Christians because it symbolizes Christ's crucifixion. There is no way for a person to "naturally" know the meaning of a cross; there is no logical connection between the object and what it stands for the way there is between smoke and fire. (The connection is historical, not logical.)

Now let us consider another matter related to visual communication that we might add to the preceding list:

4. The word *tree*

The word *tree* and the object it refers to are shown in Figures 2.5 and 2.6. Linguists tell us that there is no natural connection between a word and the object it stands for. Thus, the word *tree* and the object it stands for (defined in *Merriam-Webster's Collegiate Dictionary* as a "woody perennial plant having a single usually elongate main stem generally with few or no branches on its lower part") are not logically related. *The relationship between a word and the*

TREE

▌FIGURE 2.5
The word *tree*.

▌FIGURE 2.6
A drawing of a tree. By
Arthur Asa Berger.

object it stands for is arbitrary or conventional. This fact explains why dictionaries need to be revised all the time, because language is always changing. This same relationship between a word and its object also applies to all kinds of other phenomena, in which we learn that something (a word, a facial expression, an object, a hairstyle) signifies or stands for something else.

Let's recapitulate. We make sense of visual phenomena in a number of ways:

1. *Resemblance* (as in photographs)
2. *Cause and effect* or *logic* (as in smoke implying fire)
3. *Convention* (as in objects that have symbolic value)
4. *Signification* (as in a smile signifying pleasure)

There is a science that is of great utility in helping us understand how visual phenomena communicate—a field of knowledge called semiotics, the science of signs. Two theories are encompassed here: one is the field known as semiotics, which was developed by the American philosopher C. S. Peirce, and the other is the field known as semiology, developed by the Swiss linguist Ferdinand de Saussure. For the sake of simplicity, we'll use the term *semiotics* to cover both of these theories.

Ferdinand de Saussure describes his hopes for the science of semiotics in his book *Course in General Linguistics,* which was originally published in French in 1915. He writes (1966:16):

> Language is a system of signs that expresses ideas, and is therefore comparable to a system of writing, the alphabet of deaf-mutes, symbolic rites, polite formulas, military signals, etc. But it is the most important of these systems.
>
> *A science that studies the life of signs within society* is conceivable; it would be part of social psychology and consequently of general psychology. I shall call it *semiology* (from Greek *sēmeîon,* "sign"). Semiology would show what constitutes a sign, what laws govern them.

This can be regarded as one of the charter statements of the science of semiology, which means, literally, words about signs. As I mentioned above, the term *semiotics* is now the term of choice for this science. For semioticians, human beings are sign-creating and sign-interpreting creatures, and every aspect of our lives can be interpreted semiotically.

C. S. Peirce explains his theory as follows (quoted in the article "Peirce's Theory of Signs" by J. Jay Zeman, in T. Sebeok's *A Perfusion of Signs,* 1977:36):

> An analysis of the essence of a sign . . . leads to a proof that every sign is determined by its object, either first by partaking in the characters of the object, when I call that sign an *Icon;* secondly, by being really and in its individual existence connected with the individual object, when I call the sign an *Index;* thirdly, by more or less approximate certainty that will be interpreted

in denoting an object, in consequence of a habit (which term I use as including a natural disposition), when I call the sign a *Symbol.*

According to Peirce, then, there are three kinds of signs and the science that helps us understand how these signs work he called semiotics. Let me explain a bit more about how signs work.

What Signs Are

A sign, from the semiotic perspective, is anything that stands for something else. What does this statement mean? Only that a great deal of communication is done not directly but rather indirectly, by using various signs. For instance, there are several ways to suggest that an actor is portraying a secret agent. The actor could say, "I am a secret agent," or a narrator could tell us. Or the actor could wear a trench coat and a slouch hat, carry a small revolver with a silencer, and drive a fast sports car. All of these are signs that, taken together, suggest a secret agent.

I FIGURE 2.7
Icons for Applications on an iPhone. McGraw-Hill Companies.

ICONS, INDEXES, AND SYMBOLS.   Peirce identifies three kinds of signs: iconic, indexical, and symbolic, as the chart below shows. An *icon* is a sign that looks like or resembles the thing it stands for—which means that icons are easy to interpret; the drawing in Figure 2.2 is an icon. Because icons are so easy to interpret, signs in airports are often icons—pictures that most people, regardless of the language they speak, should be able to understand. An *indexical sign* is logically connected to what it represents; in Figure 2.3, smoke indicates fire. We have to learn about this connection and do so, often, simply from everyday life. A *symbol,* on the other hand, has conventional meaning, and there is no logical connection between this meaning and the symbol itself. It is something we have to learn, as with the cross in Figure 2.4. We can see the relation that exists among icons, indexes, and symbols in the chart that follows.

	Icon	*Index*	*Symbol*
Signify by	Resemblance	Causal connection	Convention
Examples	Photograph	Smoke/fire	Cross or flag
Process	Can recognize	Can figure out	Must learn

Peirce's theory is actually very involved, but these three central concepts can help us to understand visual communication. For example, internists

❙ FIGURE 2.8
Logos for Saturn cars. Of these four versions, the first one was chosen. All offer somewhat different "images" for the automobile, and all contain pictorial references to the planet Saturn. Courtesy Landor Associates and General Motors Corporation.

and other "cognitive" physicians (in contrast to surgeons and other "operative" physicians) work on the basis of indexical knowledge. They see various signs, and patients tell them about their symptoms; and on the basis of these phenomena, they try to determine what is causing a problem. All of us recognize the power symbols have over people—flags, the crucifix, the Star of David, college banners, logos . . . one could go on endlessly. These symbols can generate enormously powerful emotional responses in people. In fact, people often are willing to give their lives for the institutions and organizations behind these symbols.

Peirce notes that "the universe is perfused with signs, if not made up entirely of them," which means that *everything can be seen as a sign of something else* and that human beings are sign-producing and sign-analyzing beings. *Logos* are designs that are used to stand for and help reinforce the identity of a corporation or other entity (Figures 2.8). If everything in the universe is a sign or can be understood as one, it certainly makes sense to learn how to interpret and understand signs.

The situation becomes more complex because the boundaries between icon, index, and symbol are often vague. As Sandra E. Moriarty explains in "Abduction: A Theory of Visual Interpretation" (1996:169):

> A rose can be an icon (a picture), an index (a sign of summer), and a symbol (the War of the Roses). Photographs are indexical as well as iconic because they are reality grounded. In communication production and reception, the meaning may shift from one to another as the communication act progresses. For example, Sinead O'Connor's iconoclastic tearing up of the picture of Pope John Paul II . . . illustrates how conflict can be generated when an iconic representation is turned into a symbol.

An iconoclast is, literally, a destroyer or breaker of icons—but generally refers to someone who is unconventional and who goes against the grain as well as someone who destroys sacred icons. We see, then, that applying Peirce's ideas can be quite complicated.

Clifford Geertz, an anthropologist, offers us an explanation of why symbols seem so natural and why the have so much cultural resonance. In his book, *The Interpretation of Cultures* (1973:45), he writes:

> Thinking consists not of "happenings in the head" (though happenings there and elsewhere are necessary for it to occur) but of a traffic in what have been called, by G. H. Mead and others—significant symbols—words for the most part but also gestures, drawings, musical sounds, mechanical devices like clocks, or natural objects like jewels—anything, in face, that is disengaged from its mere actuality and used to impose meaning upon experience. From the point of view of any particular individual, such symbols are largely given. He finds them already current in the community when he is born, and they remain, with some additions, subtractions, and partial alterations he may or may not have had a hand in, in circulation when he dies.

Symbols, as Geertz explains, help us make sense of the world and help shape our thoughts, feelings, and behavior.

SIGNIFIERS AND SIGNIFIEDS. In *Course in General Linguistics,* Saussure discusses the relationship that exists between signifiers and signifieds. He writes (1966:66–67):

> The linguistic signs unite not a thing and a name, but a concept and a sound-image . . . I call the combination of a concept and a sound-image a *sign* . . . I propose to retain the word *sign* [*signe*] to designate the whole and to replace *concept* and *sound-image* respectively by signified [*signifié*] and signifier [*signifiant*]; the last two terms have the advantage of indicating the opposition that separates them from each other and from the whole of which they are parts.

Saussure argues, then, that a sign is divided into two parts: a signifier and a signified. A *signifier* is defined by Saussure as a sound or object that calls to mind a concept or *signified* (Figures 2.9 and 2.10). According to Saussure,

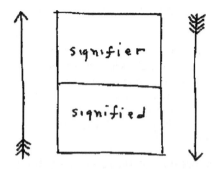

❙ FIGURE 2.9
Signifier/signified diagram. By Arthur Asa Berger.

❙ FIGURE 2.10
Signifier/signified diagram for *tree*. By Arthur Asa Berger.

the relationship that exists between the signifier and signified is arbitrary or conventional—that is, the relationship is not natural but must be learned.

Therefore, in Saussure's view, no signifier—whether a word or a drawing or any other kind of sign—is self-explanatory and implies a specific signified. A given facial expression—a wink, for example—can mean a number of different things, depending on the situation. As semiotic theorists often point out, if signs can be used to tell the truth, they also can be used to lie.

Saussure makes another extremely important point. He notes that concepts don't mean anything on their own; they are always defined in terms of how they differ from other concepts. As he puts it (1966:117), "Concepts are purely differential and defined not by their positive content but negatively by their relations with the other terms in the system."

Meaning, then, is determined not by content but by relationships. As Saussure (1966:117) suggests, as far as concepts are concerned, "their most precise characteristic is in being what the others are not." This explains why our thinking tends to be so binary, so connected to oppositions—because that's the way language requires us to make sense of things.

This idea about concepts generating meaning relationally has significance in a number of areas when it comes to visual communication. We will see, for example, that a color's impact depends to a great degree on the colors around it. And size, as we all recognize, is also relative. With this in mind, let us consider what signs can do.

What Signs Can Do

Let's look at several examples of how signs can mean different things and how we can use them for a variety of purposes. For one thing, we can lie with signs. People who dye their hair are, from this perspective, "lying" with signs—though this kind of lying is not considered of great consequence. People who lease expensive cars and represent themselves as the owner are, in a sense, lying with signs (or, in this case, status symbols). When we laugh at a joke that we have heard before so that we don't embarrass the joke teller, we are lying. Or are we merely being polite?

The Italian semiotician and novelist Umberto Eco explains the relationship that exists between semiotics and lying in his book *A Theory of Semiotics*. Eco writes (1976:7):

> Semiotics is concerned with everything that can be taken as a sign. A sign is everything that can be taken as significantly substituting for something else. This something else does not necessarily have to exist, or to actually be somewhere at the moment in which a sign stands for it. Thus semiotics is in principle the discipline studying everything which can be used in order to lie. If something cannot be used to tell a lie, conversely it cannot be used to tell the truth; it cannot in fact be used "to tell" at all.

What Eco calls our attention to is the fact that signs always have a double valence: they can be used either to tell the truth or to lie. A great deal of human behavior is based on lies, of one sort or another, accomplished by using signs.

The absence of a sign, when some kind of a sign is expected, is also a kind of sign. If you say hello to a friend and don't get a response, that is a sign. Not doing something when something is expected of you is a kind of sign for a behavior known as "aggressive passivity"; in other words, doing nothing or not responding can, in certain situations, be seen as a form of aggressive behavior. This "aggressive passivity" or "passive aggression" is often used by children to "get back" at their parents—for example, by taking forever to do their chores.

Signs are used by people as a means of getting information and drawing conclusions about things. During the Iran-Contra hearings of 1987, commentators made much of the participants' facial expressions and body language, as a means of trying to understand what the participants *really* felt or believed. In the case of William Casey, the late CIA director, however, this was impossible, because Casey was "stone-faced." Furthermore, the president, at that time, Ronald Reagan, had an extensive background in acting, and actors are people who can pretend to have feelings and beliefs that they don't really have.

Facial Expressions a Signs

In their Executive Summary of Report to the National Science Foundation, psychologists Paul Ekman and Terrence J. Sejnowski suggest that faces are "windows" into the psyche and reflect the mechanisms governing our social and emotional lives. They write that facial expressions provide information about:

1. Emotions, such as fear, anger, and enjoyment
2. States of mind, such as surprise, sadness, and disgust, and more enduring moods, such as euphoria, dysphoria, and irritableness
3. Cognitive activity, such as perplexity, concentration, and boredom
4. Temperament and personality, including traits such as hostility, sociability, and shyness
5. Truthfulness, including the exposure of concealed emotions, and clues as to when the information provided in words about plans or actions is false
6. Psychopathology, including not only diagnostic information relevant to depression, mania, schizophrenia, and other less severe disorders, but also information about how patients respond to treatment

They also suggest that facial expressions can be used in medical research and might be helpful in identifying the role played by our emotions and moods in coronary artery disease. In the field of education, they point out that a teacher's facial expressions help influence whether his or her students learn, and a student's facial expressions help teachers determine whether their messages are getting through.

They also write that it is now possible to create "automated systems for monitoring facial expressions and animating artificial models" which could revolutionize medicine, communications and many other areas.

The seven emotions, in addition to a "neutral" state, one without any emotions showing, are (in alphabetical order):

Anger	Neutral (no particular emotion)
Determination	Pouting
Disgust	Sadness
Fear	Surprise

Faces (Figure 2.11) showing five of the seven universal human emotions are found in a Ph.D. dissertation by Irfan Essa and are used with his permission.

According to Ekman, who developed what is called FACS for Facial Action Coding System, there are 43 muscles in the human face that in different combinations show our emotions, even if the emotion lasts for just a fragment of a second, and the person experiencing the emotion in unaware of having had it. Many people think they can accurately identify emotions on people's faces, but when I showed some images of Ekman demonstrating the different emotions to my students and asked them to identify each of the emotions, they made numerous errors.

I FIGURE 2.11
Faces reflecting five of the eight universal human emotions. The images below each face show the energy one uses as each emotion is expressed. Courtesy Irfan Essa.

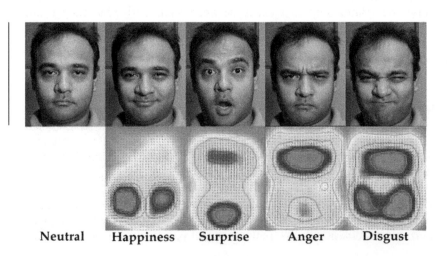

Neutral   Happiness   Surprise   Anger   Disgust

COMPUTER-ASSISTED SMILING

An article by Lucy Kellaway in *Financial Times*, July 20, 2009 titled, appropriately, "Lessons in smiling that have left me open-mouthed" contains a fascinating news items about smiling (2009:10):

> In Japan, workers are being subjected to a new sort of control—computer scanning to see if their smiles are wide enough. Every day, staff at 15 railway stations are having to bare their teeth at a computer that rates the curvaceousness of their smiles on a scale of one to 100. For those who can't muster a broad enough grin, the computer issues directions on how to improve performance.

There is another practical application of this matter of "reading" faces for emotions: playing a good game of poker. In the game of poker, players must make sure they do not give involuntary "tells," facial expressions or other signs which give away their hands. That explains why they learn to have "poker faces" and not provide any information to their opponents. But there are other matters, some of them involuntary, that can give information to opponents, such as body language, dilated pupils (showing sexual arousal), gestures, and facial coloration. Not only do poker players have to be careful not to give away information with signs, they also have to lie with signs and give their opponents false information. So poker can be seen as a game in which applied semiotics, sending signs of one kind or another, is of crucial importance. The cards are only one part of the game.

Codes

Because the relationship that exists between signs and what they mean (from Saussure's perspective) is arbitrary, we have to find ways of making sense of signs; we do so via codes. *Codes* can be looked at as ways of making sense of signs, as systems of conventions that we are taught or pick up from our culture. In fact, what we know as culture in anthropological terms can be seen as a collection of codes.

In some cases, these codes are created and systematized—as in the driving codes that we all must learn in order to get a license. These codes are collections of rules that tell us what to do when we see certain signs and when we find ourselves in particular situations. Thus, we learn that when we see a red light, we must stop our cars, and when we see a green one, we can accelerate or continue on if we have not stopped.

These codes list the conventions we have adopted in order to make it possible for us to get from one place to another with the minimum of danger and confusion. Some of the visual signs and symbols used on roads and highways are iconic, and we can make sense of them without having to be taught what they mean. But others are symbolic and conventional, and we must learn what they mean. In some cases, we have redundancy, in which a message is repeated in several ways to reinforce its impact.

These driving codes and others like them are one kind of code. They are really collections of laws and rules. There are other kinds of codes, however, that are learned more or less by osmosis as people grow up in a particular culture. These involve the whole universe of beliefs (many of which exist at a level below awareness or articulation) that tell us what things mean or what to do in given situations.

For example, we have certain ideas about what being a "blonde" means, about what having a weak chin means, about what having "shifty" eyes means, about what being short or tall or fat or skinny means. We have notions about what certain kinds of food mean and when to eat them. For instance, in the United States, we eat salad before the main course, while in France and other European countries, the salad is generally eaten after the main course. (What we call culture shock is generally the result of finding ourselves in a society where the codes or culture-codes are different from what one is used to.) We have notions of how to dress for job interviews and what certain styles, colors, and fashions mean. We should recognize here that it is also possible to misinterpret signs. Because of differences in education, region, class, and so on, people often interpret (or *decode,* to use the semiotic term) signs in widely varying ways. This aberrant decoding is a problem for people—such as writers, artists, filmmakers, and especially those who create commercials and print advertisements—who try to convey something to people but find those people interpreting it in unanticipated ways.

Clotaire Rapaille on Culture Codes

A French scholar, Clotaire Rapaille, published a book on marketing that deals with codes that are found in various countries. He explains, in *The Culture Code,* that every country has its own distinctive behavioral codes and that these codes are imprinted on children by the age of seven. "Every imprint influences us on an unconscious level," he writes (2006:7). In the book he discusses different codes found in France, the United States, Japan, and a number of other countries. These codes can be thought of as collections of imprintings and Rapaille spent many years searching for the way these imprintings function. As he writes (2006: 9–10):

> If I could get to the source of these imprints—if I could somehow "decode" elements of culture to discover the emotions and meanings attached to them—I would learn a great deal about human behavior and how it varies across the planet. This set me on the course of my life's work. I went off in search of the Codes hidden within the unconscious of every culture.

He suggests that in addition to the Freudian individual unconscious and the Jungian collective unconscious, there is a third unconscious—the cultural unconscious—that is distinctive in each country, which shapes our behavior.

As an example of how different codes function, he discusses the way Americans and French think about cheese: (206:25):

> The French Code for cheese is ALIVE. . . . The American Code for cheese is DEAD. . . . Americans "kill" their cheese through pasteurization (unpasteurized cheeses are not allowed into this country), select hunks of cheese that have been prewrapped—mummified if you will—in plastic (like body bags), and store it, still wrapped airtight, in a morgue, also known as a refrigerator.

The conclusion Rapaille reaches is that we are all guided by distinctive national cultural codes, imprinted on us before the age of seven, that shape our behavior in many areas of life. What we call "culture" can be seen as a collection of codes that govern our notions about how to store cheese and any number of other things.

Metaphors and Metonymies

Many of these codes are connected to visual matters, as we've already suggested. And much of what we know or think we know from observing various visual signs is based on associations we make or have been taught to

---

WHAT IS "FRENCHNESS"?

Semiotics is not just an abstruse philosophy but is something used in advertising, in films, in television, and every other kind of communication. People use signs to convey information and to attempt to shape attitudes and feelings in audiences. Consider the following task. You are directing a film. In that film, you want to suggest to your future viewers what we might call "Frenchness," the feeling of being in France. What visual signifiers might you use to suggest France? You might say "Let's have the action take place where you can see the Eiffel Tower. Show men wearing berets. Have little boys carrying long baguettes. Show chic women."

Here's one problem: Is the Eiffel Tower a symbol of France or of Paris? I would say Paris, rather than France. Another problem: Men in Spain and other countries wear berets, so berets by themselves certainly don't work and men wearing berets near the Eiffel Tower suggests Paris. Suggesting Frenchness rather than Paris is, actually, a difficult matter. Generally speaking, we convey information by using a number of signs that work together (form a gestalt) to generate an idea. It would be an interesting project to figure out how to convey "Frenchness" visually. And while you're at it, you might want to tackle "Italian-ness," "American-ness," "alienation," "anxiety," and "fear."

make about signs and what they signify. The technical term for these associations is *metonymy*. An example of this phenomenon would be an advertisement for Scotch whisky that shows the liquor being used by people who live in a mansion and are obviously rich and—it is suggested—have good taste. We learn to associate that brand of Scotch with what might be called "high-class" people and upscale living. The advertisement in Figure 2.12 is an example of the use of metonymy or association. Advertising makes great use of the power of **association** because this technique conveys information quickly and powerfully.

Another important method of transmitting meaning involves using **analogies**—saying or suggesting that something is like or similar to something else. Consider the two statements that follow:

1. My love *is* a red rose.
2. My love *is like* a red rose.

In the first case, we are making a very strong kind of analogy and are, in fact, suggesting equivalence. This figure of speech is known as a **metaphor.** In the second case, we are suggesting that our love is similar to a red rose, a figure of speech known as a **simile.** In both cases, the meaning is created by making an analogy.

Some scholars argue that metaphor is the basic way we have of knowing about the world and that human thinking is itself essentially metaphoric. As George Lakoff and Mark Johnson have written in *Metaphors We Live By* (1980:3):

> Metaphor is typically viewed as a characteristic of language alone, a matter of words rather than thought or action. For this reason, most people think they can get along perfectly well without metaphor. We have found, on the contrary, that metaphor is pervasive in everyday life, not just in language but in thought and action. Our ordinary conceptual system, in terms of which we both think and act, is fundamentally metaphorical in nature.
>
> The concepts that govern our thoughts are not just matters of the intellect. They also govern our everyday functioning down to the most mundane details. Our concepts structure what we perceive, how we get around in the world, and how we relate to other people. Our conceptual system thus plays a central role in defining our everyday reality.

Thus, metaphors play a central role in our thinking about the world and our functioning in it. The metaphors we have shape, it could be argued, our conception of the world and our place in it.

If, for example, you think that "love is a game" or that "love is like a game," certain logical implications will follow. You will see love as essentially a contest, with winners and losers and rules (that can be broken, in certain circumstances), and as something that ends after a certain period of "playing." This hardly seems a healthy or satisfying way to think about love.

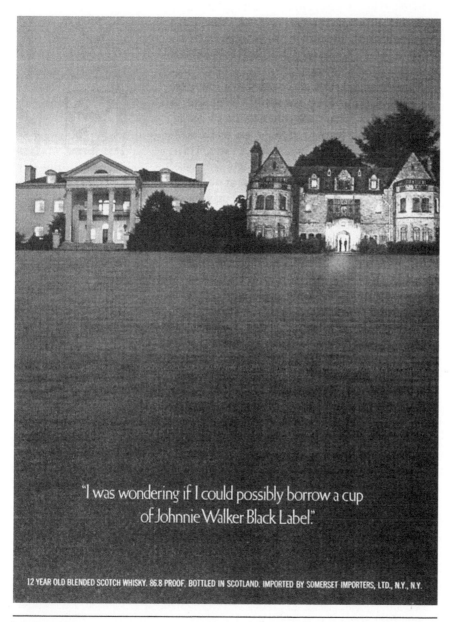

I FIGURE 2.12
Johnnie Walker advertisement. This advertisement uses the association (metonymy) of wealth and elegance to suggest sophistication and quality. *Reprinted with permission of Smith/Greenland, Inc.*

▐ Figure 2.13
Here is a visual metaphor that you might find amusing. By Arthur Asa Berger.

In a chapter on "Metaphor, Truth, and Action," Lakoff and Johnson point out that metaphors often shape our behavior. They write (1980:156) "Metaphors may create realities for us, especially social realities. A metaphor may thus be a guide for future action." Our actions, they explain, can be shaped by the metaphor which reinforces the ability of the metaphor to make our experience seem sensible and coherent. Thus, the metaphor generates a self-fulfilling prophecy.

Metaphor and simile are not confined to words and written language—they are also part of our visual language and pervade our image making (Figure 2.13). For example, in the comics, the Spiderman costume is a visual analogy; so is the characterization of Newt Gingrich as a "bomb" in *Doonesbury*. Freud's notion of "phallic and vaginal symbols," which will be discussed later, is based on visual analogies. Because metaphor and metonymy play such an important role in communication, it is only logical to find them in pictorial form as well as in our words.

It is not unusual for a given sign or symbol to have both metonymic and metaphoric aspects to it; that is, to communicate by using both associations and analogies.

Think, for example, of our old friend, the snake. We, in the West, *associate* the snake with Adam and Eve in the Garden of Eden and with our eating from the Tree of Knowledge and being expelled from Eden. Thus, the snake is connected, in Western minds familiar with the Old Testament, with deception ("The serpent beguiled me," Eve says) and a host of other negative things like having to work and having to die. At the same time, snakes are long and thin (which means their shape makes them resemble penises), and thus, they are *analogous* to or function as phallic symbols. (In certain Eastern countries, on the other hand, the fact that snakes shed their skins and become "new" again leads people to associate snakes with rebirth and immortality.)

There's a wonderful example of visual metaphors in Chapter 4 of *Alice in Wonderland*. Alice's neck has stretched out very long, and a pigeon who sees her thinks she is a snake:

"Serpent!" screamed the Pigeon.
   "I'm *not* a serpent!" said Alice indignantly. "Let me alone!"
   "Serpent, I say again!" repeated the Pigeon, but in a more subdued tone, and added, with a kind of sob, "I've tried every way but nothing seems to suit them!"

The Pigeon describes how she's hidden her eggs in many different places but has not been able to keep them from the serpents. Alice takes issue with her:

"But I'm *not* a serpent, I tell you!" said Alice. "I'm a—I'm a—"

"Well! *What* are you?" said the Pigeon. "I can see you're trying to invent something."

"I—I'm a little girl," said Alice, rather doubtfully, as she remembered a number of changes she had gone through that day.

"A likely story indeed!" said the Pigeon, in a tone of deepest contempt. "I've seen a good many little girls in my time, but never *one* with such a neck as that! No, No! You're a serpent; and there's no use denying it. I suppose you'll be telling me next that you've never tasted an egg!"

"I *have* tasted eggs, certainly," said Alice, who was a very truthful child; "but little girls eat eggs quite as much as serpents do, you know."

"I don't believe it," said the Pigeon; "but if they do, why, then they're a kind of serpent: that's all I can say."

For the Pigeon, the fact that Alice is a creature with an extremely elongated neck who admits to eating eggs is enough to classify her as a serpent, an interpretation that is visually metaphoric and, in the realm of ideas, metonymic.

The following chart summarizes the differences between metaphor and metonymy, as well as their subcategories, simile and synecdoche.

Metaphor	*Metonymy*
Analogy	Association
Meta = transfer, beyond	*Meta* = transfer, beyond
phor = to bear, carry	*onoma* = name
Love is a game	Rolls Royce = wealth
Simile uses *like* or *as*	*Synecdoche* uses part for whole or whole for part
Love is *like* a game	The Pentagon (for U.S. military)
Alice looks *like* a snake	Alice eats eggs

Obviously, it is very difficult to communicate anything with precision and certainty, because signs are so open to interpretation and misinterpretation and convey their information in so many different ways.

Condensation and Displacement

To further complicate matters, we must understand something about how the mind processes signs and symbols and other visual phenomena. Think of your dreams, for instance. In your dreams, you see all kinds of fantastic things. Sometimes, you see several different things tied together in bizarre ways. You might see a train with wings or a building floating in water.

In dreams, the mind, for its own reasons, unifies disparate phenomena and creates fantastic images.

The Bible is full of dreams and visions that feature incredible images and about which there is still much controversy. Consider, for example, the famous vision of the prophet Ezekiel (Ezek. 1.1):

> And I looked, and behold, a whirlwind came out of the north, a great cloud, and a fire infolding itself, and a brightness was about it, and out of the midst thereof as the color of amber, out of the midst of the fire. Also out of the midst thereof came the likeness of four living creatures. And this was their appearance; they had the likeness of man. And every one had four faces, and every one had four wings. And their feet were straight feet; and the sole of their feet was like the sole of a calf's foot; and they sparkled like the color of burnished brass. And they had the hands of a man under their wings on their four sides . . . As for the likeness of their faces, the four had the face of a man, and the face of a lion, on the right side, and the four had the face of an ox on the left side; the four also had the face of an eagle.

The process by which we combine elements of various signs together to form a new composite sign or symbol is called **condensation.** In another important process, called **displacement,** we transfer meaning from one sign or symbol to another, so that, for example, a rifle or a plane really stands for a phallus (if you understand what is going on and know how to interpret such matters).

These terms come to us from Freud, who discusses them in his classic book, *The Interpretation of Dreams.* He uses the terms to explain how the psyche uses images to evade what he terms the *dream censor* and avoid being wakened. By condensing images or displacing content from one image to something else, we "trick" the dream censor, so to speak. In many cases, these condensations and displacements involve sexual matters. These two techniques enable us, then, to have our sexual fantasies and, by disguising them and fooling the dream censor, to avoid being wakened.

These terms are important because much of what we find in visual phenomena involves the use of these processes, and, as in dreams, much visual communication takes place at the unconscious level. And these processes also are connected to profoundly important unconscious matters in our psyches, which explains why so many visual phenomena have the emotional impact that they do. Symbols carry a great deal of emotional baggage, on both a cultural and a personal level, and have the power to evoke powerful, and often unrecognized, responses in us.

What Freud describes as phallic symbols—rifles, umbrellas, knives, and other objects similar to a phallus in shape and function—are really good examples of displacements. Our society does not allow us to show male and female genitalia in print advertisements, for example, but it is possible (and often done, many argue) to use phallic symbols that evade the censors and call to mind various aspects of our sexuality. Consider here the symbolic significance of the monument for George Washington, the father of our country, being a large phallic shaft stretching up into the sky (Figure 2.14).

Surrealistic styles, which unite all kinds of disparate phenomena, are examples of condensation in action (Figure 2.15). And the power of surrealistic styles (found often on MTV) stems from the psychological associations connected with the various signs and symbols pulled together.

As the various paintings, advertisements, and other works reproduced in this book show, we generally find signs existing in some kind of context that includes other signs and symbols. This combination of signs and symbols is what we commonly describe as an image.

I FIGURE 2.14
Washington Monument. By Arthur Asa Berger.

THE IMAGE

From our perspective, *an image is a collection of signs and symbols*—what we find when we look at a photograph, a film still, a shot of a television screen, a print advertisement, or just about anything. The word can also be used to mean a number of other things, including a mental representation we have of something, such as "the image of the businessman in nineteenth-century American literature."

I FIGURE 2.15
What is this cow doing in this man's bed? This image, taken from L'Age d'Or, is typical of surrealism's use of fantastic images and strange incongruities that imitate dreams to express the workings of the human unconscious mind. Courtesy of Museum of Modern Art, New York, Film Stills Archive.

Images generally are visual, often are mediated—carried by the mass media—and are connected to information, values, beliefs, attitudes, and ideas people have. This connection is not a natural one, remember; we have to learn to interpret many signs and symbols, which are important component elements of images. An image is a collection of signs, and each of these signs has meaning; in any image, there are many different levels of meaning and interactions between meanings.

Think of an advertisement in which a man is shown smiling and drinking a stein of frosty beer in a tavern; from his facial expression, he seems to be having a good time. In this image (which may be accompanied by words), the bubbles in the beer, the frost on the stein, the foam, and the smile all are signs meant to convey information and generate certain attitudes in the minds of viewers.

Images, of course, do not come into existence of their own volition. They are generally created and mediated—meant to be seen and read and to have a specific function and impact. Let us now consider how images relate to media, creators, audiences, and society in general. Using the focal points model discussed earlier, we can focus on images in terms of the following elements:

1. The *artists,* who create images
2. The *audience,* which receives images
3. The *work of art,* which is an image itself and might comprise a number of images
4. The *society* in which the images are found
5. The *medium,* which affects the images

A complex interaction of these five factors makes the way images work difficult to describe. The artists or creators of the images try to use signs that the audience will interpret or decode correctly; in this case, "correctly" means the way the artists want them to. The image itself is affected by the medium in which it is found, by various artistic conventions in a given medium (for example, television is often held to be a medium dependent on "close-ups" due to the small screen), and by the audience to which the image is directed. Signs and symbols such as Uncle Sam or the Republican Elephant also often have historical significance that may be recognized by some people and not by others. These signs may allude to important cultural, political, historical, and social experiences that a stranger in the society might not recognize or understand (Figure 2.16). Because of all these complications, communicating anything clearly and unambiguously is difficult. These factors also make our communications powerful and even put them beyond the control of those who create signs and symbols. It might be suggested that communication often takes place

FIGURE 2.16
Jan van Eyck, *Giovanni Arnolfini and His Bride*, 1434. Many of the symbols used in this painting were understood in van Eyck's time but are not generally recognized now. Thus, the lighted candle in the chandelier signifies Christ's presence and the ardor of the newlyweds as well; the convex mirror suggests the eye of God seeing everything and seems to reflect the painter and another witness; the dog symbolizes marital faithfulness; the bride has her hand on her stomach (and appears to be pregnant), signifying her willingness to have children; the fruit is tied to symbolism connected with the Virgin Mary; the carving in the back of the chair is of Saint Margaret, the patron saint of childbirth; and the shoes are probably an allusion to the commandment by God to Moses to take off his shoes when on sacred soil. The signature of the painting and the date are also prominent, to record this event. When looking at a painting or any image of a symbolic nature, what we know determines how fully we can understand and interpret it. Courtesy of National Gallery Publications Limited.

between the unconscious of the creators—the artists—and the unconscious of the receivers—the audience—so that the situation becomes even more mixed up. Nobody in such a situation completely understands or fully appreciates what is being communicated and what impact it is having.

Jung offers some insights into the power of symbols. As he writes in *Man and His Symbols* (1968:3–4):

> What we call a symbol is a term, a name, or even a picture that may be familiar in daily life, yet that possesses specific connotations in addition to all its conventional and obvious meaning. It implies something vague, unknown, or hidden from us. . . . Thus a word or an image is symbolic when it implies something more than its obvious and immediate meaning. It has a wider or "unconscious" aspect that is never precisely defined or fully explained.

Symbols, for Jung, are attached to unconscious elements in our psyches and are often subliminally experienced, which helps explain why they are so pervasive in our dreams and why they have the power to move people emotionally. Symbols play an important role in our religions, our politics, and many other areas of our everyday life.

One thing is certain—images do have powerful emotional effects on people. Your self-image, for example, affects the perceptions others have of you, and their perceptions, in turn, affect the image you have of yourself. It is not unusual for people to change their images over the years and create new "identities" for themselves, as they move through their life cycles and find themselves in new situations. A person might be a hippie in his twenties, wear three-piece suits and be a "buttoned-down" businessman in his forties, and become a priest or rabbi in his sixties—three major changes in identity (and "look") in one lifetime.

Images often have a historical significance. The meaning a given image has may also change over time, as a society develops and changes its views about things. Images also play an important role in religion and the arts. Think of the importance of visual elements in our religious ceremonies, in which we find people performing certain ritual activities, wearing certain costumes, using certain artifacts, and doing so in a space full of signs and symbols. The lighting is often important in such ceremonies, because it helps generate specific attitudes—such as a feeling of awe or piety or mystery.

To see how the various aspects of images work, examine the following chart, which summarizes much of the discussion made to this point.

DECODING VISUAL COMMUNICATION		
Concept	*Example*	*Method*
Icon	Photograph	Resemblance
Index	Smoke from window	Cause and effect
Symbol	Crucifix	Convention
Signifier and signified	Bowler hat = Englishness	Convention

Condensation	Face/automobile	Unification
Displacement	Rifle = penis	Substitution
Metaphor	Spiderman's costume	Analogy
Metonymy	Huge mansion = wealth	Association

STUART HALL AND REPRESENTATION

British communications scholar Stuart Hall, editor of the influential book *Representation: Cultural Representations and Signifying Practices,* points out that **culture** is now an important subject in the human sciences.

He writes in his book *Representation: Cultural Representations and Signifying Practices* (1997:2):

> What has come to be called the "cultural turn" in the social and human sciences, especially in cultural studies and the sociology of culture, has tended to emphasize the importance of *meaning* to the definition of culture. Culture, it is argued, is not so much a set of *things*—novels and paintings or TV programmes and comics—as a process, a set of *practices*. Primarily, culture is concerned with the production and exchange of meanings—the "giving and taking of meaning"—between the members of a society or group.

He adds that culture can best be understood as the creation and transmission of meanings—that is, Hall looks at culture, and especially mass mediated forms of culture, from a semiotic perspective. As he explains in *Representation* (1997:36):

> The underlying argument behind the semiotic approach is that, since all cultural objects convey meaning, and all cultural practices depend on meaning, they must make use of signs; and in so far as they do, they must work like language works, and be amenable to an analysis which basically makes use of Saussure's linguistic concepts . . . his idea of underlying codes and structures, and the arbitrary nature of the sign . . .

In his discussion of the October 9, 1988 cover of the *Sunday Times Magazine* titled "Heroes and Villains," Hall focuses on the matter of race and the way people of color are represented in the media. The image he is interested in shows the Canadian sprinter Ben Johnson winning a race, trailed by sprinters Carl Lewis and Linford Christie. The article about these athletes deals with drug-taking by athletes, and explains that Johnson was discovered to have taken drugs and was stripped of his medal.

Hall makes a distinction between what he calls the "preferred" meaning of an image, a connotative meaning of the image, and a literal or denotative meaning of the image. The literal meaning shows Johnson winning the race. The connotative meaning of the image has to do with drugs, race, and difference. The "preferred" meaning involves both heroism (a black man won the race) and villainy (he won because he took drugs). The chart that follows summarizes these distinctions:

Literal or demonstrative meaning	Johnson wins race
Connotative meaning	Johnson is black, took drugs
Preferred meaning	Blacks are heroes and villains

The important thing to recognize, Hall asserts, is that when it comes to the representation of minorities and people of color, people interpret images in terms of Saussurean oppositions: good versus bad, civilized versus primitive, repelling because different or fascinating because exotic and strange. And often, Hall adds, people interpret images in terms of both of such oppositions.

This leads Hall into a discussion of **stereotypes.** He points out we need them to help us make sense of the world but stereotypes are inherently reductionistic and oversimplify things, setting up categories that don't hold up. How, for example, does one "classify" a mixed-race golfer like Tiger woods, or President Barack Obama, who is half black and half white?. Saussure showed that we make sense of the world by seeing things in terms of opposites and noticing differences between things. But this leads to many problems.

Hall argues that it is political power that is at the root of how races and minorities are represented in the media. Because images are ambiguous, in some cases, fortunately, the stereotyped and negative representations of people of color and other minorities are not interpreted correctly, which lessens their detrimental impact. Nevertheless, the problems caused by these negative representations remain with us.

THE POWER OF IMAGES: 9/11

The images of the airplanes crashing into the World Trade Center and then of people leaping to their deaths rather than face being burned alive and of the gigantic buildings collapsing were horrendous and shocking. In many respects, these images changed the consciousness of people all over the world about the danger of global terrorism and about the nature of the world in which we live. People everywhere are united now in being possible or actual targets or victims of terrorism and it is terrorists who now occupy the attention of police agencies and military everywhere, since terrorism is now a global menace.

I was preparing to go to class early in the morning of 9/11 when I heard an announcement on the radio that a plane had crashed into the World Trade

Center. I turned on the television set and saw images of the crash. That was the day the world turned upside down. As I watched the two planes going into the building I couldn't help but think of the similarity between the planes and viruses that infect human beings entering cells in the body. The planes seemed to be tiny viruses infecting and destroying the gigantic World Trade Center.

We make sense of new things by seeing them in terms of other things that we are familiar with, so the analogy of these planes and viruses isn't too far-fetched. Many people who saw the images of the planes crashing into the buildings thought they looked like simulations or described them as being like video games or movies.

If the planes were viruses, it would suggest that terrorists might be seen as a kind of infection or disease, such as cancer, whose aim is to destroy us. The language we use to talk about terrorists has a biological thrust to it. We talk about "sleeper cells" that are waiting for the right moment to attack us, and the fight against terrorists can be seen as similar in nature to chemotherapy or surgery, meant to rid us of this disease.

Children who watched the images in news stories were often traumatized and needed therapy, just as many adults were overwhelmed by feelings of anxiety and fear. Since 9/11, there have been terrorist attacks in Spain, in London, in Bali, and in a number of other countries. The attacks in London were captured in numerous surveillance cameras, which showed images of the four plotters at various stations and also revealed the extent to which people in London (and many other places) are under continual surveillance by video cameras.

In a curious way, the faces of Islamic terrorists have come to the fore as exemplars of "otherness," replacing other people of color, both in terms of their looks and their ideas about the role of religion in society and related matters. We know now that there are people all over the world with different ideas about just about everything we take for granted, including the sanctity of human life and the rule of law. And it is through images that are shown on television and printed in newspapers and magazines that we are increasingly aware of the existence of terrorists and the danger they pose to democratic societies.

OPTICAL AND HAPTICAL WAYS OF SEEING

Another theorist whose ideas are of interest here is the art historian Alois Riegl. He suggests that there are two opposing ways of seeing things, the **optical** and the **haptical.** His ideas are explained in Claude Gandelman's *Reading Pictures, Viewing Texts* (1991:5) as follows:

> The two fundamental categories . . . are optics and haptics. Riegl stated that one type of artistic procedure, which corresponds to a certain way of looking, is based on the scanning of objects according to their outlines. This trajectory Riegl called the optical. The opposite type of vision, which

focuses on surfaces and emphasizes the value of the superficies of objects, Riegl called the haptical (from the Greek *haptein*, "to seize, grasp," or *haptikos*, "capable of touching"). On the level of artistic creation, the optical look—if the eye belongs to a painter—produces linearity and angularity, whereas haptic creativity focuses on surfaces. Using Riegl's formula, all forms of art may be grouped under the heading "outline and/or color in plane or volume." . . . The optical eye merely brushes the surface of things. The haptic, or tactile, eye penetrates in depth, finding its pleasure in texture and grain.

The following chart (to which I've added some other relevant material from Gandelman) summarizes the differences between the two categories of seeing.

Optical	*Haptical*
Surface	Depth penetration
Scans outline	Sees texture, grain
Linear	Pictorial
Metaphoric	Metonymic

Gandelman sees the optical as metaphoric because, with that kind of viewing, one scans an object and establishes relationships among elements that aren't necessarily in contact with one another. The haptical can be seen as metonymic because it tends to focus attention on selected elements of an object (its color, grain, and so on), that is, on a part of the object rather than the whole object.

Interestingly, Gandelman argues, using Riegl's theory, that we also "view" literary texts (we scan them, with our eyes jumping from one passage to another) the same way we look at paintings and that we "read" paintings and other kinds of graphic art much the way we read books. This observation explains Gandelman's title: *Reading Pictures, Viewing Texts.* Note that the term *text* is conventionally used by critics to mean a work of art—in any medium. That is why critics often talk about "reading television" or "reading films," suggesting that television programs and films can be "read" and analyzed just as poems or novels are. The key is simply knowing the "language" these texts are "written" in—which is, to a considerable degree, the subject of this book.

CONCLUSIONS

In this chapter, we examined some of the complications involved in "seeing." It is not automatic, and we don't see without doing some thinking to make sense of what we see. We see selectively, focusing our attention on sights that interest us and paying little attention to ones that don't (Figure 2.17).

❙ FIGURE 2.17

Here we see four paintings of the same thing—Daniele's Sunroom—taken from a series of twenty paintings of the room. As the artist Jason Berger has explained, "By constantly repeating the same motif, I got a sense of digging ever deeper and extracting more and more facts." Courtesy of Jason Berger.

This is necessary, because if we paid the same amount of attention to every visual stimulus, we'd never get very much done.

One thing artists do for us is show that there are a number of different ways to perceive reality, and for painters, to paint an image that interests them. They use their creativity to show these different "takes" or versions on an image, as the paintings of Jason Berger demonstrate. Berger painted twenty different versions of a friend's sunroom, using a variety of styles.

APPLICATIONS

1. Applying your knowledge of semiotics, assume you are a television director and wish to give your viewers information and elicit certain feelings without using words. What visual phenomena—that is, what images—would you show on the screen to generate the following concepts: horror, terror, secret agent, "Frenchness," love, hate, alienation? Choose some other concepts as well. Remember, also, that sometimes the combination of visual images helps generate the concept.

2. Bring any small, simple object that you think reflects your personality to class in a brown paper bag and give it to your instructor. (This is to prevent people from knowing who brought what.) Write your name on the bottom of the bag and list the attributes the object has that you expect your classmates to find. Do your classmates interpret things correctly, or do they see things that surprise you? What do you learn from this exercise?

3. Analyze a full-page color advertisement containing people and words in terms of the various signs found in it. (Remember that words are signs also.) What signs do you find? How do they work? Do you detect any codes functioning? If so, what are they, and how do they work? (You can also use some of the advertisements reprinted in this book.)

4. Write down a dream you had in as much detail as you can. Using Freud's notions of displacement and condensation, how do you analyze the dream? If you are interested in the Jungian analysis of dreams, read Jung's *Man and His Symbols* and use his concepts to analyze the same dream.

5. Look through a magazine and find examples of linguistic and visual metaphors and metonymies (and similes and synecdoches) in advertisements. What role do you think these devices play in the advertisements?

6. Take a logo for some company and, using what you've learned about visual semiotics, redesign the logo. How does your logo work, and why is it superior to the logo the company has been using?

7. Do a library research project on facial expression. What insights about facial expression did you learn? Look in a mirror and try to make your face reflect emotions such as sadness, anger, enjoyment, anxiety, fear, and boredom.

8. What impact do you think the terrible events of 9/11 had on American culture and society? Did 9/11 affect any members of your family or any people you know? Did it affect you? If the answer to any of these questions is "yes," explain how.

9. Find an image in a news report and analyze it in terms of Hall's three meanings: the literal, the connotative, and the preferred. How do images lead to the development of stereotypes and how do they reinforce these stereotypes?

KEY TERMS FOR CHAPTER 2

association
analogies
metaphor
simile
condensation

displacement
culture
stereotypes
optical
haptical

ELEMENTS OF VISUAL COMMUNICATION

BASIC ELEMENTS

We are now ready to consider some of the fundamental elements found in visual communication. We'll start with the most basic unit, the dot.

Dots

The first element in analyzing visual phenomena is the **dot,** a small circular point in space. Dots can be used to indicate lines and thus shapes (Figure 3.1). An interesting phenomenon occurs when we see three dots that are not in a straight line. As Gaetano Kanitza explains in *The Mind's Eye* (1986:82):

> When we view three dots that are equidistant from one another and are not in a straight line, the visual system spontaneously organizes the dots into a triangle. In addition the three dots appear to be connected by straight lines. These lines are called virtual, and although they are not actually seen, they are a real presence in our visual experience.

Thus, dots can be used to create virtual shapes as well as actual ones. And, of course, when we watch television, we are actually watching dots or *pixels* (picture elements), which are used to create images—much the same way that the pointillist artist Georges Seurat did.

We are now ready to move on to the next element—the line—which has been described as "a dot that went for a walk."

The fovea is a small circular pit in the center of the retina containing roughly 25,000 closely packed color-sensitive cones, each with its own nerve fiber. . . . In man, needle-threading, removal of splinters, and engraving are some of the many activities made possible by foveal vision. . . .

Surrounding the fovea is the macula, an oval, yellow body of color-sensitive cells. . . . [T]he cells are not as closely packed as they are in the fovea. Among other things man uses the macula for reading.

The man who detects movement out of the corner of his eye is seeing peripherally. Moving away from the central portion of the retina, the character and quality of vision change radically. The ability to see color diminishes as the color-sensitive cones become more scattered. . . .

—EDWARD HALL,
THE HIDDEN
DIMENSION

Dots. Dots can be combined in various ways to form lines, and these lines can be used to create shapes. By Arthur Asa Berger.

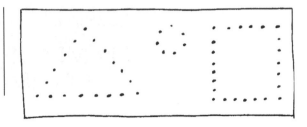

Lines

I FIGURE 3.2

The cutouts in the three circles, which look like the corners of a triangle, inevitably lead the eye to create a subjective or imaginary triangle in the mind's eye. By Arthur Asa Berger.

A succession of these dots or points in which the dots are not distinguishable forms a **line,** one of the basic elements found in visual phenomena. We use lines to indicate what things look like and what their shape is. Lines are sometimes formed on their own, but they are also formed as the edge of shapes.

Kanitza points out that "subjective contours" are formed by certain combinations of incomplete figures. Just as our visual system supplies lines between three equidistant dots, it also generates shapes. As we see in Figure 3.2, the visual system creates a "whiter-than-white" subjective triangle. This works only if we look at the figure as a whole; if we examine parts of it, the triangle disappears. Psychologists are extremely interested in the way our eyes play tricks on us and have done extensive research on optical illusions and related topics.

In a *Scientific American* article, "Geometrical Illusions," Barbara Gillam discusses how optical illusions work. She writes [reprinted in Jeremy Wolfe, ed., *The Mind's Eye: Readings from Scientific American* (1986:87)], "My own finding is that geometrical illusions depend not on apparent depth but on clues to the scale and size of objects in the visible world, clues such as linear perspective and foreshortening." What happens is that our eyes are misled and cannot deal with the cues that are found in optical illusions. She discusses three aspects of optical illusions that most researchers agree upon.

First, illusions are perceptual, not conceptual. Even if we know a figure is an illusion, we can't help but be tricked by it. Second, they are a result of our brains not being able to process the images correctly, and are not the result of our retinas not functioning adequately. Third, they are not the result of our eye movements confusing us.

When we look at actual lines in drawings and other works of art, we find that artists often develop distinctive "lines." We can see this in the work of cartoonists; some use a smooth, liquid, delicate line, while others favor a heavy, rough line. Thus, lines can have their own qualities and generate varying responses.

▌ FIGURE 3.3

Triangles, squares, and circles. These shapes are the basic elements or fundamental building blocks found in all visual communication. They are simple, elegant, and powerful. By Arthur Asa Berger.

Shapes

Lines can be generated, more or less indirectly, from shapes; but they also can create **shapes**—in outline form. According to Donis A. Dondis, in *A Primer of Visual Literacy*, there are three basic shapes: the *triangle* (an object made from three lines), the *square* (an object made from four lines of equal length at right angles to one another), and the *circle* (a figure in which all points in the circumference are equidistant from the center point) (Figure 3.3). All other shapes or figures can be thought of as being variations on these three basic shapes. Dondis suggests that these three basic shapes have their own character (1973:44):

> Each of the basic shapes has its own unique character and characteristics and to each is attached a great deal of meaning, some through association, some through arbitrary attached meaning, and some through our own psychological and physiological perceptions. The square has associated to it dullness, honesty, straightness, and workmanlike meaning; the triangle, action, conflict, tension; the circle, endlessness, warmth, protection.

Shapes, then, by themselves, have the power to generate certain feelings and responses.

In some cases, shapes are created by forming lines; but in other cases, shapes are formed as the result of other phenomena. Think, for example, of the *figure-ground* relationship—the relationship between an object and the background against which we see the object—and the famous problem it

▌ FIGURE 3.4
Figure-ground representa-tion. One can see either the faces or the vase, but not both together at the same time. By Arthur Asa Berger.

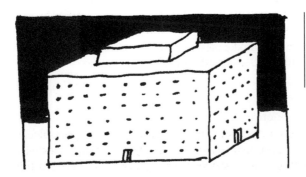

▌ FIGURE 3.5
This figure shows the importance of context in interpreting visual phe-nomena. Many images are somewhat ambiguous and depend on the con-text in which they are found for meaning. Read-ing down, the image in the center block is the number 13; reading across, it is the letter B. By Arthur Asa Berger.

presents to our minds. Figure 3.4 shows a drawing of two faces in profile *or* of a vase, depending on how we look at it. What is important to recognize is that it is impossible to see *both* the profiles and the vase at the same time. We can see either the vase or the profiles, that is, either the figure or the ground.

This figure-ground concept is important in other cases, for we often find that the ground, or context, helps determine the meaning of a figure or object, in the same way that the context in which a word is found often helps us understand how the word is meant to be understood (Figure 3.5). Thus, for example, a syringe can suggest drug abuse or medical applica-tions, depending on whether the syringe is seen in a "shooting gallery" or a hospital.

Volume

If we think of shape as a two-dimensional figure (length and width), then when we move into a third dimension—depth—we get an object, something that has *volume.* Our eyes are used to a world where objects have volume, and most of the visual phenomena we are involved with have volume—or seem to. A drawing of a building is a two-dimensional figure that tricks the eye into thinking it is seeing something in three dimensions (Figure 3.6).

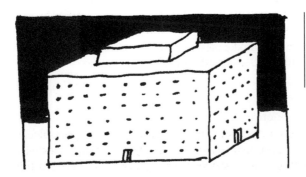

▌ FIGURE 3.6
This drawing suggests volume by adding depth to the dimensions of length and width. By Arthur Asa Berger.

ANT   HUMAN   HUMAN   MOUNTAIN

❙ FIGURE 3.7
Scale. Scale is a concept based on some kind of a comparison. Thus, a human being is gigantic relative to an ant but insignificant relative to a mountain. By Arthur Asa Berger.

Scale

Scale refers to relationships in size between shapes and objects. Unless we have a scale of reference, we cannot know how large or small something is just by seeing it. If, for example, we see a drawing of a human figure, we immediately can set the scale, because people tend to be between five and six feet tall (Figure 3.7).

Semiotics tells us, in fact, that concepts have no meaning in themselves; they make sense only because they have some relationship to some other concept (most often their opposite). In the same way, shapes and objects are indeterminate in size until placed into a relationship with some other shape or object whose size is known.

Scale carries emotional impact. The feelings we have when we are in a small room are different from those we have when we are in a gigantic space where we are "dwarfed" and seem insignificant.

One way to deal with scale is to use an optical illusion. In Figure 3.8, notice how small the center circle surround by larger circles seems in contrast to the way the same size circle looks when surrounded by smaller circles. What this shows is that context plays an important role in the way we see things and think about objects that attract our attention.

Spatiality

Our discussion of scale leads to the concept of **spatiality**, an important element in pictorial design. We have learned to associate large, open spaces with wealth and class and small, cramped spaces with the opposite; perhaps this

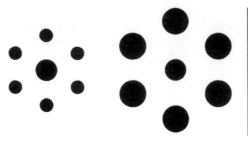

Figure A   Figure B

▌ Figure 3.8
The Ebbinghaus illusion, also known as Tichener circular. Contact plays an important role when we estimate the size of an object, as this optical illusion shows. The center circles are the same size. By Arthur Asa Berger.

association comes from the mansions and estates in which the wealthy live. Thus, the way space is used in a composition tells us something and generates specific responses. In this respect, consider the difference between an advertisement for groceries, as found in any newspaper, and an advertisement for an expensive product, as found in any upscale magazine (Figures 3.9 and 3.10). Notice how there is no white or empty space in the supermarket ad, which is crammed with lists of items and their prices. In the upscale product advertisement, on the other hand, there is a great deal of white space.

Our attitudes or feelings about what space means are quite likely based on associations and are metonymic. White space becomes associated with upper-class or upscale products and lifestyles, and so we learn to "read" the use of white space in a certain way. This reading is a coding we learn; as we

▌ Figure 3.9
Detail from a supermarket advertisement. The supermarket advertisement attempts to convey as much information about as many products as it can and thus tends to be crowded with lists. Courtesy of Safeway Stores, Inc.

Ceralene, Limoges china *Papillons*

SAN FRANCISCO • BEVERLY HILLS • DALLAS • HOUSTON

GUMP'S
SINCE 1861

I FIGURE 3.10
This advertisement from Gumps, a very upscale store based in San Francisco, has very little text. It uses a close-up of the Limoges *Papillons* china to great effect. Courtesy of Gumps, Inc.

grow up, we learn many codes that help us make sense of the advertisements and other visual phenomena to which we are exposed. We can see this in the spatiality and simplicity of the Gump's advertisement for *Papillons* china (Figure 3.10).

Balance

There are essentially two kinds of **balance**: axial and asymmetrical. With *axial*, or *formal*, balance, the elements of the composition are arranged

I FIGURE 3.11
Advertisement for See's Candies. This advertisement is very formal and uses axial balance to suggest restraint and quality. It has very little text and is organized in a symmetrical manner around imaginary vertical and horizontal axes. Used by permission of Hal Riney & Partners, San Francisco, California.

equally on both sides of imaginary axes in the composition. This design is very formal and static. With *asymmetrical,* or *informal,* balance, the situation is different; there is no desire to have balance—in fact, imbalance is deliberate, and the asymmetry generates stress, energy, and visual excitement.

We generally use the term *composition* to describe the way line, shape, volume, scale, and balance are used in a visual work, whether it be a painting or photograph or advertisement. Just as there are certain rules for writing words in the correct manner (what we call grammar and syntax), there are also rules for assembling elements in a visual work.

Figures 3.10 and 3.11 demonstrate the two approaches to balance. In Figure 3.11, notice how formal and static the advertisement with the axial balance is, how it lacks dynamics, or movement. We associate this kind of balance with antiquity, formality, sophistication, and elegance; products that desire to generate this kind of impression often use axial balance. By contrast, the Gumps advertisement in Figure 3.10 uses asymmetrical balance to suggest dynamic movement. Products that wish to convey this feeling (and this includes most products) don't, as a rule, use axial balance. If you examine the two advertisements, you will notice that they convey different impressions, in part through their use of balance.

Direction

Lines and shapes direct our eyes to move in certain directions. When we look at an image, our eyes tend to start in the upper left corner and then move around the image as we are directed by lines, shapes, and other phenomena.

Herbert Zettl uses the term *vector* for *direction* and shows how powerful vectors are in all the visual media. He defines a vector as a "force with a direction and a magnitude" (1973:386) and suggests that we must use the notion of vector fields in order to understand film and television, which present us with moving images.

In advertising, direction is often used to focus attention on certain kinds of information (textual, pictorial) that is of central importance. Our eyes are "led" to the copy and then to an image. An advertisement may exist in two dimensions and be just a moment in time; but by using vectors for directing our eyes, it is possible to give a kind of life to the advertisement, as we move throughout it. We look at different parts of it and read all kinds of different meanings into it. We do the same for paintings and photographs and most other visual phenomena.

Lighting

The kind of light we find in an image is extremely important. Our ability to see anything is a function of light; at night, as the saying goes, all cats are gray. Light can be used to direct the eyes.

And lighting shapes our perceptions of things—it shows us what things look like by illuminating shape, texture, and color and by manipulating shadows to generate certain feelings and attitudes. **Lighting** is one of the tools that artists and photographers can control and is an extremely powerful aesthetic device.

There are two basic kinds of lighting: *flat lighting,* in which the differences between light and shadow are more or less minimized, and *chiaroscuro* (kee-are-oh-skoo-ro) lighting, in which the differences between light and shadow are emphasized (Figures 3.12 and 3.13). Flat lighting reaches its extreme in hospital operating rooms, where shadows are, to the extent it is possible, eliminated. Chiaroscuro (in Italian, its two parts mean "clear" and "obscure"), with its strong lights and shadows, is associated with works of intense emotion—photographs of the dead and horror films, for instance. The following list gives the basic differences between chiaroscuro and flat lighting.

I FIGURE 3.12
Chiaroscuro lighting. This photograph has very strong
lights and darks, giving it a dramatic quality.

I FIGURE 3.13
Flat lighting. This photograph reveals more than the one
with chiaroscuro lighting but has less impact.

Flat	*Chiaroscuro*
Strong light, weak shadows	Strong lights and shadows
Rationality, knowledge	Emotion very powerful
Soap opera	Tragedy, horror film
Operating room	Graveyard

Naturally, lighting exists in all degrees of strength or intensity, depending on the purpose being served, and a given kind of lighting can be used in many different ways.

The French semiotician Roland Barthes recognized the power of lighting. In *Mythologies* (1957:15), he discusses professional wrestling and suggested, in his chapter on "The World of Wrestling," that

> the virtue of all-in wrestling is that it is the spectacle of excess. Here we find a grandiloquence which must have been that of ancient theatres.

And in fact wrestling is an open-air spectacle, for what makes the circus or the arena what they are is not the sky . . . it is the drenching and vertical quality of the flood of light. Even hidden in the most squalid Parisian halls, wrestling partakes of the nature of the great solar spectacles, Greek drama and bullfights: in both, a light without shadow generates an emotion without reserve.

What Barthes points out is that *it is the nature of the lighting that establishes, in essence, the intensity of the experience for people.* Other examples might be our association of a kind of lighting with the holy; think of cathedrals and their shafts of light.

Shadows help us gain orientation by defining space, by offering information about its contours. Shadows, which are generated by a light source falling on an object, reveal a good deal about the shape and location of objects. There are two kinds of shadows: *attached* shadows, which are on an object, and *cast* shadows, which are cast on some surface by the object. Cast shadows often reveal the shape of an object, though they can generate distortions as well.

Lighting, then, plays an important role in visual communication by directing our attention to certain things and intensifying our experiences. The fact that lighting "makes us" see and feel in a certain way must not be underestimated; it has a coercive element to it, like many other aspects of visual communication.

Lighting also can be therapeutic, and lighting therapy is often prescribed for people who suffer from midwinter depression. By exposure to simulated summer lighting conditions, relative to the time the sun rises and the amount of light people experience during a given day, these sufferers can experience relief from their symptoms.

Perspective

As strange as it might seem, what we call *linear perspective* is a relatively recent development in the arts; the ancient and early medieval painters did not know how to create the illusion of depth or of three dimensions on a two-dimensional plane, which explains why their work seems so flat—though it is often quite beautiful. Perspective was, one might say, "discovered" during the Renaissance. **Perspective** involves representing things the way they look, with parallel lines converging on some point (imaginary or real) on the horizon line via the process of psychological closure.

Psychological closure refers to the way our minds "complete" incomplete visual material that is given to us (Figure 3.14). We fill in the blanks, so to speak. We also form a *gestalt* or "whole" out of bits and pieces of information that we have—unifying them into something that is more than the sum of the parts. This process works every time we watch television, as Zettl explains (1973:137):

> The low-density (possessing relatively small amount of visual information due to the limited number of scanning lines) television picture relies quite heavily on our facility for psychological closure. Although our persistence of vision ("seeing" something for a short period after it has already been

---

VISUALIZING THE SACRED

If we take Saussure's notion that concepts have meaning by being the opposite of something else, we find that when it comes to religions we can divide the world into two opposing realms—the sacred and the profane. The sacred is all that is not profane. The great French sociologist Emile Durkheim made the same point in his book *The Elementary Forms of Religious Life*. In this book, he writes (1915/1965:52):

> All known religious beliefs, whether simple or complex, present one common characteristic: they presuppose a classification of all things, real and ideal, of which men think, of two classes or opposed groups, generally designated by two distinct terms which are translated well enough by the words *profane* and *sacred*.

The profane is our everyday world. The sacred is everything that is not profane and is signified by a number of different visual cues.

Let me offer some examples of visual phenomena connected with the sacred, recognizing that in many cases it is a combination of visual cues that communicate sacredness. I will take, for my example, a typical cathedral.

1. The spatiality of the building—a gigantic edifice with huge pillars in which the individual feels very small. Cathedrals can be described as "sacred space."

2. The dramatic lighting, as light streams in from the windows.

3. The stained glass windows, which often tell a religious narrative or show religious images.

4. The paintings and statues of religious figures from the past.

5. The relics of great religious figures.

6. The symbology, such as crosses and other religious objects, whose meaning and significance has to be learned.

7. The dress of the priests and nuns and others who are living sacred lives in the Church.

8. The illuminated manuscripts, often on display, which tell the story of the Church, its saints, their ordeals, and that kind of thing.

9. Museums in cathedrals showing religious gowns of great figures of the Church.

Cathedrals are classic examples of the way visual phenomena can suggest the sacred and intensify the experience of the sacred, but you find similar kinds of things in other religions as well, whether it is small New England churches, Buddhist temples, Jewish synagogues, or Muslim mosques. What religions do is try to suggest their singularity and unique qualities, and one way they do this is by visual means.

I FIGURE 3.14
This drawing leaves a great deal of information out, forcing viewers to rely on their eyes and previous experiences to achieve "psychological closure." By Arthur Asa Berger.

removed from our vision) helps us to perceive the scanning dot of the TV image as a complete image, we need to apply psychological closure to relate the low-information patterns on the screen into meaningful visual images.

This process, which also is at work when we look at photographs with halftones (variations in shades of gray), is automatic and not dependent on our wills or intentions.

Look at Figure 3.15. Notice how the lawn and the sky (given direction by the trees) converge on the horizon line, where we find the mansion. This is an excellent example of one-point perspective, in which our eyes are led to one point (the vanishing point) that exists on the horizon line. (There is also two-point perspective, in which we sometimes don't see the second point but can infer or imagine it from looking at the work.) This vanishing point is the focal point of Figure 3.15, and just under it, highlighted by color, we find a message in white and a Johnnie Walker sign in yellow. These two elements are outside the massive gate, which signifies power, through its size, and taste, through its delicate and beautiful ironwork.

Now examine a work that does not make use of perspective, Angelo Puccinelli's *Tobit Blessing His Son,* the work of a fourteenth-century Italian painter (Figure 3.16). Unlike modern paintings, in this painting objects distant from us are not reduced in size. This does not mean that works created before the mastery of perspective are inferior; many of these works are exquisite, but they are products of a different aesthetic system.

The placement of a horizon line generates a certain sense of spatiality (or lack of it) that has emotional consequences. The horizon line we see in the far western United States, which stretches out before us endlessly, suggests for most people an immensity and grandeur that we feel is somehow ennobling. Not being able to discern a horizon line often has the opposite effect; it can make us feel trapped and uneasy.

Proportion

Proportion involves the relationships of elements in an image or some other visual phenomenon. One of the most famous "laws" of proportion is that of Pythagoras, who is supposed to have discovered "the golden section." This law states that in a line, for example, the relationship of a small segment to a large segment should be the same as the relationship of the large segment to the entire line:

$$\underset{X}{\text{I}} \text{- - - - - - - - - - - - -} \underset{Y}{\text{I}} \text{- - - - - -} \underset{Z}{\text{I}}$$

YZ is to XY as XY is to XZ.

I FIGURE 3.16
Angelo Puccinelli, *Tobit Blessing His Son,* circa 1350–1399. This work, created before perspective had been discovered, reflects a different way of rendering reality. Samuel H. Kress Collection, Philbrook Museum of Art, Tulsa, Oklahoma.

This relationship is found all through visual phenomena—in paintings, in architecture, in advertisements—because the eye finds it naturally pleasing.

When you deal with proportion, the following factors should be considered:

Size	Large	Small
Shape	Regular	Irregular
Axis	Vertical	Horizontal
Color	Light	Dark
	Warm	Cold
	Bright	Dull

All of these factors play a role in the way we create and respond to visual images.

COLOR

Color is, it turns out, a rather complex and bewildering phenomenon. Studies by psychologists have revealed that color affects our emotions and feelings and can be used to shape people's behavior. Thus, hospitals paint

---

CHECKLIST FOR ANALYZING PRINT ADVERTISEMENTS

There is a distinction between commercials, which are broadcast on television, radio, and other electronic media, and advertisements, which are found in the various print media, such as magazines, newspapers, billboards, and posters. (On the Internet, the many static advertisements are, I would suggest, best seen as electronically disseminated print advertisements.) As a result of new technological developments, many advertisements on the Internet are dynamic and visually arresting. The following checklist focuses on print advertisements; Chapter 7 provides a checklist for analyzing television commercials.

The Mood

1. What is the general ambience of the advertisement—the mood that is created, the feelings it stimulates?

The Design

2. What is the basic design of the advertisement? Does it use axial balance, or are the fundamental units arranged in an asymmetrical manner?

3. What relationship exists between the pictorial aspects of the advertisement and the copy, or written material?

4. How is spatiality used in the advertisement? Is there lots of white (blank) space, or is the advertisement crowded—full of written and graphic material?

5. Is there a photograph used in the advertisement? If so, what kind of shot is it? What angle is it taken from? What is the lighting like? How is color used?

The Context and Content

6. If there are figures in the advertisement (people, animals), what are they like? Consider factors (to the extent that you can) such as facial expressions, hairstyles and hair color, body shape and body language, clothes, age, sex, race, ethnicity, education, occupation, relationships, and so on.

7. What does the background of the figures suggest? Where is the action taking place, and how does the background relate to this action?

---

the walls of certain rooms peach and other warm and "friendly" hues to soothe and relax people. One color researcher, Faber Birren, suggests that different personality types tend to like particular colors—active people like red, friendly people like orange, high-minded people like yellow, and fastidious people like blue-green. Birren also suggests that introverted Nordic people tend to like cool colors, like greens and blues, while extraverted Latinos tend to like warm colors, like reds and oranges.

Blonde hair has a cultural significance in the United States, where we believe that "blondes have more fun" (Figure 3.17). But the message of blonde hair is ambiguous, for blonde hair is also associated with coldness or innocence. Sociologist Charles Winick informs us, in his book *Desexualization in American Life,* that "For a substantial number of women, the attractiveness in blondeness is less an opportunity to have more fun than the communication of a withdrawal of emotion, a lack of passion." He

---

CHECKLIST FOR ANALYZING PRINT ADVERTISEMENTS

8. What is going on in the advertisement, and what significance does this action have? Assuming that the advertisement represents part of a narrative, what can we conclude about what has led to this particular moment in time? That is, what is the plot?

Signs and Symbols

9. What symbols and signs appear in the advertisement? What role do they play in stimulating positive feelings about or desire for the product or service being advertised?

Language and Typefaces

10. How is language used in the advertisement? What linguistic devices provide information or generate some hoped-for emotional response? Does the advertisement use metaphor? Metonymy? Repetition? Alliteration? Comparison and contrast? Sexual innuendo? Definitions?

11. What typefaces are used, and what messages do these typefaces convey?

Themes

12. What are the basic themes in the advertisement? What is the advertisement about? (For example, the plot may involve a man and a woman drinking, and the theme may be jealousy.)

13. What product or service is being advertised? What role does it play in American society and culture?

14. What political, economic, social, and cultural attitudes are reflected in the advertisement—such as alienation, sexism, conformity, anxiety, stereotyped thinking, generational conflict, obsession, elitism, loneliness, and so on?

15. What information do you need to make sense of the advertisement? Does it allude to certain beliefs? Is it a reflection of a certain lifestyle? Does it assume information and knowledge on the part of the person looking at the advertisement?

---

suggests that one reason Marilyn Monroe was so popular is that she didn't come across as a temptress but as an innocent and nonthreatening child.

The ambiguities we feel about blonde hair are an example of the way colors can have different cultural meanings and connotations to different groups of people. D. H. Lawrence says that in American novels blonde women tend to be portrayed as cold, unobtainable, vindictive and frigid, while darkhaired women are shown as passionate and sexually exciting.

The color black is generally associated with death in the United States. Thus, it makes sense to avoid black in hospitals and foods. Recently, soft drink companies have marketed clear sodas to suggest purity. And white, which used to stand for goodness in bread, now stands for lack of quality (and perhaps an element of sterility) and has been supplanted by darker hues, which are associated with healthfulness and naturalness.

I FIGURE 3.17
Blonde hair. Do blondes have more fun? Photo by Arthur Asa Berger.

Philosophical Speculations on Color

In his book *An Enquiry Concerning Human Understanding,* published in 1777, the great philosopher David Hume speculates about color. Hume is famous for attacking the notion of cause and effect, arguing that we never see "necessary" connections between things that happen one after another. In his book, Hume suggests that ideas ultimately result from our sense impressions—what we hear or see or feel. According to Hume (1777:17), "All our ideas or more feeble perceptions are copies of our impressions or more lively ones."

This observation led Hume to speculate on color (1777:19):

I believe it will readily be allowed that the several distinct ideas of colour, which enter by the eye, or those of sound, which are conveyed by the ear, are really different from each other; though, at the same time, resembling. Now if this be true of different colours, it must be no less so of different shades of the same colour; and each shade produces a distinct idea, independent of the rest. For if this should be denied, it is possible, by the continual gradation of shades, to run a colour insensibly into what is most remote from it; and if you will not allow any of the means to be different, you cannot, without absurdity, deny the extremes to be the same.

Hume is arguing that not only colors but shades of a particular color differ from one another. And this *must* be the case, Hume added. If it weren't, a person showing you different shades of a given color could ultimately force you to admit that quite a different color is a shade of the original color. This explains why the human eye is capable of distinguishing between an incredible number of colors and shades of colors.

The Enigma of Color

Color is an enigma. It is generated by electromagnetic waves; various wavelengths or combinations of wavelengths reflected off an object send messages to our eyes. Our eyes then interpret these wavelengths as a given color or combination of colors. If you pass a beam of sunlight through a glass prism, you will see a series of colors, called rainbow or spectral colors, that fall within the visible electromagnetic spectrum, which is between 400 and 700 nanometers.

Each color has a different wavelength and thus travels through the glass prism at a different speed: red has the longest wavelength and travels through the prism faster than blue does. The sequence is always the same: red, orange, yellow, green, blue, indigo, violet.

When we see an object that reflects back most of the light falling on it, we see it as white. When we see an object that absorbs most of the light falling on it, we see it as black. (Neither black nor white are true colors; along with gray, they are neutral or achromatic—that is, without hue or chroma.) But the process of "seeing" colors is more complicated than it seems. As Jeremy Wolfe writes in *The Mind's Eye* (1986:vii,viii):

> The first step of visual processing is to get external stimuli into the nervous system. We see "light," a narrow band of energy from the electromagnetic spectrum. At the back of the eye lies the retina, a collection of nerve cells that is, in fact, an extension of the brain. The optics of the eye form an upside-down image on the retina, and photosensitive cells convert electromagnetic energy into the electrochemical signals that are understood by the nervous system . . . The receptors in the retina give the nervous system a point-by-point assessment of the intensity of light. This input, further processed by other nerve cells in the retina, then moves down the optic nerve and into the brain. After an intermediate stop it arrives at the visual cortex, where we find cells that extract specific features of visual input. Where are there edges? What is moving? What is the size of the spot? What is the color? . . . The visual system has special mechanisms to extract information about features such as color, motion, orientation, and size. It is this information that "the mind's eye" uses to create visual perception.

Wolfe points out that he uses the term *create* deliberately, because what we see is based, it turns out, on inferences the mind makes about the world—which are based on mental input and on perceptual rules.

All of this takes place very quickly and appears to be automatic, but because seeing is based on inferences by the brain, it isn't as simple as it seems. In addition, as *The Mind's Eye* points out, other species (fish, snakes, insects) also see the world, but the world they see is quite different from ours—due, among other things, to differing eye structures.

Attributes of Color

There are a number of attributes of color that we might consider, including the following.

HUE.   Hue refers to the colors themselves (and, indirectly, their location in the color spectrum or in a color wheel). The primary hues are red, yellow, and blue, and mixing any two of them gives the secondary colors:

Red + yellow = orange

Yellow + blue = green

Red + blue = violet

Most of the colors we see are not pure hues, but combinations of several wavelengths. Color theorists often use a "hue wheel" to show colors in their rainbow order—with red at the top and blue at the bottom. This hue wheel or color wheel is made by alternating the primary and secondary colors (that is, juxtaposing the primary and secondary color triads) and adding some intermediate colors. Colors that fall opposite one another on the wheel are known as complementary colors. When these complementary colors are mixed together, they produce gray.

SATURATION.   Saturation refers to the strength, intensity, or purity of a color. Saturation is a function of the degree to which a color is not adulterated by having white or black mixed into it. (The Greek term *chroma* means "color" and is sometimes substituted for saturation.) White, gray, and black have no chroma or color saturation, and so are achromatic.

BRIGHTNESS.   Brightness involves luminance—the lightness or darkness (or tonal gradations) of an image. Brightness is related not to color itself, but to the intensity of light generated by an object. Thus, a given screen image (a still) shown on a color television set and a black-and-white television set will have the same brightness. The brightness of a color is a function of the amount of light the color reflects.

WARMTH AND COOLNESS. We describe certain colors—red, orange, and yellow—as warm and other colors—blue and green—as cool. By mixing elements of cool colors into warm, we can cool down the warm colors, and by adding elements of warm colors into cool, we can warm them up.

CONTEXTUAL RELATIONSHIPS. Colors are affected by other colors near them. A given color can be made to seem weaker or stronger, depending on the colors that are placed next to it. If a circle of bright yellow is placed in a square of gray, for instance, the yellow will look different than it would if placed in a square of bright red. In the same way that concepts derive their meaning from the context in which they are found, colored shapes have an impact based on the context in which they are found.

In his 1971 book *Interaction of Color,* Joseph Albers, a painter and color theorist, focuses on directly perceiving colors and examining their interactions. He shows, for example, that a square of gray placed on a green background appears pink and that a dark color appears light if placed on a background that is even darker. For instance, a square of light gray on a light gray background appears to be the same as a darker square of gray on a much darker background.

Albers also argues that figure and ground colors (such as a square of one color, a figure, placed in a larger square, its ground) affect each other simultaneously. In sum, with colors, as with words, as Ferdinand de Saussure points out, relationships are of crucial importance.

CONCLUSIONS

Marshall McLuhan, the Canadian communications theorist, argues that "the medium is the message." He means that a medium (such as television or radio) is more important than the content (the various programs, commercials, announcements, and so on) it carries. This position is obviously extreme, but McLuhan is correct in calling our attention to the power of the media—and, relative to our concerns, visual images—which many people tend to neglect.

As we can see from this primer in applied aesthetics, an image (such as those we see in a magazine advertisement or on our television screen) is an extremely complex phenomenon. Factors such as line, shape, dimension, lighting, design, spatiality, color, and perspective all can be looked at as conveying "messages" or being kinds of sign information that have an impact on us. Sometimes, we are aware of this impact; but sometimes, the message goes to our unconscious where, it can be argued, the message might have profound effects on us. (The "messages" we get from artists and writers often move from their unconscious to ours; they don't know the full extent of what they are doing, and we don't know the full extent of how we are

being affected.) Anyone who has ever seen an advertisement for a product
and experienced a strong desire to purchase it knows that visual phenomena
are powerful motivators. Artists, writers, and other creative people can, as
they say, "push our buttons" (Figures 3.18 and 3.19).

This chapter was written to illuminate some of the basic elements found
in visual communication; knowing about these elements might help us

understand the ways in which we can be stimulated and excited and have our buttons pushed. In the chapters to follow, you will see that these elements keep appearing and reappearing, for they are the building blocks from which all visual phenomena are constructed.

APPLICATIONS

1. Examine urban areas and malls to determine how scale is dealt with. How does scale shape our feelings in downtown "urban canyons"? How do huge malls and stores deal with scale?

2. Collect a number of images (photographs, advertisements, film stills, and the like) that have different kinds of spatiality. What generalizations can you make about spatiality and taste, class, and gender?

3. Examine lighting in different images. How do you think the lighting affects viewers? Do you notice different kinds of lighting used for different products in magazine advertisements? In different kinds of magazines?

4. When you watch television programs, focus your attention on the lighting. What generalizations can you make about the kinds of lighting used in different kinds of shows?

5. Do a research project on the psychological impact of perspective, and write a report. Why did it take so long for people to "discover" perspective? What kind of feelings do you get when you look at an early work of art that doesn't use modern perspective?

6. What do you think is the relationship between the medium and the message? What effects does a medium have on the messages it carries? Are there any cases in which a message is not affected, in significant ways, by the medium that carries it? If so, give some examples and explain why not. If you do believe that the medium affects the message, give some examples to justify your view.

7. What is your favorite color? Why? Do you think different personality types prefer different colors? If so, explain. Do you think there's a difference in the kinds of colors that people in warm and cold climates like? If so, explain.

8. Look at several packages in terms of the colors they use. What kinds of feeling do these colors generate in you? Why do you think the artists who designed these packages chose those particular colors? Redesign the package and change the colors. Explain what changes you made and why you made them.

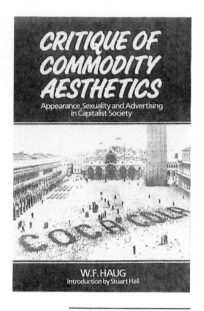

I FIGURE 3.19
The cover of this book shows pigeons being used to form the word Coca-Cola in Venice. This image preceded the Absolut advertisement and shows how images affect ones that follow after them. The Absolut advertisement is an example of intertextuality, which refers to the way earlier works influence later ones.

9. Do a research project on the psychology of color, and write a report on your discoveries. What have psychologists discovered about how colors affect us? What did you learn about yourself from this investigation?

10. Make a photographic essay on ways of suggesting "the sacred." Are there other visual images that might be used in addition to those listed in the book?

11. Color is now used in hospitals to cheer patients up. Investigate how color is used in buildings and other places to accomplish some goal. Make photographs of the way color is used in various sites and see whether the projects of your classmates reveal anything interesting about how color is used.

KEY TERMS FOR CHAPTER 3

dot	balance
line	lighting
shape	perspective
scale	proportion
spatiality	color

TYPOGRAPHY AND GRAPHIC DESIGN:
Tools of Visual Communication

Types, like all of printing, are tools in communication. Printing puts information into someone's hands, influences him to feel or think a certain way, or prompts him to take or refrain from taking a certain action. The typeface is the trigger part of that tool, so to speak, because it determines the way the message looks to the reader— pleasant, pretty, messy, painful or threatening— and this in turn affects the reader's reaction to the printed message.

–J. BEN LIEBERMAN,
TYPES
OF TYPEFACES

Every newspaper, book, and magazine we read has been designed by a graphic designer, who selects the typefaces these publications use. Every word we read reflects a choice by a typographer or designer. In a real sense, typography and graphic arts are the arts that impact most directly on the printed material we read in every medium and art form.

In his book *Typographic Communications Today*, Edward M. Gottschall writes about two competing theories of typography. As he explains (1989:11):

> Perhaps the most insistent theme in the mass of typographic design produced since the turn of the century is the tug-of-war between advocates of clarity and order in the design of printed communications and the advocates of visual vitality.
>
> Dull, look-alike pieces are not inevitable when organizing material on a grid any more than confusion and poor readability must be accepted as the price of dynamic free-form layouts.

Gottschall suggests that this tension between those typographers who stress clarity and readability and those who believe that dynamic layouts are most important really boils down to a matter of emphasis.

In truth, he adds, there's no one rule that applies to all printed communication; the secret is finding typefaces and designing typewritten material that is appropriate to what is being communicated.

In every case, the typographer must figure out how to select typefaces and how to design printed material both to communicate (that is, achieve clarity) and to be pleasing to readers or viewers (in the case of printed matter shown

❚ FIGURE 4.1
The cover of this book, which only uses typography and some simple ornaments shows that typefaces, on their own, can have a powerful aesthetic impact.

on television or in films). Typographers also must make sure that they avoid "typographic noise," which Gottschall defines as (1989: 11) "anything that reduces or interferes with comprehension of the message intended." The cover of the book on Aristotle's comedy, shown above, is a good example of typography without "typographic noise."

TYPOGRAPHY

Typography is, for our purposes, the art of selecting and arranging type or—in broader terms—using type in various graphic designs to obtain particular effects. Whenever you see any printed matter, the typefaces in which that material is set are based on someone's decision about which typefaces to use, how wide the margins should be, and so on. In the case of print advertisements, the decision is made by a specialist in type or, in some cases, by the art director in an agency.

Typefaces vary greatly—they have different looks and different meanings for people. Certain typefaces are very formal and elegant; others are casual and relaxed. Some typefaces suggest antiquity; others are very modern. The point is that, just as the size of the television screen affects television programs, so do the typefaces chosen affect how people will interpret a given message. The typeface is the medium and the words set into print are the message, to recall McLuhan's ideas. The evocative power of different typefaces is particularly important in advertising, though it also affects the way we react to books and periodicals.

Ever since Johannes Gutenberg developed movable type in 1440 and revolutionized communication by making books available to the masses (ultimately, when printing became widespread), typographers have been developing different typefaces and artists have been experimenting with graphic design.

TYPEFACES

We describe the size of type in *points* and *picas,* not inches. There are 12 points to a pica and approximately 6 picas to an inch. Thus, we talk about 10-point type or 12-point type. Then there is the matter of the design of the letters, which involves the following features:

Basic shape	Proportion of the parts
Stance (lean)	Weight or blackness
Dimensions	Contrast among parts
Size of letter	Contour or outline
Width of letter	Alignment along reading line
Quality of line	Kinds of strokes

Basic Classifications

In addition to these elements, there are many ways of classifying and describing typefaces (and there are, it is estimated, thousands of typefaces currently being used). Some of these classifications are discussed in the following sections.

TEXT VERSUS DISPLAY TYPEFACES. Text typefaces are designed to be easy to read and are used for text in books, magazines, newspapers, and other media. Display typefaces—found in titles, headings, and the like—are used to generate a graphic idea or attitude. They are very suggestive: they catch our attention and give personality to the messages they convey.

SERIF VERSUS SANS SERIF TYPEFACES. A serif is a short cross-line found at the ends of letters. Serifs originally were used in stone-cut Roman capital letters

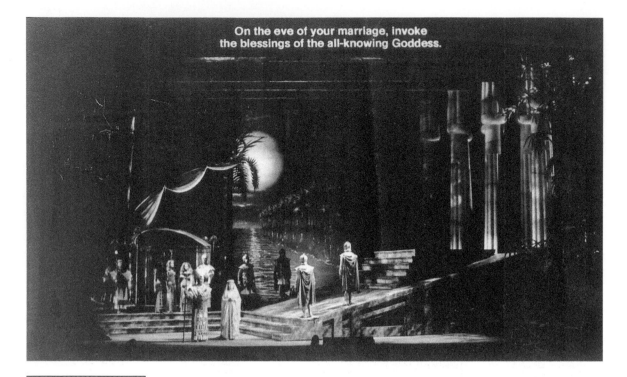

On the eve of your marriage, invoke
the blessings of the all-knowing Goddess.

❙ FIGURE 4.2

Act II of Verdi's *Aida,* "The Banks of the Nile, Outside the Temple of Isis," as seen in the San Francisco Opera's 1984 Summer Season production. Note the supertitle, in a sans serif face, on the screen at the top of the photograph. The sans serif face was used because it offers a contemporary look. These supertitles have revolutionized opera productions and made it possible for American audiences to know what is happening in operas in considerably more detail than before. Photograph by David Powers. Used with permission of San Francisco Opera.

as a means of finishing off a stroke. There are variations in the size and shape of serifs, but serif faces are a general category. Some typographers believe that serif faces are easier to read than sans serif faces because serifs help tie the letters of a word together. This book is set in 10.5/12 Berkeley, a serif typeface.

As the phrase suggests, *sans serif typefaces* lack serifs and have a cleaner, more contemporary look about them than serif typefaces. The supertitle in Figure 4.2 is an example of a sans serif typeface.

OLD ENGLISH AND ROMAN TYPEFACES. *Old English typefaces* are similar to the one used by Gutenberg in printing his Bible. He developed it out of the manuscript letter style used by medieval scribes. It is beautiful but very difficult to read for long periods of time.

Roman typefaces were developed in the fifteenth century and were modeled after the writing styles of Roman scribes. These faces developed into three classes: Old Style, with somewhat rounded serifs and little variation in line thickness; Transitional, with more open letters and rounded serifs (such as Baskerville); and Modern, with more contrast between thick and thin lines and thin, straight serifs (such as **Bodoni**). Figure 4.3 gives examples of some typefaces.

b

c

e

NEW FROM ITC

ITC Tiepolo™
Book
Book Italic
Bold
Bold Italic
Black
Black Italic

a

ITC American
Typewriter®
Light
Medium
Bold
Light Condensed
Medium Condensed
Bold Condensed

ITC Avant Garde
Gothic®
Extra Light
Extra Light Oblique
Book
Book Oblique
Medium
Medium Oblique
Demi
Demi Oblique
Bold
Bold Oblique
Book Condensed
Medium Condensed
Demi Condensed
Bold Condensed

ITC Barcelona®
Book
Book Italic
Medium
Medium Italic
Bold
Bold Italic
Heavy
Heavy Italic

ITC Bauhaus®
Light
Medium
Demi
Bold

ITC Benguiat®
Book
Book Italic
Medium
Medium Italic
Bold
Bold Italic
Book Condensed
Book Condensed Italic
Medium Condensed
Medium Condensed Italic
Bold Condensed
Bold Condensed Italic

ITC Benguiat Gothic®
Book
Book Italic
Medium
Medium Italic
Bold
Bold Italic
Heavy
Heavy Italic

ITC Berkeley Oldstyle®
Book
Book Italic
Medium
Medium Italic
Bold
Bold Italic
Black
Black Italic

b

ITC Bookman®
Light
Light Italic
Medium
Medium Italic
Demi
Demi Italic
Bold
Bold Italic

ITC Caslon No. 224®
Book
Book Italic
Medium
Medium Italic
Bold
Bold Italic
Black
Black Italic

ITC Century®
Light
Light Italic
Book
Book Italic
Bold
Bold Italic
Ultra
Ultra Italic
Light Condensed
Light Condensed Italic
Book Condensed
Book Condensed Italic
Bold Condensed
Bold Condensed Italic
Ultra Condensed
Ultra Condensed Italic

ITC Cheltenham®
Light
Light Italic
Book
Book Italic
Bold
Bold Italic
Ultra
Ultra Italic
Light Condensed
Light Condensed Italic
Book Condensed
Book Condensed Italic
Bold Condensed
Bold Condensed Italic
Ultra Condensed
Ultra Condensed Italic

ITC Clearface®
Regular
Regular Italic
Bold
Bold Italic
Heavy
Heavy Italic
Black
Black Italic

ITC Cushing®
Book
Book Italic
Medium
Medium Italic
Bold
Bold Italic
Heavy
Heavy Italic

ITC Élan™
Book
Book Italic
Medium
Medium Italic
Bold
Bold Italic
Black
Black Italic

ITC Eras®
Light
Book
Medium
Demi
Bold
Ultra

ITC Esprit™
Book
Book Italic
Medium
Medium Italic
Bold
Bold Italic
Black
Black Italic

ITC Fenice®
Light
Light Italic
Regular
Regular Italic
Bold
Bold Italic
Ultra
Ultra Italic

ITC Franklin Gothic®
Book
Book Italic
Medium
Medium Italic
Demi
Demi Italic
Heavy
Heavy Italic

Friz Quadrata
Friz Quadrata
Friz Quadrata Bold

ITC Galliard®
Roman
Roman Italic
Bold
Bold Italic
Black
Black Italic
Ultra
Ultra Italic

LIGHT, BOLD, AND ITALIC TYPEFACES. A given type family often comes in many different weights in terms of the thickness of the lines. Thus, we have bold faces, which are heavier and blacker than regular faces, and other faces that are lighter than regular faces.

I FIGURE 4.3
Examples of typefaces.
Reprinted with permission
of *U&lc, International
Journal of Typographics.*

A BRIEF GLOSSARY ON TYPE

The following list briefly defines some key typographical terms discussed in this chapter, as well as some other important terms.

Ascenders. The segment of certain lowercase letters (b, d, f, h, k, l, and t) that extends above the height of a typical lowercase letter such as e or a.

Baseline. The imaginary line at the bottom of a line of type, on which the letters seem to rest.

Descenders. The part of certain lowercase letters (g, j, p, q, and y) that descends below the baseline.

Hairlines. The thin strokes at the end of letters in serif typefaces.

Justified left. Lines of type that are flush at the left-hand margin of the page.

Justified right. Lines of type that are flush at the right-hand margin of the page.

Justified. Lines of type that are justified at both the left-hand and right-hand margins of the page.

Kerning. Adjustment of a letter so that it sets in the space of another letter.

Letterspacing. Spaces added between letters in a line to improve the look of the line.

Ligature. Two characters (and sometimes more) linked together to form a single element. Common ligatures are *fi* and *fl*.

Pica. A standard typographical measure equivalent to 12 points. This term is derived from an old printer's term for type that was 12 points.

Point. A standard typographical measure equivalent to approximately 1/72 inch. Twelve points make one pica.

Ragged. Type that has an irregular line on one or both margins. If the type is unjustified on the left, it is "ragged left"; if the type is unjustified on the right, it is "ragged right."

Sans serif. Typefaces that do not have lines crossing the main strokes or elements of a given character. Some common sans serif typefaces are **Futura** and **Helvetica**.

Serif. Typefaces that have lines crossing the main strokes of a given character. Serifs vary: they can be square or oblique, thick or thin.

Typeface family. A group of typefaces that are variations on a common design. The common variations are roman, bold, italic, condensed (the letters are narrow), and extended (the letters are broad).

Weight. The "heaviness" of a typeface. If the strokes in the letters in a typeface are thick, the typeface is "heavyweight"; if they are thin, the typeface is "lightweight."

Invented in 1501 by Aldus Manutius, italics are a slanted face, modeled after handwriting. Most typefaces have regular versions and italic ones, which are often used for emphasis. In scholarly writing, for example, we use italics to indicate the names of books and foreign words and phrases and to emphasize a word or passage in some text.

CAPITAL VERSUS LOWERCASE LETTERS. The capital (uppercase) is generally larger and taller than the lowercase letter and is used at the beginnings of sentences and for titles, proper nouns, and display purposes. It is difficult to read long passages of material set in uppercase.

Lowercase letters have a different design from capital letters and are not just smaller capital letters. Lowercase letters have ascenders and descenders that give variety and facilitate distinguishing between letters.

To see the difference between reading something entirely in capitals and reading something in capitals and lowercase type, look at the following example:

WE THE PEOPLE OF THE UNITED STATES, IN ORDER TO FORM A MORE PERFECT UNION, ESTABLISH JUSTICE, INSURE DOMESTIC TRANQUILITY, PROVIDE FOR THE COMMON DEFENCE, PROMOTE THE GENERAL WELFARE, AND SECURE THE BLESSINGS OF LIBERTY TO OURSELVES AND OUR POSTERITY, DO ORDAIN AND ESTABLISH THIS CONSTITUTION FOR THE UNITED STATES OF AMERICA.

We the People of the United States, in Order to form a more perfect Union, establish Justice, insure domestic Tranquility, provide for the common defence, promote the general Welfare, and secure the Blessings of Liberty to ourselves and our Posterity, do ordain and establish this CONSTITUTION for the United States of America.

Obviously, the second passage is much easier to read than the first passage. There is more white space around the letters in the second passage, which seems to facilitate comprehension.

Readability is not always a function of the size of the type. We can see that the passage done in capitals has larger type but is more difficult to read. Readability is connected to the way the combination of letters creates a quickly perceived word image.

POINTS. Type sizes were, at one time, identified by name, but this convention has given way to identifying them by points. (The point system was developed in France in 1737 by Pierre Simon Fournier.) A point is about 1/72 inch. Twelve points are known as a pica. When describing the size of type, we use points and thus might talk about 12-point type or 18-point type. Figure 4.4 shows examples of type size.

CONDENSED AND EXPANDED TYPEFACES. Some typefaces have very narrow letters and are known as condensed faces. These faces allow one to print more text in a given area than if one uses regular faces. There are also expanded faces, which feature very wide letters and use more space than regular faces and much more space than condensed faces.

As this brief introduction to typography suggests, typefaces play an important role in transmitting information, and the way a message is presented has a great deal of significance. Typography is a highly skilled art and

SABON

ROMAN

Excellence in typography is the result of nothing more than an attitude. Its appeal comes from the understanding used in its planning; the designer must care. In contemporary advertising the perfect integration of design elements often demands unorthodox typography. It may require the use of compact spacing, minus leading, unusual sizes and weights; whatever is needed to improve appearance and impact. Stating specific principles or guides on the subject of typography is difficult because the principle applying to
7 POINT

Excellence in typography is the result of nothing more than an attitude. Its appeal comes from the understanding used in its planning; the designer must care. In contemporary advertising the perfect integration of design elements often demands unorthodox typography. It may require the use of compact spacing, minus leading, unusual sizes
9 POINT

BOLD

Excellence in typography is the result of nothing more than an attitude. Its appeal comes from the understanding used in its planning; the designer must care. In contemporary advertising the perfect integration of design elements often demands unorthodox typography. It may require the use of compact spacing, minus leading, unusual sizes and weights; whatever is needed to improve appearance and impact. Stating specific principles or guides on the subject of typography is difficult because the principle applying to

Excellence in typography is the result of nothing more than an attitude. Its appeal comes from the understanding used in its planning; the designer must care. In contemporary advertising the perfect integration of design elements often demands unorthodox typography. It may require the use of compact spacing, minus leading, unusual sizes

ITALIC

Excellence in typography is the result of nothing more than an attitude. Its appeal comes from the understanding used in its planning; the designer must care. In contemporary advertising the perfect integration of design elements often demands unorthodox typography. It may require the use of compact spacing, minus leading, unusual sizes and weights; whatever is needed to improve appearance and impact. Stating specific principles or guides on the subject of typography is difficult because the principle applying to one job may not fit the next. No two jobs are identical
7 POINT

Excellence in typography is the result of nothing more than an attitude. Its appeal comes from the understanding used in its planning; the designer must care. In contemporary advertising the perfect integration of design elements often demands unorthodox typography. It may require the use of compact spacing, minus leading, unusual sizes
9 POINT

BOLD ITALIC

Excellence in typography is the result of nothing more than an attitude. Its appeal comes from the understanding used in its planning; the designer must care. In contemporary advertising the perfect integration of design elements often demands unorthodox typography. It may require the use of compact spacing, minus leading, unusual sizes and weights; whatever is needed to improve appearance and impact. Stating specific principles or guides on the subject of typography is difficult because the principle applying to one job may not fit the next. No

Excellence in typography is the result of nothing more than an attitude. Its appeal comes from the understanding used in its planning; the designer must care. In contemporary advertising the perfect integration of design elements often demands unorthodox typography. It may require the use of compact spacing, minus leading, unusual sizes

❚ FIGURE 4.4
Examples of typeface sizes and font variations within one type family. Not only are there many typefaces, but each typeface comes in many styles and different sizes. Reprinted with permission of *U&lc, International Journal of Typographics.*

plays an important role in shaping the way people respond to printed matter. Typographers often say that typography should be "invisible" and should not be noticed by the reader; that is, it should not call attention to itself because the purpose of printing is to produce material that is read. In such cases, it is all the more powerful.

Maximizing the Impact of Type

Let's review some of the considerations to keep in mind when laying out a print advertisement, a newsletter, or anything that has a visual/textual dimension to it.

TYPEFACE. We have already seen that the choice of typeface is important, because different typefaces have distinctive personalities. Each typeface is a means of managing impressions in the minds of readers. And the typeface must be coordinated with any drawings or photographs being used in the visual field. In the case of advertisements or other kinds of promotional literature, for example, the typefaces must fit with the product "image" that is to be created or reinforced (Figure 4.5).

CHECKLIST ON TYPOGRAPHY

The following checklist focuses on various aspects of typography to keep in mind when preparing or analyzing documents of any kind. Above all, adhere to these three basic rules: keep it simple; make things easy for the reader; and, when in doubt, throw it out.

1. Are too many typefaces used, causing clutter and distracting readers?
2. Are the lines of type too long, making them hard to read?
3. Do elements such as photographs and graphics not line up, thereby distracting readers?
4. Is the type in titles and headings too large, making pages top-heavy?
5. Is the page overcrowded with material, diminishing its emphasis and readability?
6. Is the typeface too heavy, too condensed, or too large, making it hard to read?
7. Is there insufficient contrast between the type and the background, reducing readability?
8. Is there insufficient space (or leading) between lines, making them hard to read?

TYPE SIZE. We are also affected by the size of a given typeface, because size affects the way we respond to the design of individual letters.

LEADING. The amount of white space between the lines of print is referred to as *leading*. We respond, unconsciously, to extremely minute changes in

▌FIGURE 4.5
Type not only creates words, but can be used to create an image such as this flask, which is typical of those found in scientific laboratories. American Committee for the Weitzmann Institute of Science. Used with permission.

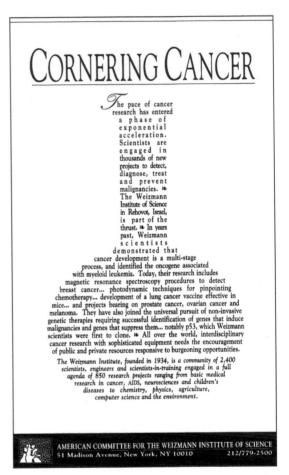

the amount of leading, because the leading can give printed material a light and open look or, conversely, a heavy, dense look (Figure 4.6).

LETTERSPACING.   Here, too, small differences have major consequences. This holds true especially for display type, where the letters are relatively large and the eye can see when letters are too close to one another, or the reverse. Experts pay great attention to these things. Although they may seem trivial, if you think of the design of an advertisement, newsletter, brochure, magazine, or other publication as a means of shaping people's perceptions, small things add up to big differences in effectiveness and impact.

MARGINS.   In recent years, the notion of having ragged-right margins (that is, margins that do not line up) has become popular. The ragged-right margin

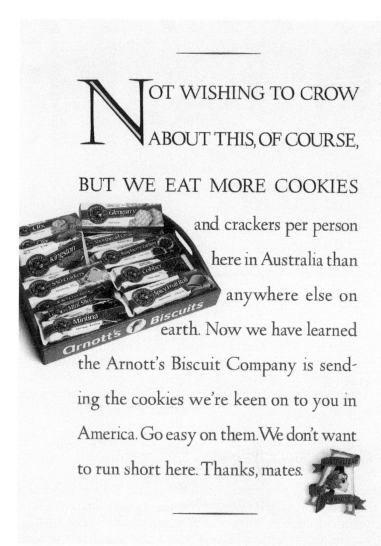

NOT WISHING TO CROW
ABOUT THIS, OF COURSE,

BUT WE EAT MORE COOKIES

and crackers per person

here in Australia than

anywhere else on

earth. Now we have learned

the Arnott's Biscuit Company is send-

ing the cookies we're keen on to you in

America. Go easy on them. We don't want

to run short here. Thanks, mates.

I FIGURE 4.6
*Arnott's Biscuits advertise-
ment. Note the amount
of leading in this adver-
tisement and the effect
this has on the image.
This advertisement was
hand-set to give it a different and more refined look
than most printed matter,
which is photoset. Used
with permission of Hal
Riney & Partners, San
Francisco, California.*

conveys a different feeling than a flush-right (or justified) margin does—it
has a less formal and, some would say, more contemporary feel to it. The size
of top and bottom margins and the way text is placed relative to photographs, drawings, or other graphic material also affects the final image.

DESIGN. This term refers to how the different elements in a visual field are
placed in relation to one another. Artists and designers have different
sensibilities (as, in the case of advertising, do clients, who sometimes affect

I FIGURE 4.7
This handsome envelope is full of beautiful stamps from Spain. Post offices in many countries nowadays prefer to print the amount of money needed for mail that is being sent abroad on a plain piece of gummed paper with a characterless dot matrix printer. But it is still possible, with a bit of effort, to purchase all kinds of attractive stamps.

the outcome), which is why a group of six art directors would each turn out different-looking advertisements, even if given the same elements to work with: a photograph and text set into type. Even something as humble as an envelope with stamps, if they are interesting and if the "image" is artfully composed, can have a very pleasing aesthetic impact (Figure 4.7).

GENERAL PRINCIPLES OF DESIGN

The material we've discussed so far has applied to visual fields in general—that is, all of the visual arts—and in this chapter to specific kinds of visual materials—advertisements, brochures, manuals, magazines, and so on. The specific topics we've mentioned can be subsumed under some more general principles of **design,** many of which have been discussed or alluded to previously. They are brought together here.

Balance

Balance refers to the way basic elements in a design relate to one another. We discussed axial or formal balance and its opposite, dynamic or informal balance, in Chapter 3. Each generates a different kind of response. In general, we must put the elements in a design into some kind of relationship that is visually effective and that accomplishes the mission of the work. Elements have different weights, depending on such things as size, shape, and color, and these weights must be tied together in some way to generate a visually functional balance.

Proportion

Here we are dealing with the size of different elements in a design. Recall from Chapter 3 that if balance involves the way elements relate to one another around imaginary vertical and horizontal axes, **proportion** involves how they relate to one another in general, relative to the size or area of the visual field being utilized—that is, the size of the advertisement, brochure, magazine, or whatever (Figure 4.8).

Let us take the example of a magazine cover. The size of the title is of some consequence. If it is too large and the typeface is too heavy (that is, out of proportion), the cover seems top-heavy and is disturbing. We all have a sense of correct proportions; when visual phenomena violate these notions or codes, we are bothered. Sometimes, of course, codes are violated on purpose, to achieve a particular effect. Tastes are continually changing when it

I FIGURE 4.8

"Thoughts" page from U&lc. The letters forming the word "DEAD" are very large in proportion to the rest of the message. This design works because the letters become a design element with a powerful aesthetic appeal. This example shows that in graphic design, all kinds of possibilities exist, and the laws of proportion, which this page violates, are extremely flexible. Reprinted with permission of U&lc, International Journal of Typographics.

comes to design, and what seems beautiful and tasteful and exciting one year can seem dull and banal a few years later.

Movement

Movement refers to the way elements in a composition lead our eyes along and force them to scan the composition for information. This movement (described by Zettl as involving what he calls "vectors") is accomplished by various means, such as line and shape and color. We know that the eye tends to favor the upper left corner in any visual field; it can then be drawn to various parts of the field by shapes and lines and other design elements.

Even when we look at a sculpture or a simple design, the eye scans in interesting ways. We tend to trace over the outline of a visual and follow lines and shapes that are presented to us by artists and designers. The fact that we seek movement and that visual phenomena can generate visual excitement and more or less "force" our eyes to move in certain directions is of considerable use not only to advertisers but also to all visual artists.

Contrast

Previously, it was suggested that concepts have no meaning in themselves but only in relation to other concepts—with opposition being the most important relationship. The same applies to visual phenomena. It is through **contrasts**—differences in size, shape, color, and so on—that elements in a visual field acquire meaning. We know, for example, that a square of red looks different with a gray background than with an orange background. The figure is affected by the ground.

In some cases, when we wish elements to stand out, we emphasize contrast and thus have something simple standing against or placed in opposition to something busy, or something dark placed against something light. Contrasts generate attention. The power of color contrasts was used by pop and op artists to generate certain effects. Very strong colors and bright color contrasts also have certain class implications or associations and thus must be used with care. For example, walls that are painted bright colors tend to be avoided by upscale people, who paint their walls off-white as a rule.

Unity

Unity refers to the way all the elements in a composition or visual field relate to one another and produce a sense of completeness and wholeness.

Related to unity is a *Gestalt effect,* a psychological and aesthetic response that is greater than the sum of its parts. In other words, the entire image may produce a response that is greater than would be produced by adding the various elements in the visual field. The opposite of unity is fragmentation, which suggests that the elements in the composition don't relate to one another, producing a sense that the work is incomplete.

In some cases, artists don't wish to generate a unified effect and so purposely use fragmentation to achieve a particular effect. *There are no absolute rules in design and composition, and the best designers and artists often violate rules.* In thinking about design, one should first consider the effect desired and then work to achieve that effect, using whatever techniques are available. So we work backward, from the desired effect to whatever can be done to generate that effect.

DESIGN EXAMPLES

Two Versions of a Page

Examine the typography and design in Figure 4.11 in terms of the following considerations.

1. The right margins for the text
2. The use of display faces
3. The size of the side margins and the location of text on the page relative to the margins
4. The margins on the top and bottom of the page
5. The lightness or heaviness of the text face
6. The size of the text face
7. The spacing between lines in the text face

The Talmud

The Talmud is a compendium of the oral law of the Jews, gathered together many hundreds of years ago and subject to the scrutiny and analysis of numerous rabbis and scholars. The typography of the Talmud is very interesting because different typefaces were used to represent the ideas of the most important commentators. On a given page of the Talmud, one might find four or five typefaces, snaking up and down the page, each reflecting an opinion on the main topic of the page, which was always printed in the largest and heaviest typeface. A typical page from the Talmud is shown in Figure 4.10.

▌FIGURE 4.9
The cover of this book shows how white space can be used to great effect. The drawing suggests how new communication technologies work on us. By Arthur Asa Berger.

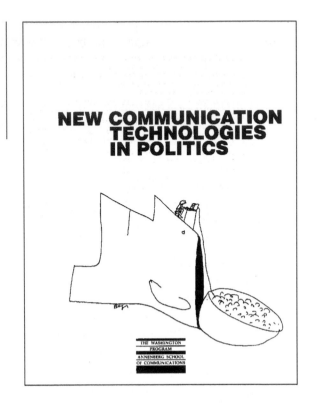

The main section is in heavy type and looks like an inverted **T**. Then, above and below it, in different typefaces, are commentaries by some of its classic interpreters. The Talmud runs to many, many volumes and is a work of extraordinary complexity and intellectual sophistication, full of astounding feats of logical deduction and brilliant insights into the human condition. It is impossible to give here more than a brief sense of what it is like or of the incredible number of interpretations of ideas and events that are to be found in it.

This use of different typefaces to suggest different views is not limited to the Talmud. The page from a business magazine shown in Figure 4.11 also employs different faces to suggest different ideas and points of view. Note also, on this page, the exaggerated size of the quotation marks and the way the typographer used ragged right for the body type and ragged left for the quoted material in the margins.

Many of the elements discussed previously, such as the use of white space, formal and informal balance, and contrast, go into the design of a book, magazine, or advertisement. There are also the aesthetic sensibilities of the audience to consider: certain designs that may appeal to "upscale" people will not appeal

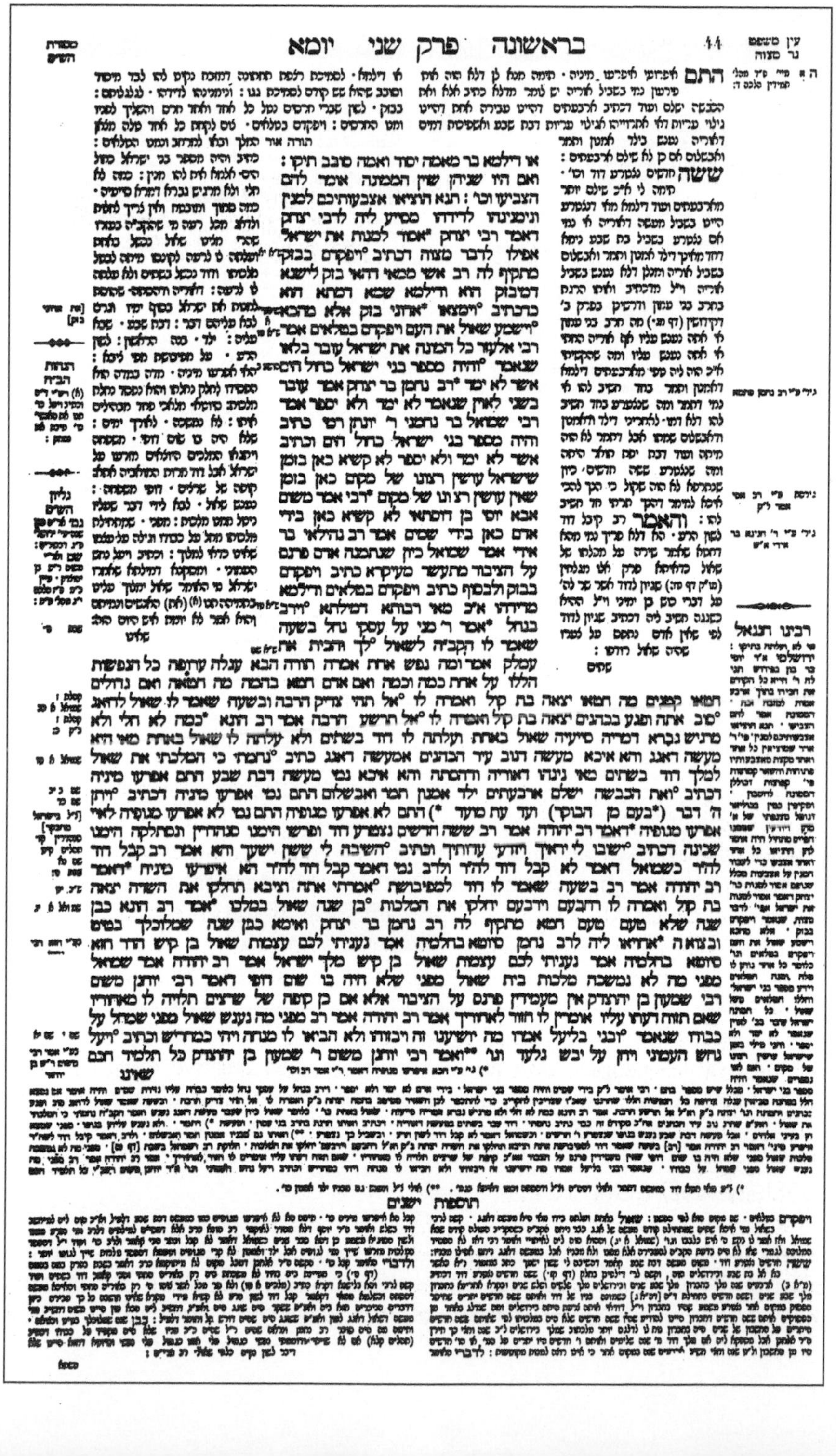
בראשונה פרק שני יומא

FIGURE 4.10
Page from the Talmud, showing different typefaces that are identified with different commentators. This shows the power of a typeface to confer an identity on someone or some institution.

❙ FIGURE 4.11

Page from *New Management*. Notice the similarity of this page and the Talmud in terms of use of different typefaces, representing different ideas on a single page. Used with permission of *New Management*.

changes its management system, we will see more powerful American competitors. 💬

Akio Morita, Chairman of Sony, put the problem most succinctly:

💬 **The problem in the United States is management. Instead of meeting the challenge of a changing world, American business today is making small, short-term adjustments by cutting costs, by turning to the government for temporary relief.Success in trade is the result of patience and meticulous preparations with a long period of marketing preparation before the rewards are available.** 💬

The key to the future lies in how our businesses are managed. Much is being studied, written, and discussed about the changes that are necessary, but too little attention is paid to the personal qualities of managerial leadership and to the dimensions missing in many of today's managers.

Missing Dimensions

While I believe in the usefulness of management science and management systems, of long-range and strategic planning, the challenges we face will not be solved by more and better systems and techniques. While there is need to continue to push the frontiers of knowledge and enhance the contributions of management science, we must not forget that much of management is still art. Effective management is a combination of knowledge and intuition, of position and personality, of environmental constraints and human will, of time and chance.

There is no single theory of management sufficient in scope to guide intelligent action; nonetheless, there are rich conceptual resources that can guide the work of management. We can identify, for example, the qualities that distinguish excellence from mediocrity in managers. The critical dimensions lie, in my judgment, in the ability to orchestrate human talent and to bring the qualitative as well as the quantitative to bear effectively on the solution of complex problems. **David Lilienthal**, founder of the Tennesee Valley Administration and former chairman of the Atomic Energy Commission, expressed the idea this way:

5

💬 **The art of management is a high form of leadership, for it seeks to combine the act—the getting something done—with the meaning behind the act.** 💬

What makes management an artistic activity? For one, effective managers are required to integrate different and conflicting theories and themes. For another, effective managers must be able to engage issues on the level of both fact and feeling, to address questions that lie in the area of overlap between science and philosophy—between the tangible and the intangible. And finally, effective managers must overcome a lack of adequate theory to assist them in integrating talent, task, values, and technology.

Viewing management as an art form does not imply any lack of regard for scientific knowledge. One cannot ignore the impressive base of scholarship in management, in decision theory, in organizational theory. But today there are too few philosophers and too many managerial mechanics—enraptured with technique, never asking questions of meaning and purpose—captives to the bottom line of quarterly earnings without a vision or set of values to guide them. There are too few statesmen. There are too many technicians clothed in power and status, but lacking in heart, mind, and spirit.

How we identify, train, and nourish individuals with the qualities for managerial leadership is the challenge faced by management practitioners and scholars. Given such leaders, our ability to address our economic future is secure. The stakes are large, and the effort imperative.

Increasingly, we must come to face the challenges confronting us with the forthrightness, intelligence, creativity and pragmatism which historically have been the hallmarks of our private enterprise system. I believe that we are beginning to engage in the kind of critical self-appraisal and analysis that can ultimately provide the necessary foundations for New Management and, ultimately, for a national renaissance. I am pleased that this new publication is dedicated to helping managers undertake these crucial changes. For if we continue this process, America can emerge from this period—reinforced and reinvigorated by the experience—with our economy, our society, and our values intact for generations to come.

"Absence of adequate tax incentives for capital investment, obsolete plant and equipment, insufficient research and development, the decline of the work ethic, poor labor relations, and problems with government all contribute to the problem. But in my judgment, management inadequacy is by far the greatest single cause."

"Much is being studied, written, and discussed about the changes that are necessary, but too little attention is paid to the personal qualities of managerial leadership and to the dimensions missing in many of today's managers."

to "downscale" people—and artists, designers, and creative directors must always make certain that what they do will be appropriate for their audience.

DESIGN AND CONTROL

The pages we have just examined reflect something that we seldom think about—namely, that design has, in a sense, the power to control people and to evoke certain responses. The size of print, the style of print, the heaviness or lightness of print, the size of margins, the arrangement of the block of type on the page—these and countless other seemingly minor matters have a profound impact on how we respond to printed matter and visual phenomena in general. When we are browsing through a magazine, do we just glance at an advertisement and then turn the page, or do we pause for a moment to examine it? And if we do pause, what do we look at first? What do we read first?

These matters are of great concern to advertisers, who spend enormous amounts of money on their campaigns. It may be true that you can't tell a book by its cover, but experience tells us you can *sell* a book by its cover.

SUPERGRAPHICS

Supergraphics reflect an interesting phenomenon: that a change in scale leads to a change in identity. Just as comic strip frames became works of art when they were blown up, painted in oils, put into a frame, and purchased by museums and art collectors, so does a word—that is, a group of letters— become an art object, so to speak, when it is enlarged into a *supergraphic*. The aesthetic components of each letter, which tend to be neglected when the letter is seen normal size, suddenly become visible.

In addition, the spaces and shapes created by huge letters are visually interesting and exciting. With supergraphics, then, we move from the printed page, where the mass of letters has an impact, to the gigantic wall, where a few letters or words and images, blown up to a great size, have an impact.

CONCLUSIONS

Some scholars believe that there are certain social, psychological, and political imperatives that flow from the development of movable type and printing. Printing, they suggest, leads to the development of a linear mode of thinking (generated by the lines of type we become used to reading) and, indirectly, to individualism and nationalism.

According to Marshall McLuhan, there are certain logical implications that stem from typography and print media. Printed media privileges the eye. Print generally comes in lines of horizontal type across a page and suggests, he argues, individualism, nationalism, logical thinking, rationality, a sense of connectedness, and detachment. Print media contrasts with electronic media, which he associates with what he describes as "all-at-onceness" and the dominance of emotions. These notions are found in his book *Understanding Media* and reflect the social, political, and economic implications that he found in each kind of medium.

McLuhan explains, in his chapter "Media Hot and Cold," that (1965:23) "the alphabet, when pushed to a high degree of abstract and visual intensity, became typography," which, in the form of the printed word, helped destroy medieval culture and economic institutions. He adds, in his chapter "The Printed Word" (1965:173–174):

> Socially, the typographic extension of man brought in nationalism, industrialism, mass markets, and universal literacy and education. . . . Print released great psychic and social energies in the Renaissance, as today in Japan or Russia, by breaking the individual out of the traditional group while providing a model of how to add individual to individual in massive agglomeration of power. . . . Perhaps the most significant of the gifts of typography to man is that of detachment and noninvolvement—the power to act without reacting.

The chart that follows shows how print media, which are "hot' media, differ from "cool" electronic media in McLuhan's thinking.

Print Media	Electronic Media
The eye	The ear
Books	Radio
Logical thinking	Emotional responses
Individualism	Community
Separation	Connection
Detachment	Involvement

When we read a book, we read individual letters, which form words and those words then form sentences. They, in turn, generate thoughts and ideas and in some cases powerful emotional responses. We read books, generally, by ourselves and not in groups, so print fosters individuality and detachment. Print also fosters logical thinking, he adds, since we learn from the books we read. We also separate ourselves from events in the world for a short while and that helps us gain perspective on things.

McLuhan offers another insight into the importance of typography in *Understanding Media*. He explains (1965:177):

> Typography has permeated every phase of the arts and sciences in the past hundred years. It would be easy to document the processes by which the principles of continuity, uniformity, and repeatability have become the basis of calculus and marketing, as of industrial production, entertainment, and science.

Books, we must recognize, are manufactured products that have to be created, distributed, and sold. So print, in the form of books like the Gutenberg Bible, also led to uniformly priced products and, ultimately, the development of modern economic systems.

We can see, then, that there are certain social, economic, psychological, and political imperatives that flow from the development of movable type and printing. This discussion is meant to alert you to the power of type and typography, which, in combination with the photographic image (in its various manifestations) and the drawn or painted image, now dominates our media and visual experience.

We need not go into such ramifications here; this brief investigation of a very complicated topic is meant to alert you to the power of type and typography, which, in combination with the photographic image (in its various manifestations) and the drawn or painted image, dominate our media and our visual experience.

APPLICATIONS

1. Duplicate four pages of text from various books. How do the different typefaces used in them generate different feelings? Consider such matters as type size, leading, weight, margin size, kind of margin (justified right or ragged right), and so on. Use this book as one of the four.

2. Write a short historical essay on a typeface that you like. Where did the typeface originate? How has it evolved? What features of the typeface appeal to you?

3. Find an example of typography that you think is particularly bad. Why is it bad?

4. Find an example of typography that you think is particularly good. Why is it good?

5. Assume a millionaire has given you a great deal of money and told you to create a new magazine. Decide on a subject matter, and choose a title. Then lay out the cover for the first issue. Using printed matter from other magazines whose style you like, dummy in a few pages to give a sense of the "look" of the magazine. What look were you striving for? Do you think you succeeded?

6. Find an image that you like, and analyze it according to the principles of design described in this chapter: balance, proportion, movement, contrast, and unity. Then do the same thing with an image that you don't like (which doesn't "work"). Why does one work but not the other?

7. Take photographs of any supergraphics in your living area, and analyze them using the criteria described in this chapter. If you were

asked to design supergraphics for the same space, what would you do differently?

8. What do you think of the notion that the linearity of print has affected society? Will electronic media change things?

9. Design a logo for yourself. Then design a business card for yourself. Experiment with using different logos and typefaces to generate different "images" of yourself.

10. Contrast the use of different typefaces, spacing, balance, and the use of white or blank space in advertisements for cars, watches, perfumes, and other similar products. What does the design of advertisements for upscale products and services suggest about the people who purchase these products and services?

KEY TERMS FOR CHAPTER 4

typography	proportion
design	contrast
balance	unity

5

PHOTOGRAPHY:
The Captured Moment

Photography is interesting because it is both a popular and an elite art. It can function simply as a record of experiences (snapshots of people in front of tourist attractions), but it can also impose an artist's vision on what is being photographed (portraits by great photographers).

THE PHOTOGRAPH

Photography was invented in 1839 by Louis Jacques Daguerre and Joseph Niépce in France and, independently, by Henry Fox Talbot in England. The Daguerre method used sensitized metal (and could not be reproduced), while the Talbot method used a paper negative process that led, eventually, to modern photography as we now know it. The American George Eastman, who founded Eastman Kodak, made further refinements that led to roll film, which was introduced in 1881 and led, ultimately, to the modern motion picture.

Film photography involves the following processes:

1. Using a camera to take a picture on light-sensitive film
2. Developing or processing this film and making a negative
3. Using this negative to make prints on light-sensitive paper

The result of this process is the film photograph, the dominant form of permanent image in the modern world, until recently.

A *photograph* can be defined as an image, in the form of a positive print, taken by a camera (a device with a lens and shutter) and reproduced,

Human visual perception is a far more complex and selective process than that by which a film records. Nevertheless the camera lens and the eye both register images—because of their sensitivity to light—at great speed and in the face of an immediate event. What the camera does and what the eye can never do, is to *fix* the appearance of that event. It removes its appearance from the flow of appearances and it preserves it. . . . The camera saves a set of appearances from the otherwise inevitable supercession of further appearances. It holds them unchanging. And before the invention of the camera nothing could do this, except, in the mind's eye, the faculty of memory.

–JOHN BERGER,
ABOUT LOOKING

permanently, on a photosensitive surface. Cameras range from cheap throw-away models to very expensive German and Japanese models with powerful lenses and many automatic features.

DIGITAL PHOTOGRAPHY

The development of **digital** photography has altered the way photographs are taken and stored. Digital cameras can store an enormous number of images on devices called storage cards, whose capacity varies depending on the type of card. The number of images a card can store also depends on the resolution of the images. It is now possible to purchase digital cameras with eight or ten megapixels (MPX) and numerous functions for around $100. These cameras can hold thousands of images on their cards at low resolutions and many hundreds of images at the highest resolutions. It is relatively easy to load the images into one's computer and send them, over the Internet—to friends or to stores or Websites that can print them out at around ten cents each. In addition, many cell phones now have cameras with high enough resolutions to take good photographs and videos. So, digital photography now has revolutionized the news industry, as videos taken by people with cell phones are often used by television stations or posted on the Internet on sites like YouTube. Anyone with a cell phone that can take photographs or make videos is now a potential photojournalist. For example, the popular Canon Powershot A85, a four megapixel (MPX) camera, can store around 250 images, at the highest resolution and degree of compression, on a 512 MB card. At the lowest resolution it can store an amazing 5,200 images. It is relatively easy to load the images into one's computer and send them over the Internet—to friends or to stores or Websites that print them out for less than it costs to print on a home printer. At many drugstores, for example, it is possible to get prints of digital images for less than twenty cents an image and on the Internet the price is as low as ten or twelve cents an image.

DIGITAL PHOTOGRAPHY AND OIL PAINTING

A California artist, Denis McNicoll, uses digital cameras and Photoshop to generate images that he uses to make oil paintings. Figure 5.1 shows a number of photographs he made of flowers. He used Photoshop to assemble the discrete images into a composition that pleased him. Then he made a painting based on the Photoshop images of the flowers. Artists often use drawings or photographs as the basis of their paintings but now, thanks to the power of digital cameras and programs such as Photoshop, artists can assemble discrete images into compositions, which they can then employ to make paintings.

(a)

(b)

❙ FIGURE 5.1
Digital photographs used
to make an oil painting.
Courtesy of Denis
McNicoll.

(c)

Digital cameras have revolutionized photography and now most of the new cameras being sold are digital cameras. They have dropped in price considerably as economies of scale enable camera makers to continue bringing out cameras with new features. There are Websites on the Internet, such as www.dpreview.com and www.dresource.com that evaluate the new digital cameras and link viewers to stores that sell the cameras being reviewed.

As a result of the capacity of these new digital cameras, and the ease with which images can be stored, people using digital cameras tend to take a large number of images because it is very easy to delete them. By using the LCD displays on digital cameras, photographers can know, instantly, what kind of picture they have taken and if they are not satisfied, they can retake shots. Many digital cameras come with an automatic setting, which means they are point-and-shoot cameras that do not demand any knowledge of technical aspects of photography; the camera sets the aperture and shutter speed automatically, for example. Even though it is easy to take photographs and owners of digital cameras take hundreds and hundreds of them, photographs still fall into a certain number of genres. It is this matter that I discuss next.

GENRES IN PHOTOGRAPHY

The term **genre,** French for "kind" or "type" or "category," is used to classify works in a given medium. We distinguish between a medium—such as print, radio, television, film, or photography—and the genres or kinds of works found in each medium. For example, television is a medium that includes (and also affects) genres such as soap operas, commercials, news shows, sports programs, talk shows, and so on. In the same light, photography is a medium that includes a number of different genres. Some of the most important genres of photographs are discussed here.

Art Photos

Works of fine art by gifted photographers who exploit the aesthetic elements of photography to their fullest (to create works that are considered "high" art) are now found in the photography collections of many museums. The great photographers traditionally worked in black and white—in part, because color photography had not been developed when some of them were doing their work. Even now, many art photographers prefer to work in black and white, though this is slowly changing. Also, new developments in digital cameras and image manipulation are having an impact on photography (Figure 5.2).

Snapshots

Photographs taken by ordinary people, typically showing their children growing up, sights seen in their travels, and special events, are a form of personal documentation (Figures 5.3, 5.4, and 5.5). (Portraits can be art photographs, but more often, they are simply formal versions of the snapshot.) Because these snapshots are taken by amateurs, the persons being shot often are somewhat stiff, and the spatiality and other design elements in the picture are not very good. When people travel, they generally photograph themselves in front of "the sights" to document that they have been there

▌FIGURE 5.2
Church of High Fidelity
from the book *Churches
ad hoc* by Herman
Krieger. This art photo has
an element of whimsy to
it. Used by permission of
Herman Krieger.

and to remind themselves, when they look at their photos or slides later, of their experiences.

If you look through travel brochures you find many iconic images, which can be defined as images of certain buildings or sites that, because they are so beautiful or striking, become identified with the countries in which they are found. The term "iconic" is now generally understood to mean an important example of something. The Taj Mahal in Agra, for example, is certainly an iconic building and one of the most famous buildings in the world. It is almost always shown in brochures about travel in India. The building was described by the poet Rabindranath Tagore as a "teardrop on the face of eternity." It was built by Emperor Shah Jahan as a memorial for his wife, Mumtaz Mahal. She died in 1631 while giving birth to their four-teenth child. The building was completed in 1653 and is a UNESCO World Heritage Site.

Iconic buildings play a large part in tourist advertising, and later on in touristic experience. That is because many tourists think about cities and countries in terms of iconic images of buildings they've seen and want to be photographed in front of these buildings, to show that they were there. The Taj Mahal, the Eiffel Tower, the Leaning Tower of Pisa, and many other

▌FIGURE 5.3
In a typical tourism photo-graph, a tourist is shown standing in front of a visually interesting site—offering proof that he or she was there. By Arthur Asa Berger.

▌FIGURE 5.4
The Taj Mahal in Agra, India. By Arthur Asa Berger.

❚ Figure 5.5

A formal portrait of President Bill Clinton. Used by permission of the White House.

❚ Figure 5.6

"Snapshot" of President Ronald Reagan. Informal portraits convey a considerably different impression of people than do formal ones, as the formal portrait of President Bill Clinton in Figure 5.5 demonstrates. Reagan is portrayed here in a natural setting, has powerful arms, is informally dressed, and has a larger-than-life quality about him. Technically, this photograph isn't really a snapshot, but rather an informal shot that gives the feeling of being a snapshot and may be seen as an example of Reagan's ability to give people "illusions" about himself. Used by permission of the White House.

buildings function as important signifiers of the cities or the countries where they are located.

THE IMAGE-FREEZING MACHINE VS. THE DEATH OF PHOTOGRAPHY

In his article "The Image-Freezing Machine" social psychologist Stanley Milgram argues that when tourists take photographs of beautiful scenery, their picture-taking interferes with their enjoyment of the scenery. He also suggests that in many cases people go to certain countries essentially because they provide a good background for their photographs. Travel, he suggests, has become transformed by photography and our assessment of our vacations is often based on the beauty of the images in the photographs we take (see Figure 5.3).

Milgram makes another point about photography—photographs don't merely "reflect" reality but also affect reality. As he writes (*Society*, November/December 1976:12):

> There is a universe of events that we smell and a universe that we hear; there is also a universe of events whose existence is embodied in photographs. Thus each year we eagerly await the official Chinese Communist May Day photograph to see who is photographed alongside the chairman and who has been displaced. The official photograph is not only a reflection of the political reality, but itself solidifies that reality and becomes an element in it. The question, therefore, is to what degree events that exist in photographs exert an effect outside the photographs. Does a photograph act back on and shape the real world?

The answer Milgram gives is "yes." Photographs, he suggests, do two things: they reflect reality and they affect reality. And this power of photographs is amplified by television, which shows us images that not only reflect reality but also often have a powerful emotional and political impact. We must remember that the images we see in photographs and other photographic media do not mirror reality but reflect someone's view of reality; there is always an element of selectivity involved, always someone deciding what to shoot and what not to shoot. What you don't see is often more important than what you do see when it comes to images of events of importance.

The development of digital photography has led to what art historian Nicholas Mirzoeff describes as the "death of photography." He writes, in his book *An Introduction to Visual Culture* (1999:88):

> After a century and a half of recording and memorializing death, photography met its own death some time in the 1980s at the hands of computer imaging. The ability to alter a photograph digitally has undone the fundamental condition of photography—that something must have been in front of the lens when the shutter was opened, even if questions remained as to the authenticity of what was recorded. It is now possible to create "photographs" of scenes that never existed without the fakery being directly observable. As in early 1982, the special effects company Lucasfilm declared that their work implied "the end of photography as evidence for anything."

We now know that photographs do not always mirror reality but can be used to create their own realities—something we are exposed to when we see many films, nowadays.

THE POWER OF LANDSCAPES

On a cruise in Antarctica's waters and on a camping trip in the middle of a desert in Egypt, I experienced the power of landscapes. The two experiences were quite opposite to each other. When cruising in Antarctic waters,

❙ FIGURE 5.7a
Antarctic seascape. By Arthur Asa Berger.

❙ FIGURE 5.7b
Egyptian desert landscape. By Arthur Asa Berger.

passengers seemed mesmerized by the frozen and empty wastes of the Antarctic landscape and the incredible beauty of the continent. Their faces reflected a kind of ecstatic wonderment as they crowded onto the decks of the cruise ship and snapped photographs as fast as they could. The same kind of blissful excitement happened on a two-day camping trip in the Egyptian desert, where the remarkable rock formations and the vastness of the desert profoundly affected everyone and also led to a kind of frenzied picture taking.

Although Antarctica was cold and the desert was hot, they were similar in that both landscapes were wildernesses—empty, quiet, and pristine, and they afforded visitors to both places an opportunity to see primeval areas that hadn't changed in countless centuries and to experience the power of landscapes. The reason, I believe, is that nature has the power to call forth in humans powerful emotions, and sites like Antarctica, the desert, gardens, beaches with yellow sand and blue skies, and picturesque villages resonate with emotions and feelings buried deep in our psyches.

Because we treasure these kinds of moments, we wish to capture them on film and video, so we can relive, to the extent that is possible, or at least remember, our experiences in such places. To say that these kinds of places are nothing but "photo opportunities" doesn't recognize the remarkable emotional impact of our experiences and the meaning that our photographs and videos have for us.

Photojournalism

In newspapers and magazines, photographs are used for their documentary and illustrative powers. These photographs show us the important events and people we read about and augment the information we get from the printed word. As Kevin G. Barnhurst points out in his 1994 book *Seeing the Newspaper,* there's a considerable amount of debate about the role of photojournalists. Some analysts focus on their role as chroniclers of reality, while others suggest there is an ideological content to their work—whose pictures they take, what angles they use, when the pictures are taken, and how they are used to "tell" a story.

Barnhurst (1994:43) discusses an exhibition of press photos held at The Museum of Modern Art in 1973 in which the curator, John Szarkowski, assigned certain "roles" to the photos:

> Seen as a whole, press pictures contain a kaleidoscope flow of particular faces within a few permanent roles. Szarkowski, with the aid of Diane Arbus, among others, selected the most "compelling" and "original" pictures, judged by their formal and iconographic contribution to the vocabulary of roles. The organization of the exhibit demonstrated a few of these roles: participants in a ceremony, the loser and the winner, victims of disaster, the bizarre, partakers in the good life, the contestant, the hero.

There is, then, a hidden structure to photojournalism—a set of roles that reveal themselves in the kinds of photographs that are taken. Presumably, these roles are the newsworthy ones in our society. Whether these roles are the most significant, as far as revealing what is going on in the social and the political realms, is another question.

Photodocumentaries

The photodocumentary is a visual form of sociology and anthropology meant to capture images of importance that social scientists and others can use to get a sense of what a group of people is like (Figures 5.8 and 5.9). We now consider it important to have a record of how people live: their homes, their clothes, the objects they have in their homes, the foods they eat, the rituals they participate in, and so on. Scholarly journals published by visual anthropologists and visual sociologists are devoted to furthering the development of these disciplines. The camera is now an extremely important element of fieldwork for anthropologists and has revolutionized the way anthropologists work. (The same could be said for the Super 8 film camera and now the video camera.)

Commercial Photography

Photographs in advertisements, packaging, record covers, posters, and bill-boards probably represent the dominant use of photography in contemporary society. The average American is exposed to huge numbers of these photographs each day.

As the result of the power of the photograph to record reality, oil painting has changed, and artists no longer focus so directly on reality. It can be argued that the photograph indirectly led to such movements as abstract expressionism and op art, genres concerned not with being realistic and imitating reality, but rather with expressing emotions and feelings through the use of color, design, and related techniques.

THE PROBLEM OF OBJECTIVITY

In an article entitled "The Elemental Fascination of Portrait Photography," the art historian Dore Ashton writes (1989:B60):

> There is a considerable body of literature verging on the philosophic concerning the photographic image. But I think it is worth pointing out that nothing serious has ever been written about photography that does not, in one way or another, concede that any photograph is only part of a truth. In the exceedingly interesting struggle to define just what photography is, most commentators have sooner or later come up against the problem of interpretation. They have discovered that the photograph, once thought to be the most faithful of representations of reality, is just as dependent on conventions of seeing and epochal conditioning as is the non-mechanical work of art.

Variables in Photography

A photographer must make many decisions when doing a portrait. These variables show how complicated photography is and why we no longer can view photographs as merely a record of reality.

1. *The viewpoint.* How close should the photographer be? How much background should be included in the shot? Where will the photograph be taken?
2. *Framing.* Will the composition be balanced or unbalanced? What composition elements will be included in the photograph?
3. *The angle.* Should the photograph be taken from above, from below, from the side, or from straight on?

4. *Lighting.* How will the subject be lighted? What light effects will be used? Should the lighting be flat or chiaroscuro?

5. *Focus.* How sharply will the photograph be focused? Should some elements of the photo be blurred or in soft focus?

6. *The pose.* What should the person being photographed be doing? Will any props be used? What facial expression should the subject adopt?

Consider the difference between the poses in Figures 5.10 and 5.11. The mug shot is designed for a practical purpose, but the portrait is meant to reflect something about the person being photographed. Consider also the impact of an acrobatic and seemingly gravity-defying pose such as Buster Keaton's in Figure 5.11.

Because there are so many variables in photography—in terms of camera angles, use of light and dark, texture, and focus—we must recognize that a picture is always an *interpretation* of reality, not reality itself. A dozen photographers taking pictures of the same scene would come up with a dozen different views of it. The photographs would be similar as far as the subject matter is concerned but different as far as the actual photographs are concerned. Photography, though it is a mechanical process, does not automatically reproduce reality.

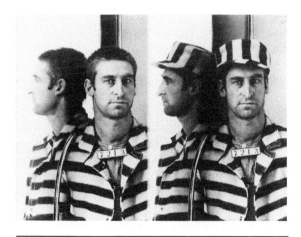

I FIGURE 5.10

Mugshot No. 7213. The purpose of a mug shot is purely practical—to shoot what a person looks like as clearly as possible. Courtesy of the Museum of Modern Art, New York, Film Stills Archive.

I FIGURE 5.11

What is it about this film still of the famous film comedian Buster Keaton that is so intriguing? His striking, maybe even acrobatic, pose? His deadpan facial expression? His body language? Something else? This photo leads us to consider how it is that photographers are able to capture our attention and affect our emotions. Courtesy of the Museum of Modern Art, New York, Film Stills Archive.

❙ FIGURE 5.12
Portrait of Alaina Albertson. Notice the expressiveness of this woman's smile, her alluring pose, and the way her gaze focuses on the viewer. Used by permission of the San Francisco Ballet.

Evidence and Glamorization

In a mug shot, photography is used to record a person's likeness in as simple and uncomplicated a manner as possible. In the portrait, photography is used to capture the essence of someone's personality and character—one might sometimes say to "glamorize" the person. These two poles—*evidence* and *glamorization*—are the extremes between which photography operates.

In Figure 5.12, a beautiful young woman (who happens to be a ballerina) is shown smiling and, from her pose, looking right at us. She is tousling her hair, a nonverbal form of communication that has erotic implications. Her face is expressive and radiant, and the pupils of her eyes are slightly dilated (or enlarged), a sign generally held to be an unconscious indicator of sexual interest and excitement.

Desire can also be evoked by making allusion to certain scenes or stories or individuals that are part of our collective frame of reference and signify romance, love, and related matters: Cleopatra, Romeo and Juliet, Helen of Troy, Marilyn Monroe—the list is endless. As Tony Schwartz (1974:24–25) writes in *The Responsive Chord:*

> The critical task is to design our package of stimuli so that it resonates with information already stored with the individual and thereby induces the desired learning or behavioral effect. Resonance takes place when the stimuli

put into our communication evoke meaning in a listener or viewer. That which we put into the communication has no meaning in itself. The meaning of our communication is what a listener or viewer gets out of his experience with the communicator's stimulus.

In other words, the photographs we see every day are stimuli that "activate" us by setting off the appropriate responsive chord. These photographs (and advertising in general) exploit what is already in our heads, the cultural lore we have stored up as a result of our education and experiences.

Connected with this desire is a latent dissatisfaction with ourselves the way we are, as well as our hopes for a better self in the future (when we have purchased whatever product or service is being advertised). And so we live our lives, suspended in a sense, between the mug shot of everyday reality and the portrait and the life of glamor and romance that it promises us.

The Pose: Figure and Ground

Some photographs are taken randomly, as a shot suggests itself in the course of a given day or experience. But others—in particular, the portrait—are posed. We all like to think that we can "read" personality or character just by looking at a person's face, as if that face recorded or stored up, in some magical way, that person's experiences. Although we may often be able to do this to a degree, in many cases poses are a representation not of character, but of personality. The term *personality* comes from the word *persona,* which means "mask." Our personalities are masks that we present to the world, and the photograph may be capturing this mask and not our "real" selves.

How do we read a photograph for personality or character? (Or should we ask, "How do we misread a photograph?") First, background helps define the person in a portrait. Lawyers are frequently portrayed in their libraries, with rows and rows of law books behind them, suggesting the knowledge (and with knowledge, power) that this person has. We find portraits of poor people in their shacks, with only the barest of furniture or possessions; this ground helps define the figures. So the ground helps define the figure, just as the figure helps define the ground. This background and the objects in it provide us with information that helps us gain an understanding of the person being portrayed.

Second, the person's appearance influences our interpretations. We all have notions about what having blonde hair or a weak chin or being gap-toothed or very thin or fat or short or tall signifies. "Conventional wisdom" tells us what facial features and body shapes mean, and we apply this "wisdom" (which, of course, is often wrong) to the people we see in portraits. Facial expression is another way of conveying information—through such things as a smile, a frown, a look of puzzlement, or stoic resignation.

We all can empathize with others because we reveal different emotions via our facial expressions.

Third, body language helps us read photographs. We are now aware that a whole world of nonverbal communication exists and that we are always communicating, whether we say a word or not. Thus, body language generates messages that we all can interpret. In addition to facial expression and body language, people use various props (in the theatrical sense of the term) to generate impressions. Some of the most important props include the following:

1. *Hairstyle.* Crewcuts, punk, long hair, the "Ollie North" look—all convey information about a person. With women, long, straight hair conveys a different impression than does short, curly hair. And as time progresses and hairstyles become popular or fade, we read people via hairstyles, which suggest that someone is "with it" or "square." In their book, *Reading People,* Jo-Ellan Dimitrius and Mark Mazzarella discuss the meaning of radical hair cuts, colors and styles and say they suggest (1999:55):

   Nonconformity

   Rebelliousness

   An adventurous nature

   An unconventional job and lifestyle

   A desire to appeal to a particular peer group

   Trendiness

   Disregard for personal appearance

   A need to be different and noticed

   Cultural influence (age, race, social group).

   We can find many different meanings in these hairstyles; young people tend to be more experimental with their hair. The book is full of lists of ways to interpret other phenomena associated with creating an identity, such as body language and fashion.

2. *Eyeglasses.* The style of eyeglasses tells us about the taste or lifestyle of the person wearing them. Now that contact lenses are so popular, a person who chooses to wear eyeglasses might be trying to create a certain impression.

3. *Fashion.* We have learned in recent years that fashion provides information and that there are various ways one dresses for "power." Think of the difference between a dark, pin-striped three-piece suit and jeans and a T-shirt.

4. *Jewelry.* The kind of jewelry one wears is a means of impression management. What does it mean when men wear earrings? What if a woman wears many pairs of earrings? Think about class rings and wedding rings. Jewelry or its lack is an important prop.

5. *Makeup.* A woman with a great deal of makeup seems to be quite different from a woman with no makeup at all (the "natural" look). Long, polished nails convey a certain image—associated with glamor—in our minds.

6. *Briefcases, attaché cases, bags, and so on.* These objects also generate impressions and are used by people for the purpose of impression management.

When we look at a photograph of a person or a group of people, we must decipher a great deal of visual detail if we are to get the full meaning of the photograph (Figure 5.13). We use our faces, our bodies, our clothes, and objects to create certain impressions in other people. To read photographs correctly requires background information or what might be called "consumer cultural literacy." If you do not recognize, for example, that a briefcase has the logo of an expensive Italian fashion house, you've missed something its owner wanted to convey.

I FIGURE 5.13
This long shot from the film *Citizen Kane* achieves its dramatic quality by framing the figure in the door against a background of light. The image also is enhanced by the decorative nature and the huge size of the room. Courtesy of the Museum of Modern Art, New York, Film Stills Archive.

TECHNICAL ASPECTS OF THE PHOTOGRAPH

A number of different technical matters should be considered when taking a photograph. We'll start our discussion of these with the most important—focus.

Focus

Focus refers to the clarity of an image or part of an image. We use the term **depth of field** to refer to objects in focus in an image. This depth of field varies, depending on the kind of lens we use in the camera. We get greater depth of field with wide-angle lenses than with narrow-angle lenses. We can use focus to emphasize certain things and deemphasize others or to generate certain impressions. Thus, a soft focus is associated with romantic and related emotional states and is often used in cosmetic advertisements, which sell magic and fantasy. By contrast, very sharp and clear focus is connected with science and pure rationality.

Grain

The term **grain** refers to the prominence of the minute dots that make up a photograph. Grainy photographs are associated with snapshots and photographs taken by chance or in difficult situations. Thus, we associate grain with realism and honesty. We do not use grainy photographs as a rule; and so when they are used, it suggests that something unusual has transpired or is being communicated.

Shot Angle

Angle refers to where the camera is relative to the subject of the photograph. A shot that "looks up" to the subject conveys a different impression (such as reverence?) than one that "looks down" on (and is superior to?) the subject. When we photograph people, the **shot angle** is quite important. A full-face shot conveys a different impression than does a three-quarter-face shot or a profile.

With the full-face shot, we find that the person being photographed is, in a sense, looking us directly in the eyes; and thus, this pose suggests honesty and candor. The three-quarter-face shot has been interpreted by Roland Barthes to suggest a person of vision, who is looking beyond us to the future. The person in the profile shot becomes an object of scrutiny, someone looked at. We find this angle in mug shots and in certain portraits, where a person's profile strikes the photographer as the best way to portray the subject.

Kinds of Shots

Here we are concerned with how far the camera is from the subject. The following list presents some of the most important shots, assuming that we are photographing a person, though we could be photographing an object or a building or a general landscape:

1. *The extreme close-up.* This might portray only part of a person's face.
2. *The close-up.* This generally would include the face but not much else of a person.
3. *The medium shot.* This would show the face and part of the torso.
4. *The long shot.* This would include the entire body and some of the surroundings.
5. *The extreme long shot.* Here the figure would be relatively small, with much of the surroundings shown. This shot functions as an establishing shot and suggests the context in which a given person or group of persons is to be found.

Each of these shots has a particular function and conveys a certain kind of message. The extreme close-up is very personal and intimate and is meant to give us insights into the personality of the person being photographed. As we move away from the camera in a perpendicular line (known as the *Z-axis*), we become less involved with personality and more involved with background or context. Close-up, medium, and long shots of a building are shown in Figures 5.14, 5.15, and 5.16, respectively.

Color

Photographers can use different kinds of coated lenses to manipulate color. They can deepen or emphasize certain colors and minimize others. Thus, color is one more variable that photographers can play with to create the effects they wish—such as making food in photographs look so mouthwateringly good.

Composition

When photographers print their negatives, they have an additional opportunity to manipulate images. They can create a **composition** that pleases them

❙ FIGURE 5.15
Medium shot of the White House. In this shot, we see the
entire White House but nothing else. Used by permission
of the White House.

❙ FIGURE 5.14
Close-up of the White House. Here we see just a portion of
the White House. Used by permission of the White House.

❙ FIGURE 5.16
Long shot of the White House. Here we see the fountains
in front of the White House and a bit of the environs. We
are considerably farther away from the White House than
we were in the medium shot. Used by permission of the
White House.

by selecting only a certain portion of the negative to use, a process known as
cropping. A given negative can yield any number of different photographs,
depending on the aesthetic interests of the photographer.

By playing with focus and depth of field, shot angles, kinds of shots,
grain, color, and composition, photographers are able to create many different effects and generate many different meanings in a given situation.
Photography is not a reflection or an imitation of reality, but an interpretation of reality. Therefore, seeing isn't always believing, because photographs
only reveal, ultimately, what photographers want their photographs to
reveal.

With developments in computer imaging, photographs can now be
manipulated in remarkable ways, and changes made to them cannot be

detected by the human eye. As a result, photographs no longer can be thought of as evidence, because with computers almost anything is possible. Again, seeing is not believing, and what you get is not always what someone saw.

As has been suggested earlier, what we see is, to a great degree, affected by what we know—the degree of cultural literacy we have and the extent to which we can understand allusions and references to things, can evaluate the socioeconomic significance of props and objects, and are in tune with the same codes as the photographer (or, in the case of advertisements, the copywriter and art director responsible for a given advertisement).

ADVERTISING PHOTOGRAPHY AND OIL PAINTING

In *Ways of Seeing,* the English art critic John Berger points out that many of the devices found in advertising photography come from oil painting. He writes (1972:138):

> Compare the images of publicity [the English term for advertising] and paintings in this book, or take a picture magazine, or walk down a smart shopping street looking at the window displays, and then turn over the pages of an illustrated museum catalogue, and notice how similarly messages are conveyed by the two media. A systematic study needs to be made of this. Here we can do no more than indicate a few areas where the similarity of the devices and aims is particularly striking.

A partial list of the items mentioned by Berger (1972:138) follows. Notice the degree to which information *in the mind of the observer* is crucial to interpreting these images correctly:

> The gestures of models (mannequins) and mythological figures. The romantic use of nature (leaves, trees, water) to create a place where innocence can be refound.
>
> The exotic and nostalgic attraction of the Mediterranean.
>
> The poses taken up to denote stereotypes of women: serene mother (madonna), free-wheeling secretary (actress, king's mistress), perfect hostess (spectator-owner's wife), sex-object (Venus, nymph surprised), etc. [Figure 5.17]
>
> The special sexual emphasis given to women's legs.
>
> The materials particularly used to indicate luxury: engraved metal, furs, polished leather, etc.
>
> The gestures and embraces of lovers, arranged frontally for the benefit of the spectator.
>
> The physical stance of men conveying wealth and virility.

┃ FIGURE 5.17
This 1976 painting, *Mary,* is by Marilyn Powers. How would you characterize Powers' style? Do any of John Berger's stereotypes apply to *Mary?* Courtesy of Marilyn Powers.

All of these images come from the world of oil painting, which had the mission (before the development of photography) of celebrating private property and suggesting, as Berger puts it, that "you are what you have." This task has now been taken over by photography and, through the institution of advertising (a $200-billion industry in America), is spread to the masses.

What advertising does, Berger suggests, is make us marginally dissatisfied with our lot so that we pin our hopes on a better future, obtainable through purchasing products and services that will enhance our sense of well-being. For the working classes, advertising promises (1972:145) "a personal transformation through the function of the product it is selling (Cinderella); middle-class publicity promises a transformation of relationships through a general atmosphere created by an ensemble of products (The Enchanted Palace)." These implied promises are tied to the power of the image to create desire as well as to generate a certain amount of anxiety, and the two are linked together. Wherever we find desire, we also find anxiety.

THE IMAGE AND CAPITALISM

We can push this analysis of the image and society up one rung on the ladder of abstraction by examining the ideas of Susan Sontag. She suggests in *On Photography* that capitalist societies need photographic images (1973: 178,179):

> A capitalist society requires a culture based on images. It needs to furnish vast amounts of entertainment in order to stimulate buying and anesthetize the injuries of class, race, and sex. And it needs to gather unlimited amounts of information, the better to exploit natural resources, increase productivity, keep order, make war, give jobs to bureaucrats. The camera's twin capacities, to subjectivize reality and to objectify it, ideally serve these needs and strengthen them. Cameras define reality in the two ways essential to the workings of an advanced industrial society: as a spectacle (for masses) and as an object of surveillance (for rulers). The production of images also furnishes a ruling ideology. Social change is replaced by a change in images. The freedom to consume a plurality of images and goods is equated with freedom itself. The narrowing of free political choice to free economic consumption requires the unlimited production and consumption of images.

From Sontag's perspective, the photographic image has rather ominous and sinister dimensions. Whether her analysis is correct is a matter for debate; but she does point out the power and usefulness of the photographic image and the complex role these images play in modern societies.

It is estimated that the average person in London is photographed on video cameras three hundred times each day. These cameras are placed throughout London to help the police fight terrorists, but they also enable the police to document the activities of ordinary citizens in considerable detail. It can be argued that Londoners have lost their privacy as a result of these cameras.

Susan Sontag's notion that visual images, especially those found in advertising, play an important role in capitalist societies, is also made by Marita Sturken and Lisa Cartwright in their book *Practices of Looking: An Introduction to Visual Culture*. They write, in their chapter "Consumer Culture and the Manufacturing of Desire" (2001:189):

> Images are not free. Visual images play a primary role in the commerce of contemporary society. For instance, works of art are considered to have financial worth and fuel the commerce of the art market, and news images are bought and sold because of their value in depicting current and historical events. Images also have a primary role in the functioning of commerce through advertisements. This means that images are a central aspect of commodity culture and of consumer societies dependent upon the constant production and consumption of goods in order to function. Such advertising images are central to the construction of cultural ideas about

lifestyle, self-image, self-improvement, and glamour. Advertising often presents an image of things to be desired, people to be envied, and life as it "should be."

Visual images plan an important role in the creation of print advertisements and televised commercials that are so ubiquitous in capitalist societies and in the critiques that Marxists and others make of capitalist consumer societies. Their notion about the role of advertising in generating envy and desire calls to mind the discussion, earlier in *Seeing is Believing,* of René Girard's theory of mimetic desire.

THE PHOTOGRAPH AND NARCISSISM

The photograph is used as a record of our existence and that of our loved ones. Thus, when we have young children, we take many pictures of them as they develop. We also take pictures of ourselves on trips as proof, so to speak, that we actually made the trip and as a way of indirectly indicating that we exist and are participating in history. This explains why we often take snapshots of our loved ones (or induce others to take pictures of us and our loved ones) in front of hotels, statues, palaces, churches, temples, and other sites of significance.

There is also an *autoerotic* element to the photographs we take of ourselves. If modern societies subject us to the stresses John Berger and Susan Sontag write about, there is some measure of consolation in retreating into ourselves, into what might be described as an imagistic form of narcissism. Like Narcissus, the mythological figure who fell in love with his own reflection, our photographs do have a powerful self-referential eroticism about them. We may not go as far as Narcissus, but we do have strong feelings about our image, as presented to us by photographs.

That might explain why we complain so often about photographs taken of us that they "don't look like" us, aren't flattering, or don't do justice to us. One reason for this stems from the difference between the idealized image of ourselves that we "see" in the mirror and the harsh reality of the photograph. It is, of course, possible to have a photograph that really doesn't look like oneself; this happens from time to time.

And some photographs are terribly unflattering, due to the lighting or camera angle and that kind of thing. But more often than not, it is not the photograph that lies to us, but we who lie to ourselves. Or we lie to others by using photographs of ourselves that were taken many years back. It is quite natural to wish to present ourselves to others in the best possible light, which—in the instance of a portrait—often means (ironically) the least possible light.

Many people have an oversimplified notion of what narcissism is. There's more to narcissism than self-absorption. In Charles Brenner's book,

An Elementary Textbook of Psychoanalysis, we find a discussion of narcissism in a chapter on the psychic apparatus. Brenner writes (1974:98):

> In psychoanalytic literature the term "object" is used to designate persons or things of the external environment which are psychologically significant to one's psychic life, whether such things are animate or lifeless.

This leads to a discussion of the self-directed libido (it can be defined as sexual drives) which Freud designated as narcissism. He based the term on the Greek legend of Narcissus, who fell in love with himself and perished, looking at his reflection in a stream. Narcissism can be defined as a disproportionate concern with oneself and one's image. In the realm of consumer cultures, narcissism signifies a desire for the good things of life and, as is often the case, an obsessive desire for things that can be purchased, leading sometimes to fixations on specific products.

But, as psychologists explain, we all need an element of narcissism in order to develop adequate self-esteem and to accomplish things in our lives. It has been argued that many of our greatest creative artists, dancers, and musicians are narcissists. They have succeeded by channeling their narcissism in constructive ways.

Many manifestations of narcissism can be connected with images of one kind or another, and particularly with photographs, with which we faithfully record the trips we've taken, the way our children look, and many other things connected with our existence. The photograph is used . . .

CONCLUSIONS

There is a paradoxical aspect to the photographic image. It promises us truth but all too often is used to subvert and distort the truth. Pictures may not lie, but liars (that is, those who manipulate the truth with their images) take pictures—so we find ourselves necessarily ambivalent about the images that photography brings us. As Kiku Adatto points out in *Picture Perfect: The Art and Artifice of Public Image Making* (1993:23):

> Over a century and a half after its invention, the promise and the paradox of photography are with us still. From video cameras mounted on Air Force jets, we record smart bombs descending upon their targets in the Persian Gulf and watch a war on television. At the same time, suspicious of pose, we wonder whether, for all the satellite hookups and video wizardry, we are really witnessing the truth of the war.
>
> The modern revolution in the technology of picture-making has extended the potential of the camera for authentic documentation, but also has created the potential for the image to subvert reality on an unprecedented scale. We have played out the paradox of the artifice of imagery to a

degree unimaginable to those who called the camera the "pencil of nature." They aspired to the "perfect picture," and judged the image by its fit with the world. In our image-conscious culture, we have reversed the words. We seek moments or events that are "picture perfect," and judge the world for its fitness as an image.

We see this reversal Adatto writes about in the selection of photographs used in newspapers and magazines and, most particularly, in the stories covered by television news. It is now the images, more than anything else, that determine what stories will be carried ("If it bleeds, it leads").

It turns out that much of the film footage we saw of the "smart bombs" did not tell us the whole truth. In fact, according to a government study, they were no more effective than ordinary weapons—though they were enormously more expensive. We saw only the successes of these smart weapons, not their many failures.

The photograph is, then, an extremely enigmatic and complicated item. It has enormous power, which means that we must always consider the ethics involved in taking photographs and using them. We use the photographic image in numerous ways, and photographic images pervade our modern society—making it what it is and, some would say, giving us images of ourselves that shape our sense of identity and our sociopolitical order.

Certain people (often in what we describe as nonliterate cultures) believe that if you have an image of a person, you have some kind of occult power over that person. We may laugh at such "superstitions," but if we consider the power of the photographic image more closely, these notions may not be so wrong. In the beginning was the word; shortly after that came the image; and when we put the two together, all kinds of remarkable things started to happen.

APPLICATIONS

1. Do you consider photography to be a fine art? If so, why? If not, why not?

2. What do you think is the difference between a snapshot and a photograph?

3. If you have access to photographs taken of you when you were growing up, examine them. What might they tell you about yourself and your family?

4. People frequently claim that photographs taken of them don't really look like them. Do you think this is correct? If so, how do you explain it? If not, why not?

5. Why is it that photographs have the power to evoke strong emotional responses in people? How would you explain this?

6. It has been suggested that photographs are very useful documents for people who want to find out about a culture. How can we use photographs this way? What do we look for? Find some photographs that you think have cultural significance and analyze them. What do you find?

7. Do you think a photograph can capture the essence of a person or merely the image of a person? Explain your position and justify your answer.

8. To what degree does what we know and bring to a photograph affect the way we respond to and interpret the photograph? If you had never heard of the Holocaust and were shown pictures of people in the concentration camps, would the pictures have the same impact? Explain your answer.

9. Pretend you are a tourist and take a series of photographs that a tourist would take in your hometown or some area near you. Now pretend you are a visual anthropologist and take another series of photographs that an anthropologist would take in the same place. What differences do you find in the two series of photographs?

10. Assume you are commissioned by a photography magazine to take some portraits of your friends. Take some portraits in which you pose your subjects and try to capture their personality and character. Then answer these questions: What problems did you confront in taking these photographs? How well were you able to capture the personality and character of your subjects?

11. Use your camera to document a typical day in your life. What does this exercise reveal about you and your everyday life? Assuming your classmates do this exercise, what do their photographs reveal about their lives? Did you discover anything about your life or the lives of your friends that was surprising? How did you make sure you weren't giving a false impression of your everyday life? How did you decide on which photographs to take?

12. Choose some subject that interests you and that has interesting pictorial possibilities and do a photo-essay on it. What is it like to write about a topic that you have also photographed? Was your photo-essay shaped primarily by what you wanted to show or what you wanted to say? Explain your answer.

13. If you have a digital camera, how has it affected the way you take photographs? How do you store your photographs and what programs do you use to crop your images and manipulate them in other ways?

14. Do you think digital cameras have changed the way tourists take photographs when they are traveling? Explain your answer.

15. Do you think the images of 9/11 would have had a different impact if they been only photographed rather than televised and photographed? Do photographs of 9/11 affect people in ways televised images cannot? Explain your answer.

KEY TERMS FOR CHAPTER 5

genre   grain
digital   shot angle
focus   composition
depth of field

FILM:
The Moving Image

Movies are a very complicated—and in recent years, a very expensive—art form. With the development of computer animation, just about anything in the way of special effects can be done in a movie now. In the final analysis, however, movies tell stories. If a movie doesn't tell a good story and have characters that audiences find interesting, all the special effects in the world can't make people go see it.

MOTION PICTURES

Movies have had a curious history. In their earliest days, they were regarded as miraculous but rather primitive amusements. Later, they were seen as entertainments, but not as a serious or significant art form. Now, the motion picture is considered an extremely important art form. Many films are seen by scholars as great works of art, and many directors are treated as great creative artists (or, as the French put it, "auteurs"). So the motion picture has come a long way, from popular art form to elite art form. In recent years, with the development of semiotics, the motion picture has been studied not only in terms of what it reflects about society and what ideological messages it carries but also, and perhaps primarily, in terms of how meaning is generated by what might be described as the grammar of film—the various kinds of shots and editing techniques that directors use to give shape to their vision.

A motion picture can be defined as a succession of discrete frames, projected at a rate of twenty-four frames per second (normal speed), that offers

Like painting and sculpture, film employs line, texture, color, form, volume, and mass, as well as subtle interplays of light and shadow. Many of the rules of photographic composition followed in the motion picture are similar to those applied in painting and sculpture. Like the drama, film communicates visually through dramatic action, gesture, and expression, and verbally through dialogue. Like music and poetry, film utilizes subtle and complex rhythms, and like poetry, in particular, it communicates through images, metaphors and symbols. Like pantomime, film concentrates upon the moving image, and like the dance, that moving image has certain rhythmic qualities.

—JOSEPH M. BOGGS,
THE ART OF
WATCHING FILMS

the illusion of motion—because an afterimage lingers in the eye that connects all the images together.

There are several variations on the speed at which scenes are filmed. Scenes filmed at greater-than-normal speed (but projected at twenty-four frames per second) seem to move slowly; this is called slow motion. When the reverse happens, and scenes are filmed at slower-than-normal speed and projected at twenty-four frames per second, we have fast motion (sometimes called "speeded" motion). There is also a device known as the "freeze-frame," where one image is continued for a period of time, stopping motion. This powerful effect is often used as a transitional device.

The basic unit of film is the **frame,** which is a discrete image. (Unlike film, television does not have frames.) The existence of discrete frames (or *stills*) makes it possible for film scholars to examine films in considerable detail and to reproduce certain frames of significance (Figure 6.1). Frames contain an enormous amount of material—they are really analogous to the photographic images discussed in Chapter 5. But the complete motion picture involves combinations of frames and is based on what might be called *shots* (to be discussed shortly).

❙ FIGURE 6.1
F. W. Murnau, detail of a frame from *Nosferatu*, 1922. Notice how this shot conveys horror. We look up at the vampire figure; he has sunken eyes, a deathlike expression on his face, and long, hideously curved fingernails. Courtesy of the Museum of Modern Art, New York, Film Stills Archive.

Films are not shot in sequence; different scenes are shot in different order, but all are merged into the proper sequence at the end of shooting— a process known as *editing* (Figure 6.2). Editing involves deciding how to arrange the segments of the film as a means of shaping the emotional responses of the viewers. A given amount of film footage, from the original shoots, can be shaped in many different ways, depending on the aesthetic sensibilities of the film editor.

In one sense, a film can be regarded as a work designed to generate certain desired emotional responses in viewers. This is somewhat of an oversimplification, but it points out the fact that filmmakers seek various effects; in fact, they often start with a given desired effect and work backward, trying to figure out how to achieve the effect.

FILM IN SOCIETY AND SOCIETY IN FILM

When we see a film, though we may not be aware of the fact, we are also seeing portrayals of certain types of people and of the societies in which they live. The performers are involved in narratives, which can be seen as the "figure" against the "ground" of society and culture, or, in many cases, certain subcultures within society at large. This is why films are of such interest to social scientists, because there are always characterizations of social and political institutions in films. While the focus of a film might be on the actions of the characters, these characters are social beings whose activities reflect the societies in which they live.

Thus, for example, films are studied in terms of what they reveal about such topics as racism, sexism, the abuse of power by politicians, the nature of love and heroism, and many other topics. When we follow the activities of characters in a film, our sense of what motivates them and our evaluations of their behavior are tied to social conventions and aesthetic values at a given point in time.

Let me list some of the more important perspectives that can be used in analyzing films, many of which are employed at the same time by film critics:

Sociological criticism. This looks at the way films reflect institutions and society in general.

Psychoanalytic criticism. This criticism analyzes the events in a film in terms of psychoanalytic theory and its notion of the role of the unconscious in shaping behavior.

Semiotic criticism. Semioticians focus on the important signs in a text, such as the facial expressions of characters, the way they look and dress, the backgrounds in scenes, and other such things.

❙ Figure 6.2
Sergei Eisenstein, *The Battleship Potemkin*, 1925. These frames, taken from the great Russian film, show how directors edit films—they vary the shots to provide information and to shape the emotional responses of viewers. Courtesy of the Museum of Modern Art, Film Stills Archive.

Historical criticism. The focus here is on what the film reflects about the historical period in which it takes place.

Ideological criticism. In this kind of criticism, the basic belief systems of the characters, especially as they relate to power, are the primary subject of interest. Many ideological film critics are also interested in the role of film and other media in shaping the consciousness of those who see films.

Cultural studies. In the last thirty years, a new "metadiscipline" called cultural studies, which combines all of these methodologies, has become popular in academic circles, especially since many of the methodologies described above are interrelated and draw upon one another.

CONVENTIONS OF FILM EDITING

There are certain conventions or codes of editing that we all learn by experience, from watching numerous motion pictures. These conventions include the following:

1. *The wipe.* A new image replaces a previous one by a defined horizontal, vertical, or diagonal line that "wipes" the old image off the screen. This creates a sharp break with past action.

2. *The dissolve.* One image gradually fades or "dissolves" into a new image. This less radical break with past action often is used to suggest the passage of a good deal of time.

3. *The fade-out* or *fade-in.* The image gradually fades away to black (an empty screen) or fades in from an empty screen. Often, fade-outs and fade-ins are combined, but this need not be done.

4. *The flip-frame.* The frame appears to flip over into a new scene.

5. *The cut.* A sequence is stopped, and a complete new image is shown. When a number of cuts are used to suggest a number of things going on at the same time (simultaneity) and excitement, it is called quick cutting.

6. *The defocus shot.* A scene ends by moving out of focus and a new scene begins out of focus and moves into clear focus. This device links the two scenes in the viewer's mind.

All of these devices are analogous to punctuation in writing; they are the means by which the director indicates (though not overtly) to viewers how they should relate scenes to one another. Someone unfamiliar with these editing conventions is likely to misinterpret the film. As we grow up and watch films, we all learn, through trial and error, what the conventions are and how to respond to them.

SHOTS AND SHOT RELATIONSHIPS

We have already discussed shots in the chapter on photography. Because of the nature of film, however, some additional topics need to be dealt with here.

The Zoom Shot

Film makes possible the **zoom shot,** in which we use a lens to move in, smoothly, closer and closer on a subject, from a long shot or medium shot, until we arrive at a close-up (Figure 6.3). The zoom shot has the effect of intensifying an image, of making it possible to inspect an object or a person's face more closely. It is a message from the director that we must pay special attention to something and look for something that will be revealed to us. There is a suggestion of intimacy. Inexperienced directors sometimes become "zoom crazy" and use the zoom so often that it loses its novelty and impact.

In the same way, a reverse zoom, in which the lens moves away from a close-up of an object or a person, conveys the opposite emotion. Here we are being asked to take a larger view, to look at the big picture. Thus, this shot is meant to give us a picture of relationships and the overall structure of a situation. It suggests reason and distancing, not emotional involvement.

The Reaction Shot

Here the camera focuses on the reaction of a character to something said (the dialogue) or an event in the film. The *reaction shot* reveals, visually, how an important figure in the story has responded to something. This shot is meant to shape our perception of and emotional response to the dialogue or events that have just transpired.

Montage

This concept was developed by the film theorist and director Sergei Eisenstein, who used it in a number of different ways. In essence, Eisenstein argued in *Film Form* (1949:49), **montage** "is an idea that arises from the collision of independent shots—shots even opposite to one another . . ." Thus, we derive meaning in film from seeing shots in combination. One shot is, for all practical purposes, a photograph, but when shots are *combined* in certain sequences, we are led to have certain ideas or emotional responses. This explains, in part, the power of MTV, which often is exciting and experimental in its use of shots and editing.

As Eisenstein writes in his book *The Film Sense* (translated and edited by Jay Leyda, 1975:4:)

> Our films are faced with the task of presenting not only a narrative that is *logically connected*, but one that contains a *maximum of emotion and stimulating power*. Montage is a mighty aid in the resolution of this task. Why do we use montage at all? Even the most fanatical opponent of montage will agree that it is not merely because the film strip at our disposal is not of infinite length, and, consequently, being condemned to working with pieces of restricted lengths, we have to stick one piece of it on to another occasionally.

There is a psychological property found in film, Eisenstein adds, which is (1975:4) "the fact that two film pieces of any kind, placed together, inevitably combine into a new concept, a new quality, arising out of that juxtaposition." The basic element of film is the shot. It is only when we attach a second shot to the first one that two shots together start generating meaning.

Montage can involve such visual matters as graphic elements, planes, volumes, spatiality, and images of motion. By playing off one shot (or aspects of that shot) against another, we produce the meaning or effect that Eisenstein considers to be the basis of montage and, ultimately, of film (Figure 6.4). This calls to mind the notion of the Swiss linguist Ferdinand de Saussure, who argued in his *Course in General Linguistics* (1966:117) that "concepts are purely differential and defined not by their positive content but negatively by their relations with the other terms of the system." An image by itself can be made to mean anything, and it is only when we see this image or shot placed in relationship to another image or shot that we get a specific emotion or idea.

COLOR IN FILM

Originally, films were black and white. When color film was introduced, it was something of a novelty, and seeing a color film was a special occasion. Films would advertise, for example, that they were in technicolor; and color films, because they were unusual, had a distinctive appeal and quality. Now,

I FIGURE 6.4
Sergei Eisenstein, frame from *The Battleship Potemkin*, 1925. This image is one of his most famous. It shows a woman after she has been shot, with her blood spurting out. This and other images from this great film conveyed Eisenstein's sense of the horror of life under the czar. Courtesy of the Museum of Modern Art, New York, Film Stills Archive.

with few exceptions, all films are made in color. This means that black-and-white films now are unusual and signify that a film is a documentary or an "art" film or was made many years ago.

From our discussion in Chapter 3, we realize that color can generate powerful emotional responses, especially when combined with other elements of film. So color (or, in some cases, the lack of color) is one more tool used to enhance and intensify our responses to images.

Because of the arbitrary relationship that exists between a signifier (such as the use of color) and what is signified (such as madness), we should not automatically assume, however, that black and white is a preferred medium for showing the "darker" elements of the psyche. It has been pointed out, for example, that the extremely rich coloration of the film *Blue Velvet* signified emotional disorientation and pathology equally as well as did the use of shadows and distorted images in black-and-white films from earlier times.

SOUND

The first films did not have sound and relied on the images and captions or printed words to carry the narrative. The coming of sound, with *The Jazz Singer* in 1927, changed film dramatically, for now it was possible to use dialogue, sound effects, and music to shape the viewers' responses.

Spoken Dialogue

The conversation that characters carry on in a film is dialogue. Dialogue generally is tied to scenes, not to frames (which are single images). When the scene—which is a segment of a story with certain characters in a particular place—changes, so does the dialogue.

The dialogue tells us what people are doing and often, by inference, what they are thinking. Thus, dialogue helps the visual images carry the story along. Without sound, we can still get a pretty good idea of what is happening in a film, but our understanding is crude and simplistic. Often, a pattern of shots and countershots or reaction shots (or reverse-angle shots) matches the pattern of conversation in a scene. Using these conventions, directors let us know what the different characters are thinking (or seem to be thinking) and how they are responding to the conversation. It should be noted that film dialogue, like most conversation, is characterized by sentence fragments, interruptions, and overlapping speech. We do not, as a rule, always wait for others to stop speaking or speak in complete and beautifully structured sentences. And the dialogue generally is used to add something to the visual image, not to repeat the information the visual image offers us; the dialogue should add to the narrative but not replace the image.

We also must recognize that the language used in dialogue and the quality of a character's voice tell us a great deal. The human voice has an intrinsic capacity to generate emotions and thus adds to the power of the image—which explains why the motion picture is such a powerful medium.

Narration

In some films, such as documentaries, we find narration, in which a speaker (or several speakers) off the screen provides us with information relevant to the images we are seeing. Often, we have both narration and dialogue, as a narrator sets a scene for us and then the characters involved act out the scene. Sometimes, the narrator is also part of the action and steps in and out of the film to offer his or her comments. The narrator, as someone who is distanced from the action (even if only momentarily), can tell us things, offer opinions, and act as a kind of omniscient presence.

Narrators fill in gaps in a film's story line, provide important background information, tell us what we should think about various characters (and often what various characters are thinking), frame plots, and provide a tone to a film. As such, they are very useful in all kinds of films—whether they be dramatic films or documentaries or mixtures such as docudramas. The presence of a narrator suggests that a story or film is realistic and that it has documentary elements in it.

Sound Effects

Sound effects, which imitate the sounds associated with given phenomena, make a film seem realistic and natural. They also function as cues that shape our emotional responses. Thus, for example, a film about space might augment a scene of a rocket blasting off with the awesome power of an associated series of sounds. In the same vein, if the sound we hear does not correspond to our expectations and does not "go" with the event, we are immediately aroused and made suspicious.

There is some question about whether specific sounds always have a predictable effect on people. Semiotics would suggest that this is *not* the case: a given sound—such as a shriek—can be used, depending on the situation, to suggest joy and happiness or dread and terror. Recall that Saussure explained that a sign (which he defined as a sound or object) was arbitrarily or conventionally related to a given signifier or meaning. So any sound can be made to mean anything.

In *How to Read a Film,* James Monaco (1977:180, 181) cites a French film theorist, Christian Metz, on the "five channels of information in a film: (1) the visual image; (2) print and other graphics; (3) speech; (4) music; (5) noise (sound effects). Interestingly, the majority of these channels are auditory rather than visual." And, he continues, there are only two continuous channels in this list—the visual image and noise/sound effects.

Sound in film is all-pervasive and helps create locales (room sound) and a sense of time. And, as we have developed technology with stereo, Dolby systems, and the like, the power of sound in film has been augmented.

Music

The music heard in the background of films plays a very important role, and many producers argue that the music in a film can mean the difference between a hit and a flop. Music is used to key the responses of viewers to particular scenes. This is done through the use of *motifs*—passages that become linked to certain kinds of events.

What generally happens is that we are taught to associate certain musical motifs with certain events or kinds of events. These motifs then can be used to trigger certain responses in us—we are, so to speak, conditioned, and we respond accordingly (the same way Pavlov's dogs were taught to associate a bell with being fed and thus were conditioned to salivate when they heard the bell). Music has the power to speak directly to our emotions, so it helps intensify and dramatize scenes and augments the visual images. A good example of this is found in Philip Glass's synthesized musical score for the postmodern film *Koyaanisqatsi* (Figure 6.5).

I FIGURE 6.5
This is a scene from *Koyaanisqatsi,* a postmodern film made by Godfrey Reggio in 1983. Courtesy of the Museum of Modern Art, New York, Film Stills Archive.

As with sound effects, in almost all cases it is the association that is crucial, not some intrinsic quality in the music itself that automatically generates a specific emotional response in everyone who hears it.

SPECIAL VISUAL EFFECTS

A number of things can be done to affect the visual image, from simulated events (what we commonly describe as special effects) to holding the camera by hand and getting a certain look. In some cases, we keep the camera stationary and move the camera head or use a zoom lens; in other cases, we move the camera and its support in various ways.

The Hand-Held Camera

When a camera operator holds a camera and shoots with it, there is an unsteady, jerky quality to the resultant image suggesting that this is the kind of film we might get from a spectator at a scene who just happened to have a camera on hand. The lack of precision or absolute clarity engenders a sense of realism and truthfulness. So directors often use hand-held cameras when they want to counter the kind of image they get from using mounted cameras.

Camera Movement

A *pan* involves a camera head traveling horizontally across a person, object, or scene, while a *tilt* involves a camera head traveling vertically across a person, object, or scene. A *roll* involves a camera flipping an image of a person, object, or scene about, which is much more disorienting than the other kinds of shots. A *truck* (left or right) involves the horizontal movement of the camera and its support in front of a given scene; a *dolly-in* or *dolly-out* involves the actual movement of the camera and its support either toward or away from a scene; and an *arc* is a movement, semicircular in nature, of a camera and its support around a given scene.

Each of these shots creates a different effect. For example, the pan is a kind of inspection of a terrain, the tilt is more focused and direct, and the roll disorients and surprises the viewer.

Deep and Shallow Focus

Deep focus refers to a large depth of field, in which objects close to the camera, as well as those a considerable distance from it, are in clear focus. This clarity imparts a very strong sense of realism to a scene. Orson Welles used

deep focus to stunning effect in his masterpiece *Citizen Kane* (Figure 6.6).
Shallow focus, which involves having only a small part of an image in focus,
directs the attention of the viewer to something in particular, by having it in
focus and everything else out of focus.

The Jump Cut

With the **jump cut,** the editor slices out the middle or some part of a sequence
and cuts or "jumps" from one section of it to another. This process helps shape
the rhythm of the scene and speed it up. We learn the convention of the jump
cut from comic books. The artists cannot provide all the intervening shots, so
they jump from one scene to another and allow us to fill in the gaps in our own
imaginations via the process of psychological closure (Figure 6.7).

POSTMODERNISM'S IMPACT ON FILM

Postmodernism is difficult to define but is related to such trends and ideas
as the blending of different styles and genres (often seen in buildings) and the
depreciation of narratives (reflected in the mass media and in some philosophical thought). One of the most succinct definitions of postmodernism is that

of the French scholar Jean-François Lyotard, who writes in his book *The Post-modern Condition: A Report on Knowledge* (1984: xxiv), "Simplifying to the extreme, I define *postmodern* as incredulity toward metanarratives."

Postmodernists argue that around 1960 there was a great shift in belief and modernist thought, which was based on large, all-encompassing theories and beliefs and was replaced by postmodernist thought.

What Lyotard meant by this was that in postmodern periods people no longer believe in the great systems of thought, the "metanarratives," as reflected in political ideologies, religious beliefs, and philosophy, that had shaped their beliefs and behavior in modernist periods. These large, all-encompassing metanarratives have been replaced by many different, smaller, and in some cases, personal narratives that guide us. But this leads to a problem that he described as a crisis of legitimation.

We don't know, Lyotard suggests, what to believe, and have no guidelines to help us. Some philosophers have suggested that in postmodernism, "anything goes" since there are no widely accepted codes to guide us. Postmodernism is also associated with the development of the mass media, the growth of consumer cultures (some see postmodernism as a form of late capitalism), and, in the arts, the pastiche, the blurring of lines between reality and images, and the mixing of aesthetic styles.

❙ FIGURE 6.7
Detail from Gilbert Shelton's *The Fabulous Furry Freak Brothers*, "Getting Out the Vote." Filmmakers have learned a great deal about varying their shots from studying frames in comic strips. Used with permission of Gilbert Shelton.

Thus, postmodern films tend to lack an easy-to-follow linear narrative structure. It's best to think of these films in terms of montage—the juxtaposing of images and fragments of narratives to generate responses from viewers without much regard for sequence and plot line, as we traditionally recognize them.

According to Jack Solomon, *Koyaanisqatsi,* a 1983 film by Godfrey Reggio, is a classic example of postmodernism. As Solomon writes in *The Signs of Our Times: The Secret Meanings of Everyday Life* (1990:213):

> It has no characters, no dialogue, no words, no subtitles, no narrative, nor anything recognizable as a plot. Without commentary or overview, the cameras simply juxtapose such violently contrasting images from the natural and the industrialized worlds as Indian hieroglyphics, a slow-motion rocket launch, time-lapse photography of cloud patterns, scenic aerial views of the American Southwest, atomic blasts, shots of the litter-filled streets of New York, endless replays of the demolition of a decaying housing complex, scenes from Las Vegas . . .

The film also features a minimalist score by avant-garde composer Philip Glass that, as Solomon puts it, "pulses in rhythmic correlation with the imagery."

After eighty-seven minutes of "sensory assault," the film concludes by flashing some definitions of the term *koyaanisqatsi* on the screen. As Solomon recounts (1990:214), *koyaanisqatsi* is a Hopi term that means "1. crazy life, 2. life in turmoil, 3. life out of balance, 4. life disintegrating, 5. a state of life that calls for another way of living." The film uses a variety of images to generate this feeling in viewers and offers a filmic mosaic of the world suggesting that it is in turmoil and that life is chaotic. We can wonder whether *Koyaanisqatsi* is a mirror reflecting a society in a state of disintegration or is a kind of lamp projecting this view of the world, a view held by its maker but not necessarily an accurate portrayal of contemporary society.

In any case, *Koyaanisqatsi* and a number of films such as *Blue Velvet, Blade Runner, Crimes and Misdemeanors,* and *sex, lies, and videotape* are generally held to be postmodern in nature. That is, they are thought—or so postmodernist theorists argue—to reflect the postmodern, nonlinear, image-crazy world in which we live.

Earlier I discussed the film *Blade Runner,* whose replicants, which look exactly like human beings, pose a problem of the relation between illusion and reality. One of the most significant challenges to our ability to know what is real or, in other words, to know the "truth" about events comes in Akira Kurosawa's masterpiece *Rashomon.* In this film we can only be sure of two things. First, we know that a bandit rapes the wife of a samurai in a grove, as the samurai, who has been tied up and is immobile, watches. Second, we know that the samurai dies.

Everything else is a problem. It turns out that what happened in the grove was observed, secretly, by a woodcutter. But how the samurai died and who killed him is very problematic, to put it mildly. For in *Rashomon,* all of the characters involved in the story give radically different versions of what happened in the grove in testimony before a court.

The bandit says he killed the samurai after a fierce battle. The wife says she killed her husband in a trance caused by the hatred emanating from his eyes. Music, that reminds one of Ravel's *Bolero* (the music was written to suggest the work) plays as she advances on her husband, knife in hand. Her husband, the samurai, says that he was brokenhearted by his wife's behavior after she'd been raped, and so he stabbed himself and committed suicide. His testimony is given through a woman who goes into a trance and speaks with the voice of the samurai. And the woodcutter says that both the bandit and the samurai were terrified when they fought, with their knees shaking madly, though he says eventually the bandit did kill the samurai.

What *Rashomon* does is pose the problem of whether we can "know" reality. This film was a sensation when it was shown some fifty years ago and is, I would suggest, one of the most important postmodern films ever made. Postmodernism argues that the fundamental and basic belief structures that have sustained us for many years are no longer valid. As Jean François Lyotard explained, postmodernism means "incredulity toward metanarratives." We used to think that we could know reality, but postmodernism, with its attack on our ability to know the truth about reality and separate simulations from real things, makes us doubtful about what we can know and what we should do.

Sociologist Norman K. Denzin devotes the second part of his book *Images of Postmodern Society: Social Theory and Contemporary Cinema,* to postmodern films. He discusses the following films as postmodern:

David Lunch, *Blue Velvet*

Oliver Stone, *Wall Street*

Woody Allen, *Crimes and Misdemeanors*

Steven Soderbergh, *sex, lies, and videotape*

Spike Lee, *Do The Right Thing*

Wim Wender, *Paris, Texas*

Denzin mentions other postmodern works by the filmmakers he discusses and also deals with postmodern films such as *Brazil, Blade Runner, Speaking Parts, Zelig,* and *The Fly.* In his concluding chapter he writes (1991:155), "The postmodern is a cinematic age; it knows itself through the reflections that flow from a camera's eye." This means, he adds, as analysts of films, we must find ways of making sense of those films and narratives in other media that define the current postmodern age.

| FIGURE 6.8
Scene from D. W. Griffith's classic film, *The Birth of a Nation,* 1915—a controversial film about race relations in America. Courtesy of the Museum of Modern Art, New York, Film Stills Archive.

THE POWER OF THE FILM IMAGE

When we see a film in a theater, we find ourselves "captives" (in a sense) in a large room with others, where we sit in darkness watching huge images on a gigantic screen. The very scale of these images itself has an impact; that is why you get a much different feeling when you see a film in a theater than you do when you see that same film in your home (Figure 6.8). And the quality of the audio system in the theater is also much better, which intensifies the experience.

But there is something about movies, wherever we see them, that also strikes responsive chords in us. It is the fact that we generally are watching stories featuring human beings, with whom we can empathize and to whom we often have (and often unconsciously) a sensual or erotic response. As Martin Esslin suggests in *The Age of Television* (1982:30):

> Drama is basically erotic. Actors give the spectators who watch them a great deal of pleasure simply by being interesting, memorable, or beautiful specimens of humanity. Quite apart from their artistic or intellectual accomplishments, actors are people who exhibit their physical presence to the public. . . . In a sense all actors are exhibitionists: they enjoy being seen, being found appealing and worth looking at. Conversely audiences of dramas are also, in a certain sense, voyeurs.

I Figure 6.9
Aristotle said that comedy is based on making men ridiculous. Could he have been thinking of Woody Allen's outfit in his film *Sleeper* (1973)? Courtesy of the Museum of Modern Art, New York, Film Stills Archive.

The power of this generally submerged and subliminal erotic relationship we have with actors and actresses is such that it is easy to identify with them and to internalize their values and beliefs. In some films, or at least in some scenes in films, a comic response rather than an erotic one is generated. This is the case in *Sleeper*, in which we find Woody Allen in an absurd costume (Figure 6.9).

There is an element of what is called *scopophilia* (loving by looking) at play here, which helps explain why facial expressions play so important a role in drama. We are all fascinated by others and want to know as much as we can about them, their personalities, their hidden selves. Thus, we scrutinize their facial expressions (and take note of everything else, I might add) as a means of getting to know characters. In discussing television, Esslin writes (1982:29), "The ability of TV to transmit personality is, undoubtedly, the secret of its immense power. For human beings are insatiable in their interest about other human beings." The same could be said about films.

It may also be that the sense of isolation and separation many people feel in modern societies exacerbates their hunger for relationships (even if only mass-mediated pseudorelationships) and makes movies and television dramas much more important aspects of their lives than they might otherwise be.

Social scientists use the term "para-social relationships" for the feeling many people have that they really know actors and actresses.

THE NATURE OF DRAMA

Films generally tell stories; that is, they are narratives in which we find characters pursuing their own interests, often in conflict with one another. Thus, the element of action is added to that of personality (and, often, demonstrates personality), enabling us to make a "willing suspension of disbelief" and enter into the drama, forgetting that we are spectators watching actors and actresses pretending to be certain characters doing various things. In dramas, there usually is a conflict (or many conflicts) between characters (who may be heroes and heroines and villains and villainesses) and a satisfactory resolution to the conflict.

Narratives can be defined as stories, generally involving a sequence of actions, conflict, jeopardy, and some kind of a resolution that is satisfactory to those who read or see theatrical versions of these narratives. The stories can be serious, comic, or some combination of the two. The jeopardy can be serious or comic and in some cases, a combination of the two.

Narratives depend on their audiences having a store of information that allows them to understand the story and get caught up in the action. Narratives are not limited to works of fiction; we find narratives in our dreams, in our conversations, in news stories shown on television, and many other areas. But it is the narratives found on television and in the cinema that are of most interest to us here.

Aristotle's discussion of tragedy offers some important insights and rules about theater that shaped people's beliefs on the subject for thousands of years. In addition to stressing the vital role of plot and character, Aristotle also recognized the importance of dialogue (diction), film design, editing, pacing, and special effects (spectacle) and music and sound effects (melody). All of these combine to generate the emotions we feel when we watch a film.

The pacing of many films, the rapidity of the action sequences, and the nature of the dangers presented to the heroes and heroines excite us. Such excitement is inherent in films such as *Raiders of the Lost Ark* and others in that genre, in which one action scene leads to another one in rapid succession (Figure 6.10). These are very similar in structure to commercials full of quick cuts. The very rapidity of the cutting generates a sense of excitement.

In many respects, film and television dramas are like dreams, in which all kinds of remarkable things occur (Figure 6.11). According to Freudian theory, our dreams occur in the form of discontinuous images that we "put together" when we recall them, via a process known as *secondary elaboration*.

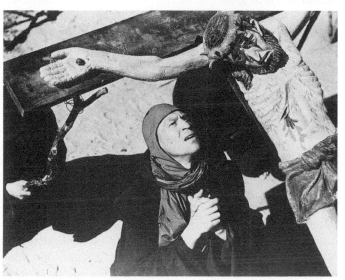

In his masterpiece, *The Interpretation of Dreams,* first published in 1900, Freud writes (1965:82) "dreams think essentially in images" and (1965:83) "dreams construct a *situation* out of these images . . . they "dramatize" an idea . . . in dreams . . . we appear not to *think* but to *experience;* that is, we attach complete belief to the hallucinations." Freud suggests that when we are awake, our minds generate ideas and thoughts using verbal images and speech, but when we sleep, in dreams, we use images.

Freud then discusses two commonly used means of interpreting dreams. The first, which he calls "symbolic" dream interpretation, involves replacing the content of a dream with another content, similar in nature to the dream, that is more intelligible. This involves, in a sense, retelling the dream. The second technique, which he describes as "decoding" dreams, involves using books with fixed meanings for symbols and does not take dreamers or their particular circumstances into account. Neither of these techniques is acceptable. That is because dreams are very complex and the symbols used in dreams can have many different meanings. Semiotically speaking, we could say a signifier can have many different signifieds.

For Freud, the interpretation of a dream must be connected to the dreamer and the various problems and psychological difficulties the dreamer faces. In dreams everything can be important, so Freud has his patients learn not to disregard things in their dreams that seem to be irrelevant or trivial. We can say the same thing about films and other kinds of narratives.

A Russian scholar, Yuri Lotman, in his book *The Structure of the Artistic Text* writes (1977–23), "The tendency to interpret everything in an artistic text as meaningful is so great that we rightfully consider nothing accidental in a work of art." This means we must be mindful of everything we find in television programs and films, and seemingly trivial or irrelevant images or dialogue can actually play an important role in these texts.

We learn from Freud's discussion of dreams that when we interpret a film we do not retell it and we must not assume that every symbol found in the film has a fixed meaning. We always have to tie symbols in films to the characters in them and their motivations and actions.

A dream would be very much like a series of jump cuts or comic strip panels, for which our minds fill in the gaps. What makes dreams (and films) powerful is that they are full of symbols that speak to repressed or unconscious elements in our psyches and that evoke powerful responses. Generally, these symbols have a sexual content that is hidden or masked by the processes of displacement and condensation. If there are erotic aspects to watching films and television, as Esslin suggests, there are even more powerful sexual aspects to our dreams—the dramas that we create in our own minds as we sleep. In our dreams, we are not only the producers and directors but also the actors and actresses.

CONCLUSIONS

Film is a very powerful and complex medium. In recent years, with the development of semiotics (often in alliance with psychoanalytic theory and Marxist theory), we have become interested in how films generate meaning

---

ANALYZING FILMS, TELEVISION PROGRAMS, AND OTHER NARRATIVE TEXTS

In answering these questions, relate each of these topics to dominant visual images and image sequences found in the film, television program, or other narrative text that makes use of images.

1. What do you think is the *subject* of the text? Are there other important subjects treated in the text?
2. What is the *plot* of the text—that is, what are the main events that take place in it? Does the plot interest you? If so, why?
3. What *themes* are dealt with? Some typical themes are the redeeming power of love, the destructive nature of jealousy, the nature of evil, and the value of freedom.
4. What are the *most important images or image sequences* found in the text? How do they shape the meaning of the text and affect the emotions of those watching the text?
5. Who are the *main characters* in the text and what is their symbolic importance? What do they look like?
6. *When* does the text take place? *Where* does it take place? What is the importance of the *setting*? How does the setting shape our notions about what's going on in the text?
7. What are the most important *ideas* dealt with in the text? What are the most important values that are supported?
8. How good is the *dialogue*? Is it fitting? Are the characters properly motivated? Are they believable?
9. Which *techniques* are used in the screenplay? Are there flashbacks and flash-forwards? What about the lighting? The use of sound effects? Is there suspense? Is their jeopardy?
10. What *genre* is the text? Is it science fiction, horror, love, crime, detective, spy, western, action-adventure, comedy, or some combination of these or other genres? What visual cues are given to help us recognize the genre of the text?
11. What is the *tone* of the text? What "attitudes" toward life and people are reflected in it? Is the tone appropriate to the story?
12. Did you *like* the text? If so, why? What were its strongest features? What were its weakest elements? How does your evaluation of the text relate to the topics in this chart? What did you learn about life from seeing the text?

In analyzing film, it is important to remember that film is a collaborative effort involving the work of producers, directors, scriptwriters, performers, camera men and women, film editors, costume designers, lighting experts, set and production designers, music writers, and musicians. It takes a lot of money and the efforts of large numbers of people, generally speaking, to make a film. And, like all kinds of art, it is a very risky business. Even with famous directors and casts full of famous actors and actresses, films often end up as aesthetic and financial disasters.

for people and have discovered that it is a very complicated process. We used to think that a given film had a given meaning and that it was the function of the film critic to point out that meaning. Now we know that everyone doesn't interpret a given film the same way. What we see and get out of a film is related to what we know and have experienced in life.

Thus, if a film is full of parodies of other directors' work and includes allusions to historical events and we don't recognize the parodies or the allusions, we will not get as much out of that film as will someone who does recognize them. That is why it is now fashionable to talk about audiences "reading" films and to suggest that audiences must play a significant role in making sense of a film. The film does not bear the entire burden; instead, it cooperates with us, so to speak.

This shows why an understanding of the principles of visual communication is so important. When we study a film (or that important genre of film or television we call the commercial), the more we know about lighting and camera angles and kinds of shots and color and symbolism, the better we will be able to understand how it works and, finally, what is good and bad about it.

Of course, when we go to the movies simply to enjoy ourselves, we just watch the film and hope to be entertained by it. But later on, if we discuss the film with friends or study it, we can employ the repertoire of visual communication concepts we have learned to make sense of the film and our responses to it. It is also true that the more we know about how film (or any form of visual communication for that matter) works, the more our appreciation of film is enhanced. So the more you know, the more you can appreciate forms of visual communication—or literature, music, and all other art forms.

APPLICATIONS

1. Make a list of the five best films you've seen in the last year or so, ranked from one to five. What are your criteria for evaluating a film—that is, what makes a film "good"? Do you think certain criteria should be generally accepted, or are such things essentially a matter of opinion and personal taste? Compare your list with those of your classmates to see whether there is any agreement on which were the best films.

2. If you think a film is wonderful and a friend thinks the film is terrible, what is the "truth" of the matter? Is one of you likely to be correct and the other likely to be incorrect, or can you both be correct? Why is taste an unreliable guide to aesthetic judgments?

3. Videotape a film and then play it without the sound for a while, so that you can concentrate on such matters as facial expressions, lighting,

editing, and kinds of shots. Rewind it and play it with sound. Do you have a better understanding of how the film was made and how it achieves its effects?

4. What makes a film a "classic"? In what ways do "classic" films differ from ordinary films?

5. Can you think of ways in which films have been influenced by television's visual techniques? Be specific about the films and the techniques.

6. Suppose you were asked to teach a course on contemporary American culture (since the 1960s). Which films would you use to give your students an understanding of our culture in all its variety? Justify your choices.

7. Take a film that you like and use the different methods mentioned in the discussion of film in society to analyze the film. Does analyzing a film this way increase your appreciation of the film or ruin it for you?

8. Watch the film *Rashomon* and write a short paper in which you determine which of the characters is telling the truth. Also, use the material on analyzing films and television programs to deal with the film. Did you find *Rashomon* boring? If so, why? The film won numerous awards. Why do you think it received these honors?

9. Try to remember a dream you've had. Write it down in as much detail as you can and then try to interpret it, focusing on its images and symbolic content. Can you connect the dream to anything that happened to you in recent days? Freud believed that dreams are connected to wishes we have and represent a kind of wish-fulfillment. Does your dream involve some kind of a fulfillment of a desire?

KEY TERMS FOR CHAPTER 6

frame

zoom shot

montage

jump cut

postmodernism

TELEVISION:
The Ever-Changing Mosaic

If you spend four hours a day watching television (approximately the national average), by the time you reach age sixty-five, you will have spent about nine years in front of the "boob tube." Was that the best expenditure you could have made of those nine years? In this chapter, we explore television's curious power and investigate the medium everyone "loves to hate."

THE TELEVISION IMAGE

Watching television is considerably different from watching film. The film image is like a discrete photograph, loaded with information and very high in resolution. When we watch a film, we see twenty-four of these frames per second, each of which appears very briefly and then is followed by another. Because of the lingering afterimage, we get the effect or, should we say, have the illusion of motion.

The television image is altogether different. It is best described as a mosaic, made up of a large quantity of dots (**pixels**) that are constantly changing. As Marshall McLuhan put it in *Understanding Media: The Extensions of Man* (1965:313):

> With TV, the viewer is the screen. He is bombarded with light impulses that James Joyce called the "Charge of the Light Brigade" that imbues his "soul-skin with subconscious inklings." The TV image is visually low in data. The TV image is not a still shot. It is not photo in any sense, but a ceaselessly forming contour of things limned by the scanning finger. . . . The TV image

Essentially, television is more like radio than it is different from it. As with radio, the concept of flow is all-important; the product of both media is continuous and continuing, with both the smaller unit of the show and the larger unit of the day's or evening's programming. Moreover, because of the relatively poor quality of the televised image (as compared with theatrical film), TV depends heavily on its audio component. The curved screen, the lack of definition and contrast, the difficulties of broadcast reception, all work to minimize the effectiveness of the TV image. Visually, the density of information is low, which is made up for in part by a relatively compressed density of programming and sequencing. The segue and lead-in of radio are also of prime significance in the grammar of television: dead space and dead time are to be avoided at all costs: the flow must continue.

–JAMES MONACO,
HOW TO READ A FILM

❙ FIGURE 7.1
Photo of television image at 1/1000 second.

❙ FIGURE 7.2
Photo of television image at 1/500 second.

offers some three million dots per second to the receiver. From these he accepts only a few dozen each instant, from which to make an image.

McLuhan probably underestimated the number of dots we use to make images, but his point is correct: a television image is a constantly changing mosaic of dots, and viewers must make sense of them (Figures 7.1, 7.2, and 7.3). We can do so with great facility and ease, but the point is, we *must* do so.

It is this difference between the amount of data given by the television image and the screen image that led McLuhan to suggest that differences in media are more important than the differences in the programs or genres they carry. As he put it, "the medium is the message." McLuhan has a highly controversial theory that distinguishes between "hot" media and "cool" media. A *hot medium,* he tells us (1965:22), "is one that extends one single sense in 'high definition.' High definition is being well filled with data." When there is high definition, McLuhan adds, there is low participation. A *cool medium,* on the other hand, has low definition, offers relatively few data, and fosters high participation.

A list of hot and cool media, as McLuhan sees things, follows.

Hot	*Cool*
Film	Television
Radio	Telephone
Photograph	Cartoon
Printed word	Speech

❙ FIGURE 7.3
Photo of television image at 1/125 second.

Lecture	Seminar
Book	Dialogue

The television image, because it is so low in data relative to the film image, is cool and encourages (or should we say requires) participation and attention.

The very nature of the television image, then, has a significance and an impact on viewers. According to McLuhan, television is more involving than film, requires more effort from the viewer, and is used in different ways by viewers. However, studies reveal that people do not, in fact, always watch television with undiluted attention; the set is on in a lighted room, and people watching it often converse with one another, eat, read, and do all kinds of things. And viewers watch more than three and one-half hours of television per day in America. (The television set is on almost seven hours per day in a typical home.)

From McLuhan's perspective, this is important because he believed that the medium of television has altered our sense ratios, or patterns of perception, and that this development has had a profound impact on us (and people in other countries as well, because this alteration varies from culture to culture). As he wrote (1965:45):

> There is . . . no way of refusing to comply with the new sense ratios of the TV image. But the effect of the entry of the TV image will vary from culture to culture in accordance with the existing sense ratios in each culture. In audio-tactile Europe TV has intensified the visual sense, spurring them toward American styles of packaging and dressing. In America, the intensely

visual culture, TV has opened the doors of audio-tactile perception to the non-visual world of spoken languages and food and the plastic arts.

McLuhan's theories were very controversial when he launched them in the early 1960s. Now they are not so frequently discussed, but they explain a good deal and, if taken with a grain of salt, help us understand why different media affect us the way they do.

THE TELEVISION SCREEN

Television Versus Movie Screens

When we go to the movies, we sit in a large room and watch huge images on a very big screen. Movie screens vary in shape—depending on how the films are shot—but they are all large, and some are even gigantic. The television screen, on the other hand, is relatively small. Many sets have a twelve-inch screen (measured diagonally), though the most common size screen is a good deal larger than that, ranging from nineteen to twenty-five inches. There are even larger screens, but they are much more expensive and not as widely used.

The small television screen means that images are relatively small, which is why many people argue that television is a close-up medium. As Martin Esslin writes in *The Age of Television* (1982:30,32):

> Television is the most voyeuristic of all communication media, not only because it provides more material in an unending stream of images and in the form most universally acceptable to the total population, but also because it is the most intimate of the dramatic media. In the theatre, the actors are relatively remote from the audience, and the dramatic occasion is public. In the cinema, also a public occasion gathering a large audience into a single room, the actors are nearer to the spectators than in the theatre, but in close-ups they are larger than life. Television is seen at close range and in a more private context. *The close-up of the television performer is on a scale that most nearly approximates direct human contact.* [My italics]

Thus, the close-up image on television, uniquely, gives us the illusion of being with others, which has profound psychological implications. It is television, more than any other medium, that can generate pseudocompanionship, an electronic intimacy that is illusory and unreal.

From this perspective, our sense of "knowing" characters on television and our erotic feelings about them should be much stronger than with characters from films, especially if we watch television programs that are serial in nature and expose us to these characters daily (or weekly) for extended periods of time.

NEW TELEVISION SCREENS AND THE AGONY OF CHOICE

The previously dominant 4:3 format for television screens (four inches of width for three inches of height) is now being replaced by wide-screen 16:9 format television screens, whose ratios are the same as most movie screens. As a result of new display technology, buyers of television sets can now also choose between a variety of different kinds of television sets such as LCD (liquid crystal display), plasma, rear-projection, or the old picture tube television sets. Some of the new plasma sets are fifty inches in size and rear-projection sets can be even larger, reaching sixty-one inches in size. As companies refine their technologies, the size of television screens keeps getting larger and larger.

Another feature of television sets today is HDTV. High Definition Television broadcasts have 1080 lines of resolution and are designed for screens with a 16:9 aspect ratio. HDTV thus provides much more visual information than conventional television. As a result of a ruling by the Federal Communications Commission, all television sets sold in the United States must be able to receive HDTV (High Definition TV) signals by March 2007 and television stations must broadcast in high definition by April 2009.

Those who wish to purchase television sets now have to decide between a number of competing technologies. Until recently, the only decision one made when purchasing a television set involved which brand to get and which size to choose. Now, there are different television technologies and it is difficult to determine which one is most suitable for one's specific needs. Whereas the old tube television sets sold for a few hundred dollars or so, depending on the size and brand, the new sets often cost several thousand dollars. For example, in December 2005 a forty-two-inch Hewlett Packard Plasma HDTV sold for $3,299 and a fifty-two-inch Sony LCD HDTV was advertised for $2,499.

The small screen also means that action on television takes place on the **Z-axis,** the axis that extends from the viewer through the television screen and that is perpendicular to it. On a huge film screen, action can move horizontally across the screen (on what is known as the **A-B axis**) and not lose impact. On the tiny television set, things are different. The only way to deal with large spaces is via the Z-axis, which means action generally moves toward and away from the viewer. The viewer is therefore more directly involved in action. Figures 7.4 and 7.5 show the difference between A-B axis action and Z-axis action.

It is possible to suggest, then, that the small size of the television screen involves viewers in two ways: via the close-up, which approximates human conversational distance, and via the Z-axis, which situates viewers so that action almost always takes place moving toward or away from them.

Watching a film on television is different, then, from watching the same film in a theater. The film does not focus as directly on the viewer and the

▌ FIGURE 7.4
This drawing shows the A-B axis. It is a simplification of the Johnnie Walker advertisement shown in Figure 2.12. By Arthur Asa Berger.

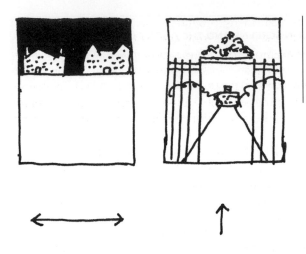

▌ FIGURE 7.5
This drawing shows the Z-axis. It is a simplification of the Johnnie Walker advertisement shown in Figure 3.15. By Arthur Asa Berger.

Z-axis or rely so heavily on close-ups, so that the impact of the film, when it is seen on the television screen, is different from its impact when seen in a theater. The quality of the image is also different, and this has an effect on the film's impact. The film image, which is very powerful and full of information, is turned into a television image and thus diluted.

The previously dominant 4:3 format for television screens (four inches of width for three inches of height) is now being replaced by wide-screen 16:9 format television screens, whose ratios are the same as most movie screens. As a result of new display technological developments, buyers of television sets now can choose between a variety of different kinds of television sets such as LCD (liquid crystal display) television sets, plasma television sets, and rear projection television sets whose images are very powerful.

This does not mean we cannot get a good deal of pleasure from watching a film on television; the incredible development of the videocassette rental industry for films shows that people like to watch films on their home systems. But they are not having the same experience as seeing the film in a theater, with a large screen and a powerful stereophonic audio system. (The amount of money people save on tickets and baby-sitters by renting video cassettes likely is of primary importance; convenience may also be a factor.)

Talking Heads

There is an element of conventional wisdom in the television industry about avoiding programs with "talking heads." If all one has is a program with no variety of camera shots and the talk from these talking heads is dull and uninteresting, the program will, indeed, be dull.

But it isn't as simple as that. Many programs that involve, for the most part, talking heads are extremely interesting and diverting. On the Public Broadcasting System, for example, one of the most popular programs for many years has been "Washington Week." In this program, reporters sit around a table and talk about politics. There is nothing in the way of action but because the topic of the program—politics—is of great interest to many people, there doesn't have to be any action. In fact, any action would be counterproductive.

In the summer of 1987, the Iran-Contra hearings took place before joint House and Senate committees; and millions of people watched, transfixed, as a collection of incredible characters came before the cameras to tell fantastic stories about their actions and activities. These recalled the McCarthy hearings of the 1950s and the Watergate hearings of the 1970s—other occasions when millions were enthralled by "talking heads."

During the Iran-Contra hearings, witnesses contradicted one another and revealed amazing things about what was going on in the White House and how U.S. foreign policy was being conducted. The hearings "created" a new American hero (at least for some people), Oliver North, whose hairstyle was promptly imitated by large numbers of young men and whose appearance also seems to have had, at least in the short run, benefits for the Contras and military recruiting.

In these hearings (and in all talking heads programs), the camera played an important role and was very active—scanning the committee, zooming in on witnesses who were testifying, showing important evidence that had been enlarged and posted on the walls of the committee hearing room. An active camera can generate energy and force viewers to think in certain ways (thus, the zoom-in suggests that we pay attention because something important is going on). The camera work can add an element of drama to a given program.

If one of the functions of television is to bring personalities to viewers, there's nothing in the talking head format that prevents this from being done. In the final analysis, it is the quality of the people who are talking and what they have to say that is crucial. And a great number of formats on television employ little more than talking heads: game shows, talk shows, interviews, and political speeches.

TELEVISION GENRES

Three television **genres** are particularly interesting in terms of visual communication: the commercial, the news program, and music videos. The commercial is also important because it is the cash cow that finances television. In fact, some media critics have suggested that television programming exists mainly to furnish an audience for the commercials, the most important genre carried by the medium.

We must make a distinction between a medium, such as television, and its program genres: commercials, news shows, sports programs, science fiction programs, talk shows, soap operas, situation comedies, crime shows, and so on. Many critics pay little attention to the impact of a medium on a genre, which means they neglect a matter of considerable importance. It is as much an oversimplification to argue that "the program is the message" as it is to argue that "the medium is the message." We must always keep in mind the conventions of genres when we talk about television shows.

In the chart that follows, I offer some suggestions about some genres that help us understand how they are structured. These are conventions that people who watch certain kinds of programs expect, with minor modifications from time to time, when they watch a television show or go to a movie.

Genre	Romance	Western	Science-Fiction	Spy
Time	Early 1900s	1800s	Future	Present
Location	Rural England	Edge of civilization	Outer space	World
Hero	Lords, upper-class types	Cowboy	Space man	Agent
Heroine	Damsel in distress	Schoolmarm	Space gal	Woman spy
Secondary	Friends of heroine	Townpeople, Indians	Technicians	Assistant agents
Villains	False friend	Outlaws	Aliens	Moles
Plot	Heroine finds love	Restore law and order	Repel aliens	Find moles
Theme	Love conquers all	Justice and progress	Save humanity	Save free world
Costume	Gorgeous dresses	Cowboy hat	Space gear	Trench coat
Locomotion	Cars, horses, carriages	Horse	Rocket ship	Sports car
Weaponry	Fists	Six-gun	Ray gun, laser gun	Pistol with silencer

In recent years we have mixed genres together, and television shows such as *Survivor* blend together elements from game shows, beach-bunny bikini shows, soap operas, spectacles, and mysteries. Reality television is a misnomer, for these shows are highly edited and turned into dramas that involve deceit, manipulation, and revenge.

The Commercial

Let me turn now to the commercial, probably the most important genre shown on television. In 2008, advertisers in America spent around $170 billion on all media and close to $58 billion on television and cable advertising. Of this, advertisers on media using images spent:

$18 billion on national broadcast television

$15.2 billion on national cable television

$17.8 billion on the Internet

$23.6 billion on magazine advertising

These figures, obtained from Zenith Optimedia (personal correspondence) mark a considerable decrease in advertising expenditures from earlier periods. In 2004, advertisers in American spent a total of about $245 billion, when the economy was doing better and companies spent money on advertising more easily. Money spent on advertising on the Internet grew from $5.6 billion in 2004 to $17.8 billion in 2008, an enormous increase. I should point out that these figures are estimates; there is no one source of data on advertising expenditures that everyone accepts.

Fifty-seven billion dollars spent on broadcast and cable television is a substantial amount of money and translates into an enormous number of commercials.

Each commercial is a big investment on its own: the average thirty-second network commercial costs around $350,000 to create and millions of dollars to air. As a result of the high cost of air time, commercials are getting shorter and shorter, which means they must compress their messages into thirty or even fifteen or ten seconds. This compression has an impact on the visual aspects of the commercial.

In the first chapter, I discussed some of the ways in which commercials can utilize hard-wired elements in our brains to obtain their effects. I mentioned such phenomena as our tendency to return the gaze of others (direct-eye response), our natural inclination to empathize with others, our involuntary response to expressions of emotion, to sexuality, and to images of the beautiful, and the fact that we often identify and imitate others—especially celebrities and authority figures. When you add the techniques used by editors to vary the kinds of shots we see and the pace at which we see them, and add the way editors use lighting, camera techniques, and music, you see that commercials are often quite complex, and sometimes influential, works.

One thing that the commercial did was to get rid of (in most cases) the establishing shot—the long shot that gives viewers a sense of context. Films traditionally used establishing shots regularly. We would see an extreme long shot of a building; then the camera would pan along the street to the building, up the building to a window, and into the window where the action would begin. The commercial plunges viewers right into the middle of the action and gets them involved immediately. Films have now adopted this convention and, like commercials, now frequently "start in the middle."

Many commercials can be described as microdramas, in which a traditional plot is compressed to thirty seconds. In these microdramas, the product is a miraculous agent that resolves problems and allows the characters to, we surmise, live happily ever after (Figure 7.6).

To sell as quickly and convincingly as possible, actors and actresses in commercials use a great deal of facial expression and body language. If you turn off the sound and simply watch commercials, you can see that many of the characters really exaggerate their facial expressions and body language. The exaggeration counters the brevity of their performances and the disbelief that viewers bring to commercials. The performers also use their voices, all kinds of props, their sexuality, humor, and anything else they can to convince viewers to buy a given product or service.

Analyzing the Commercial

The commercial is television's most important genre—and, in certain respects, its most interesting. Commercials cost an enormous amount of money to produce and to air. The people who make commercials are some of the best and most creative individuals in the advertising and film and video world. We can learn a great deal, then, from studying these minidramas to see how they obtain their effects. What follows is a list of some of the more important topics to consider in analyzing commercials. Consider the storyboard in Figure 7.7, as well as the one in Figure 7.6, while you read this list.

NARRATIVE STRUCTURE.   What happens in the commercial? What is its plot—if a plot exists? What techniques are used to captivate viewers? Are there flashbacks or flash-forwards? Is there a narrator? Is there action? Is there conflict?

CHARACTERS.   Who are the characters in the commercial? What are their characteristics? What relationships seem to exist among them? Are they appealing? Are they funny? Are there hunks and glamor girls? If so, what function do they have? How are we supposed to relate to these characters? What about their faces (and use of facial expression), the style and color of their hair, the shape of their bodies, their age, the clothes they wear, and the

FIGURE 7.6
Storyboard for Levi's commercial—"Stranger." This storyboard shows some of the significant images found in the microdrama. Because the commercial was an animated film, it was possible to show images exactly as they would be broadcast in the commercial. Reproduced with permission of Levi Strauss & Company and Foote, Cone & Belding.

possessions they have? What kind of voices do they have? How might they help sell the product or service being advertised?

DIALOGUE. What kind of language is used? What techniques of persuasion are used to sell viewers: humor, scare tactics and the generation of anxiety, sexuality and "seductiveness," appeals to authority or to vanity, pleading, and so on?

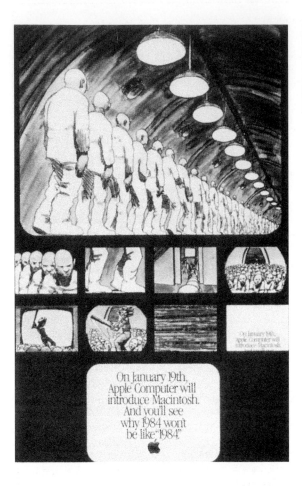

I FIGURE 7.7
Storyboard for "1984" microdrama commercial by Chiat/Day Advertising, Los Angeles. Reproduced by permission of Apple Computer, Inc.

SETTING.   Where does the action take place? When does it take place? What significance does the setting have? Are there any props of importance—furniture, paintings, machines, gadgets, cars, and so on?

VISUALS.   What kinds of shots are found in the commercial? Is there a variety of shots: close-ups, extreme close-ups, long shots, and so on? What shot angles are used, and what effect do they have?

What about the editing? How is the commercial cut? Is there hardly any cutting at all, or is there a great deal of quick cutting? If there is quick cutting, what impact does it have? Are such things as dissolves, distortion, compression, or fade-outs used? What impact do these phenomena have?

Also, how is color used? What colors are found in the commercial, and what role do these colors play? What kinds of effects are generated by the colors? How is the color related to the lighting?

CHECKLIST FOR ANALYZING TELEVISION COMMERCIALS

The following checklist focuses on the most important elements to keep in mind when viewing and analyzing television commercials.

The Narrative Structure

1. What happens in the commercial? What is the narrative line?
2. What dramatic techniques are used in the commercial? Is there humor? Surrealism?
3. Is there a narrator? If so, what is the narrator's function?
4. Is there action? What is the significance of the action?
5. Is there conflict? If so, what kind? And how is it resolved?

The Characters

6. Who are the characters? What roles do they play?
7. What do the characters in the commercial look like? Consider their facial features, their hair color and style, their bodies, their use of body language, the clothes they wear, and so on.
8. What relationship seems to exist among the characters?
9. What are the demographics of the characters in terms of age, sex, race, ethnicity, educational level, occupation, and so on?
10. What are the voices of the characters like? Do they have accents?
11. How do the attributes of the characters in the narrative help sell the product?

The Dialogue

12. What kind of language is used?
13. Does the commercial use rhetorical devices such as metaphors, associations, or alliteration? What about exaggeration, comparison and contrast, jingles, or humor?

The Setting

14. Where does the action of the commercial take place?
15. What significance does the setting have? How is the setting used to give viewers certain impressions?
16. Are any props of importance used?

The Visual Images and Sound

17. What kinds of shots are used? How many different scenes are there in the commercial?
18. How is the commercial edited? Are there numerous quick cuts? Lingering dissolves? Zooms? How are close-ups used?
19. How is color used?
20. How is lighting used?
21. Are there any intertextual elements in the commercial, such as reference to well-known films, works of literature, and the like?
22. How is sound used? Is there music? If so, what kind, and what effect might it have?

The Viewers

23. How does the commercial use information viewers already have to sell them on the product or service being advertised?
24. How does the commercial relate to popularly held beliefs, myths, ideas, attitudes, values, and archetypes?

The Product

25. What function does the product have? How do people use it?
26. What does the product and the commercial tell us about social and political considerations? For example, does it reflect problems such as alienation, anxiety, generational conflict, stereotyped thinking, or boredom?

VIEWERS' STORE OF KNOWLEDGE.   What generally held beliefs, attitudes, values, ideas, myths, heroic archetypes, and so on are reflected in the commercial?

Because commercials are so compressed, they are forced to draw on and use information and ideas their viewers already have in their heads. The primary function of the commercial is to generate a response, to create "desire," not to convey information. Commercials make use of the stock of information we all have picked up, often through our experiences and the mass media, for their own purposes.

It is useful to think of commercials as "sign systems" and to consider every aspect of a commercial as a sign to be interpreted. Thus, all of the topics discussed in this book can be used to interpret and understand the fascinating (and often irritating) art form we know as the commercial.

Television News

News programs (as well as documentaries and certain videos) are at the opposite end of the "disbelief spectrum." Numerous surveys indicate, for example, that large numbers of Americans get most of their news from television news programs and think that the news shows are more believable than stories in newspapers. We know, however, that while the camera doesn't lie, the person who controls the camera can "lie" or, at least, determine what is presented to the viewing public.

In a famous study of a 1950s parade in Chicago for General Douglas MacArthur after he had been fired by President Truman, Kurt and Gladys Engel Lang showed that what was presented on television news programs was quite different from what really went on. The actual parade was a rather dull affair, and not too many people were there, but, by using only certain shots, the television news directors led viewers to believe that it was an exciting event with mobs of people. As we noted in the discussion of photography, cameras don't lie, but liars use cameras.

News programs are also interesting for those interested in visual communication because they use a large number of graphics, captions, and similar devices. Television news is visual and aural; but there is still a need for the written word and for various kinds of signs, charts, and graphs, because they can show relationships very well and compress a great deal of complex information into a relatively simple visual display.

The news program (at least the national news) is generally a very sober affair that strives for realism. But events on television news programs often are dramatized so that they entertain as well. In other words, the producer of a news program can make the news "exciting" by injecting dramatic elements into stories—who is winning or losing, who is lying or telling the truth, or what important consequences will stem from a given event. Visually, national newscasts all have a similar look: we see the anchor or anchors sitting at a desk with screens in the background. The anchor narrates the news, and the program switches back and forth between the anchor and the field reporters, who are usually shown on screen, interviewing important figures or showing some scene of consequence.

Because television is a visual medium, many critics have suggested that television news focuses on stories that have a visual dimension to them and neglects many important stories that don't. Whatever the case, the typical national newscast runs for thirty minutes (with six or more minutes taken up with commercials), and it cannot go into great depth for any story, which is why some media analysts have suggested that television news is essentially a headline service. Viewers interested in details, background, and analysis must go to a print medium, such as a newspaper or magazine (or to a program like "The News Hour with Jim Lehrer" on public television).

Televised Hearings

Televised hearings, court proceedings (such as the O. J. Simpson trial), and similar events represent one of the more important new genres in television. These hearings have often played an important role in our political order, affecting the careers of important politicians and, at times, even presidents.

Televised hearings generally attempt to avoid manipulating images with camera work, lighting, and so on, but sometimes, by chance, the camera placement has significant effects. In *Picture Perfect: The Art and Artifice of Public Image-Making,* Kiku Adatto recounts a story in which the filmmaker Steven Spielberg was visiting Washington during the Iran-Contra hearings. Adatto writes (1993:13):

> As he watched the hearings with some Democratic congressmen, he offered them a lesson in camera angles. "Watch this," Spielberg said, as he turned down the sound and directed the congressmen's attention to [Colonel Oliver] North's image on the screen. "The camera on North is shooting up, from about four inches below his eyes. This is the way they shot Gary Cooper in the western, *High Noon,* to make him look like a hero." When the camera panned to the committee members questioning North, Spielberg pointed out, the lighting was dim. Seen at a distance, they looked sinister. Spielberg told the assembled Democrats: "It doesn't matter what Oliver North says. He has already won the battle because he looks like a hero and everyone else looks like a villain."

We can see, then, that matters which might seem to be trivial, such as camera angles and lighting, play an important role in hearings and similar media events, because images often convey messages to viewers that are more significant than what is being said by the person being videotaped.

Music Videos

This genre is particularly interesting for students of visual communication because we find that MTV has a particular look to it. The music videos broadcast on television are, in fact, commercials for the recordings produced by various musical groups. Depending on the available money and the artistic inclinations of the producer, the videos generally either show the band making the song or turn the song into some kind of a dramatic piece.

What is interesting about music videos is that so many of them have surrealistic qualities. *Surrealism* is a visual style that is dreamlike and nonlinear (full of flash-forwards and flashbacks), makes use of fantastic images and distorted perspectives, and is full of special effects (Figures 7.8, 7.9, and 7.10). The term *surrealism* comes from painting and describes the work of a group of highly experimental artists such as Joan Miró, Salvador Dalí, André Breton, and René Magritte, who worked in the 1920s (and later) and who wanted to represent the unconscious mind with their paintings.

We find surrealistic elements in many music videos—a surprising combination of avant-garde visual aesthetics and rather ordinary, formulaic musical aesthetics. One of the problems with music television is that after watching it for an hour or so, it tends to blur in your mind. There's been so much visual excitement that you suffer from a bad case of "information overload."

These music videos, one might argue, take the experimentalism and vitality found in the commercial and push these phenomena to their furthest limits. They have, in turn, greatly influenced the look of regular commercials and also have impacted the psyches of the teenagers (and others) who watch them.

In her essay "The Look of the Sound," Pat Aufderheide describes how these videos relate to young people in America (1987:118):

> With nary a reference to cash or commodities, music videos cross the consumer's gaze as a series of mood states. They trigger moods such as nostalgia, regret, anxiety, confusion, dread, envy, admiration, pity, titillation—attitudes at one remove from primal expressions such as passion, ecstasy, and rage. The moods often express a lack, an incompletion, an instability, a searching for location. In music videos, those feelings are carried on flights of whimsy, extended journeys into the arbitrary.

These music videos, Aufderheide argues, reflect a basic tension found in American youth culture—a sense of instability and incompleteness. These feelings push young people into a quest to "buy and belong" that forces

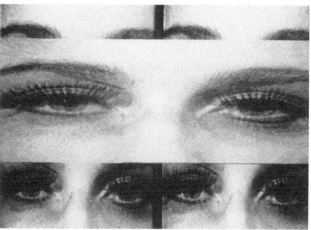

▌ FIGURE 7.10
Lynn Hershman, still from
"Birdie," 1987. This surrealistic image was created
using a Proteus computer.
Reproduced by permis-
sion of Lynn Hershman.

them to "become a piece of the action in a continuous performance." Is it healthy, one might ask, to have young people, who are searching for stable identities, spend so much time watching a genre that is full of discontinuities and random chaos, as well as images that, all too often, are sexist, sadistic, and excessively violent?

One of the more interesting aspects of music videos is that their visual elements are used to enhance the music, rather than the music being used to enhance the visual images—the opposite of what is found in films and television. The music is what is basic. These videos create narratives (stories) that often use innovative choreography, costuming, animation, and avant-garde editing techniques (quick cuts, unusual montages, hand-held cameras, dramatic colors and lighting, and so on). In short, music videos represent an exciting, distinctive genre that dramatizes music, often in visually interesting and arresting ways.

VIDEO ARTISTS

It is hard, at times, to know where to draw the line between what we call commercial television and video art. The video artists, like all artists, have their private visions and use video to make personal statements, to create videos that they think are beautiful and thought-provoking. Unlike commercial television, these videos are not meant to please the general public, though videos sometimes are shown on television stations (generally public television). They are often highly imaginative, can be experimental in form (in the way they manipulate images, color, music, and narrative structure), and frequently have sociological and ideological dimensions to them.

Ironically, music television and other television borrows from these video artists—in the same way that the surrealists influenced other artists and impacted other media. The moral is that art styles and movements have an impact and influence that is quite widespread.

ZAPPING OR CHANNEL SURFING

The final irony, relative to the television image, stems from the development of the remote-control channel switcher. Increasingly large numbers of people use these channel switchers for "zapping" or channel surfing, a process by which they jump, back and forth, from channel to channel. Estimates suggest that about a third of television watchers zap regularly and that more than 50 percent of teenagers do so.

What this means is that people are watching not so much television programs as television itself. (This is a big problem for advertising agencies, which are selling audiences to advertisers. If people flip at the first sign of a commercial, or even before that, the whole television advertising industry is in trouble.) Not only is the television screen a mosaic, but people are also turning television itself into a kind of mosaic and simultaneously watching (to the extent that the term *watching* applies) a dozen or more programs at the same time.

This reduces television to its elemental form—visual images—and people who zap essentially turn television into a set of visual images (and auditory stimuli) at the expense of program form and continuity. We have a micro-mosaic reaching its audience in the form of what we might call macro-mosaic, a huge surrealistic collection of bits and pieces of many different programs and stories that become a person's television program. People who zap make their own television programs out of the programming available at a given time—an electronic montage. Thanks to the remote-control device, we can all become video artists (Figure 7.11).

TIVO AND VIDEO RECORDING DEVICES

The development of TiVo and other digital recording devices with the ability to zap commercials has been a big blow to the advertising industry. These devices enable owners to prerecord programs and fast-forward

I FIGURE 7.11
This image is a pictorial rendering of channel surfing. By Arthur Asa Berger.

through commercials when the programs are played back on television. In response to this, advertisers are now resorting to product placement, which involves having characters in television programs do things like eat certain brands of food, use certain brands of products, and drive certain models of cars.

In addition, now companies are "purchasing" the integration of their products into scripts, so the products play a more important role than they did when they were by chance placed in the script. What this means is that commercials and traditional television genres such as action-adventure shows, crime shows, game shows or whatever, are now merging, and traditional genres are losing their distinctive identities. How television viewers respond to this kind of purchased integration of products into scripts remains to be seen.

CONCLUSIONS

Television is the medium everyone loves to hate. It has been described as a "vast wasteland" and is the object of endless condemnation by elitists, many of whom take pride in never watching it. It is also the object of countless studies by psychologists, sociologists, and other social scientists, who investigate its effect on everything from our family lives to our sex lives to our political behavior.

One of the most important shortcomings of many studies of television is that they pay no attention to the visual and aesthetic aspects of the medium. The basic model for most studies comes from social psychology and is concerned with the impact of television on attitudes, beliefs, and values—which can then be used to predict everything from consumer behavior to voting behavior. This model, which neglects the power of images, sound, and other aesthetic factors (such as the kinds of shots used, the cutting, and so on), is simplistic and not adequate to deal with television in all of its complexity.

Fortunately, this emphasis is changing, and as interest in visual communication progresses, we can hope that new and better ways of studying television will emerge.

APPLICATIONS

1. Watch commercials without the sound so that you can pay attention to their technical aspects. What do you find of interest?

2. Assume you have been asked to create a commercial for some product. Create a storyboard for the projected commercial (with six or eight frames), and be prepared to explain to a potential client why you did what you did. How will your commercial help sell the product?

3. Create a new television genre by mixing various television genres, and write a one-paragraph description of the show, for newspapers, that would summarize the show for potential viewers. You can use up to three genres. In what way is your new genre distinctive and unique? Why would audiences like it?

4. Tape three network news programs and compare them in terms of the order of topics, the topics covered, and related concerns. Are there important similarities? If so, why? Are there important differences? If so,

how do you explain this? (You can do the same for local news programs also. See if you can figure out how the show with the highest ratings differs from its competitors.)

5. Make a list of the topics covered in a network news program, and compare it with the first page of *The New York Times*. What do you find? Is television news just a "headline" service? What does that mean?

6. Using everything you've learned about visual communication, analyze a music video that you find interesting. Consider such matters as the images, the cutting, the lighting, the use of color, the way performers are shot, the way women are shown (and their roles), the way men are shown (and their roles), the lyrics, and anything else that you think is of interest. What factors contribute to the video's appeal? And why have music videos been so successful overall?

7. Add other genres to the chart on genres. Deal with genres such as horror, action-adventure, sitcoms, news programs, and reality shows.

8. How has the fact that Americans are exposed to many more commercials than people in other countries affected our psyches and our society? If you could do something to change the role advertising plays in the United States, what would you do?

KEY TERMS FOR CHAPTER 7

Z-axis shot
A-B axis shot

shot

COMICS, CARTOONS, AND ANIMATION:
The Development of an Art Form

Comics have evolved from lowly "kid's stuff" appearing in newspapers into graphic novels and animated films of considerable power and brilliance. They are also valuable repositories of our social and cultural beliefs and practices.

THE COMIC STRIP

Comic strips have been prominent features of American newspapers since the early 1900s, and some media scholars have suggested that, in many respects, the comic strip is an American idiom. Describing the comic strip as an American medium would be more proper. Over the years, a huge number of comic strips have been created, many of which are now seen as "classics" and are being reprinted in large art books.

We now recognize that the comic strip has an aesthetic quality of its own and that the strips are important repositories of our values and beliefs. For this reason, historians and sociologists have made increasing use of the comics as a kind of documentary record of American culture—especially in the early part of the twentieth century. Many comic strips lasted fifty or sixty years; in some cases, a strip has been kept going after the original artist died by bringing in a different artist. This is the case with *Blondie,* which started in 1930. Chic Young, the creator, died in 1973, but the comic strip is being published.

Normal dialogue appears in balloons with an unbroken outline, with the tail pointing to the speaker. A perforated line indicates whispering. If the words are written in very small letters within a big balloon, it means the speaker is astonished or ashamed. A cry has a spiky outline, and the famous "telephone voice" has a zig-zag shape, with a zig-zag arrow disappearing into the telephone. Balloons indicating cold or conceited voices have little icicles sprouting from their undersides. Thought balloons are connected with the thinker by a series of little circles which look like bubbles, and if a speech balloon has a little arrow pointing outside the picture, the speaker is "off."

– Rheinhold Reitberger and Wolfgang Fuchs, Comics: Anatomy of a Mass Medium

Reading the Comics

A **comic strip** can be defined as a form of pictorial art that has the following attributes:

1. Continuing characters
2. Frames that show the action
3. Dialogue in balloons (generally speaking)

Although we call them "comics" or "the funnies," there are many comic strips that are serious—so the term really is misleading. (The French use the term "designed bands," which implies that not all comics are humorous.) In fact, many of our greatest comic strips—*Dick Tracy, Little Orphan Annie, Buck Rogers, Tarzan*—are not humorous. A number of years ago the United States Post Office issued a set of stamps featuring some of our "classic" comics (Figure 8.1). Comics are also an art form that many artists and writers find useful for telling stories, as the page from *Streetcar Romance* shows (Figure 8.2).

We can make a distinction between comics and cartoons: cartoons do not have continuing characters or dialogue shown in balloons. And some cartoons—political ones—are not always funny or meant to make people laugh, though many are humorous as well as critical.

There are, it turns out, a number of conventions we have to learn if we are to read the comics correctly. Let's look at them.

1. *The way characters are drawn.* In some comics, the style is realistic. But in others, it is highly stylized and meant to be funny; these characters have big noses, big ears, silly looks on their faces, and so on. The way the characters are drawn is a clue as to how to classify the strip—as funny or as serious.
2. *Facial expression.* Being a visual art, comics make considerable use of facial expression to show the feelings or emotional states of the various characters. Exaggerated facial expression is one way comic strip artists can inject humor into their strips.
3. *The role of balloons.* Comic strip artists use various methods to let us know how to respond to the dialogue of the characters. Sometimes, the words are shown in heavy print or in some other typeface. We often find exclamation marks used. There is another convention that is important here: thoughts are shown in scalloped balloons, and so comic strip artists can show what people are saying and thinking by using different kinds of balloons. Sound effects are often shown in zigzagged balloons, which gives the artists one more way of generating effects.

4. *Movement lines.* Artists show movement and speed by using lines that indicate movement, and sometimes puffs of smoke to show how fast someone or something is moving.

5. *Panels at the bottom or top of the frame.* These panels are used to maintain continuity and to tell readers what to expect or what is going on at a given moment.

6. *The setting.* A given setting provides readers with a sense of what is going on and how seriously to take things.

▌FIGURE 8.2
This self-published comic book has the basic elements found in comic strips. *Streetcar Romance.* Script by Donelle Merton; art by Sarah Kortum.

7. *The action.* Each frame in a comic strip is the equivalent of a frame in a film, except that dialogue is shown in the comic strip, thoughts are revealed, and narration is provided through the printed word. The comic strip provides points of action that readers must fill in or complete in their own minds—quite similar to the "jump cut" of film.

Comic strips are often collaborations between writers and artists, though the old humorous comic strips generally were drawn and written by the same person. The artists who draw these strips use a variety of shots and shot angles in telling their stories. The artists must be mindful of the strip or the page (in the case of comic books) and make certain that they maintain visual interest by varying the kinds of shots and shot angles. (In this respect, the storyboards used in planning television commercials are very much like comic books: the storyboards show six or eight basic shots and indicate the dialogue that goes with each shot.)

As we grow up and become accustomed to reading the comics, we learn the various conventions connected with this medium. As with film, you have to learn how to "read" comics to be able to understand them fully.

Reading the comics, then, is not as simple as we might think. In addition to the various conventions we have to master, we must keep in mind that there is a complicated interplay between the visual elements of the comic strip and the linguistic ones. As Roger Sabin points out in *Adult Comics: An Introduction* (1993:9):

> A strip does not "happen" in the words, or the pictures, but somewhere in between, in what is sometimes known as "the marriage of text and image." The strips may just be a mix of words and pictures, but the permutations of the two are almost endless—limited only by the imaginations of the creators. In short, strips have their own aesthetic: they are a language with their own grammar, syntax and punctuation. They are not some hybrid form halfway between "literature" and "art" (whatever those words might mean), but a medium in their own right.

Sabin's point is important, because many critics see the comics as, by definition, childish subliterature. That is, because we start reading comics when we are young children, many critics assume that comics must be childish. These critics are unaware that the comics are a distinctive medium and that the mixture of images and words found in the comics has enormous resonance and power. Comics are a wonderful medium for telling stories—and for teaching—and, in fact, the two often go together.

The Power of the Comic Strip

Why is this simple medium so powerful? For one thing, we spend many years with comic strips and their characters. *Peanuts,* for example, started in

---

JAPANESE COMICS

There was an interesting phenomenon in Japanese comics (*manga*) in the sixties known as *kawaii*, which translates into "cuteness" in Japanese. Cute women are generally shown in these comics with large, round (that is, non-Asian) eyes and relatively little in the way of breast development. The opposite of these cute girls were the *utsukushii*, beautiful and well-developed women who also looked rather Western. Over the years, things changed and by the nineties these "cute" girls had kept their facial features (the large, Keane-like eyes) but had fully developed bodies. They were often involved in sexually explicit and violent sexual scenarios, involving bondage and in some cases rape. We find rape fantasies and other violent sexual fantasies in many comics read by middle-class workers in Japan—a country with relatively low levels of violence. It may be that these sexually explicit and violent comics help middle-aged and middle-class Japanese males deal with various kinds of repression and other anxieties from which they suffer.

1950, and many people have been following that strip for fifty years or more. The more we follow the strip, the more significance various events that happen in it have for us, because these events relate to the characters and their personalities, and we have been observing both for long periods of time. The comic strip is an iterative (repetitive) medium or "art form," as some put it. Thus, the more we follow it, the more it means to us, until finally, as in the case of *Peanuts*, its characters merge into our folklore and, in a curious way, into our lives.

So the comic strip (or certain ones, at least) involves us for long periods of time, even though we may read a given episode in a matter of seconds. In addition, the comic strip has the power to create fantastic and fascinating personalities, with whom we become "involved." In certain humorous ones, we find personalities who spend decades "locked" in comedic combat with one another—Beetle Bailey and Sarge in *Beetle Bailey,* Krazy Kat and Offissa Pupp in *Krazy Kat,* and the Spook and the Jailors in *The Wizard of Id,* to name just a few.

The great characters in comic strips develop their personalities over many years, and we develop attachments to these characters and expectations about them. Think of *Doonesbury* and its remarkable cast of characters, who, year after year, keep appearing and reappearing in various guises and situations.

The remarkable capacity of the comic strip to generate memorable characters is another reason comics are so powerful. We continually search for personalities with whom we can identify (and to whom we can relate, even if only through a medium). Thus, the comic strip, which can generate personalities who have extraordinarily long lives (as fictional characters go), has much more impact on people than we might imagine.

In addition, the art style of some cartoons is extremely expressive and often quite individualistic. (A French scholar, Robert Benayoun, even wrote a book, *Black and White in the Comics,* which deals with the visual attributes of the comic strip.) The use of grotesques (visually and psychologically) gives the comic strip a unique power. The *grotesque* is an art style that uses exaggerated and often distorted physical characteristics to make a point. The physical ugliness of grotesques is often allied, especially in the work of *Dick Tracy* creator Chester Gould, with their moral ugliness and criminality. Indeed, Gould created a veritable bestiary of criminal characters, such as Flat Top and the Mole, with whom he peopled his strip (Figure 8.3).

Psychologically, comics are filled with grotesques in the sense that we find numerous monomaniacs, obsessives, and single-minded types—who live only to scrounge their next meal, to escape from prison, to harass some

(a)

I FIGURE 8.3

(a) This image of Dick Tracy was on a postage stamp, but it could also have been done by an artist like Andy Warhol. Many pop artists made paintings based on comic strips and advertisements. (b) The frames from Gilbert Shelton's *Tricky Prickears* parody *Dick Tracy.* Used with permission of Gilbert Shelton.

(b)

character, or whatever. Most of these grotesques are found in strips where their obsessive quality becomes amusing and makes possible humor based on frustrating them. In some cases, we have momentary monomania—as in *Peanuts,* where Lucy congenitally fails to catch fly balls or snatches the football away just before Charlie Brown can kick it.

THE COMIC STRIP AS A TEACHING TOOL

In addition to providing entertainment, the comic strip has been used for teaching purposes. For example, a textbook on archaeology, *Archaeology: The Comic,* created by Johannes H. N. Loubser, offers readers an introduction to archaeology in the form of a large-format comic book (Figure 8.4).

Educators have discovered that writing textbooks in the form of narratives—novels, detective stories, and comics—is a good way to induce students to

❙ FIGURE 8.4
This book uses the comic strip format to teach the basic principles of archaeology. Used with permission from David Yurkovich.

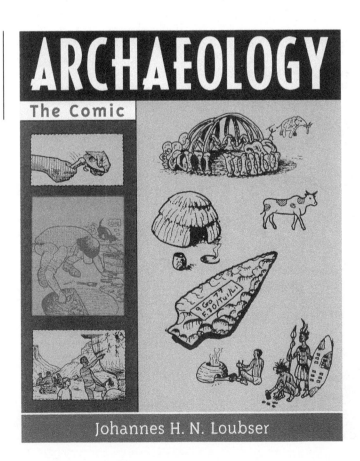

learn about various subjects and a growing number of professors have taken to writing textbooks using these formats.

The military has also learned that creating manuals in the form of comic books has been effective and has produced a number of manuals to teach various subjects. The comic strip is a format that Americans are familiar with and used to reading, and they associate comic strips with pleasure and entertainment. So it makes sense to use this format for educational purposes.

GRAPHIC NOVELS

In recent years, the comic strip and comic books have morphed into something new, the graphic novel (Figure 8.5). These graphic novels—novels told in comic strip form—are much longer than traditional comic books and often

I FIGURE 8.5
Page from a graphic novel. Courtesy of AltaMira Press, a division of Rowman & Littlefield Publishers.

are used to tell stories that are considerably different from the kinds of stories about superheroes, like Spiderman or Superman, found in comic books.

The graphic novels are serious works of art but because they use a format that has been traditionally reserved for popular culture, the comic strip frame, many people find it hard to give them the status of being "high" art. Some of them, such as *Maus*, deal with important themes, such as the Holocaust, while others represent more elevated treatments of traditional comic book stories.

When the comic strip moves into animation, we discover how powerful the graphic image can be. Some animated films, by great animators, can be considered works of high art and are universally recognized as brilliant achievements. A good example would be *Swept Away*, which has achieved the status of a modern classic.

THE CARTOON

A **cartoon** is usually confined to one frame and does not have continuous characters, though it may use certain types over and over again (or, in the case of political cartoons, which are often not meant to be funny, certain political figures). The cartoon uses not balloons but captions underneath the frame to make its point. There are two types of cartoons: humorous cartoons (Figure 8.6), which often satirize conventions in a given society as well as certain character

❘ FIGURE 8.6
Notice the degree of stylization in this image taken from the Beatles' movie *The Yellow Submarine.* Courtesy of the Museum of Modern Art, New York, Film Stills Archive.

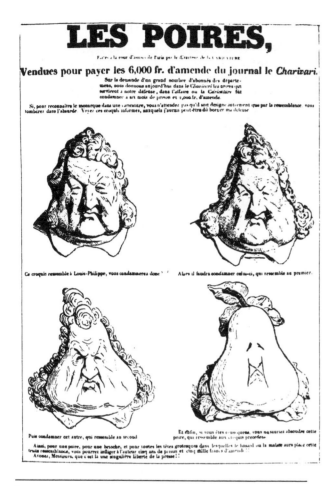

L. C. Gregg in the Atlanta *Constitution.*

FOR PRESIDENT!

I FIGURE 8.7
Philipon, "The Pears," *Le Charivari*, January 17, 1831. The artist used the image of a pear, playing on his face and physique to caricature France's King Louis-Philippe. Censors of the king eventually forbade artists to draw any pearlike figures.

I FIGURE 8.8
L. C. Gregg, "For President," *Atlanta Constitution,* circa 1904. This political cartoon is an optical illusion in which Teddy Roosevelt's image was created by using various objects, a technique employed many centuries earlier by the Italian artist Arcimboldo. The objects are all connected with militarism, death, and war and generate a negative impression of Roosevelt.

types, and political cartoons (Figures 8.7 and 8.8), which make a point about some political situation and which may or may not be funny.

The cartoon often relies heavily on information known to readers and thus functions by striking a responsive chord—by making us see something we didn't see before or recognize the cupidity and stupidity of humans and their institutions. Sometimes they can be used to provide valuable information in an amusing and nonthreatening manner (Figure 8.9). Cartoonists also may develop a recognizable "line" or style and a stance or point of view.

PANTS MADE TO A DIFFERENT VISION.

▌FIGURE 8.9
This advertisement uses humor and whimsy to sell Levis. Reproduced with permission of Levi Strauss & Company and Foote, Cone & Belding.

Many of the common techniques of humor are available to the cartoonist—who can set characters up and manipulate them for comic effect. Cartoonists use techniques such as revelation of ignorance, mistakes, exaggeration, coincidence, satire, parody, and reversals. Therefore, although the elements of the cartoon are rather simple, the possibilities for expression are almost limitless.

Visual Humor in Cartoons

A number of important techniques of visual humor can be used in cartoons.

EXAGGERATION.   Here the artist makes funny drawings in which feet are very big, noses are elongated, bodies are very large (relative to the size of heads or simply in general), ears stick out, and so on. Exaggeration is a standard technique used by humorists; in this case, the exaggeration is physical—and may reflect the zany psychological characteristics of the characters.

CARICATURE.   This is a form of portraiture in which a character's likeness is preserved but great liberties are taken with his or her face (Figure 8.10). This technique is often used in political cartoons to ridicule a person. Often, the person portrayed is put into some embarrassing situation—usually of political or social significance and frequently unflattering in nature.

We should not underestimate the power of caricature. It is used by many political cartoonists, often with devastating results, as most newspaper editorial pages demonstrate.

I FIGURE 8.10
John Updike, *Caricature of Art Berger,* circa 1954. This caricature was drawn by the author John Updike. Note the simplicity of the drawing and the way Updike exaggerates the features of the subject. Compare the caricature with the photograph of the subject to see what the caricaturist has seized on to emphasize in his drawing.

MISTAKES.   Here we find characters misunderstanding gestures or making other mistakes that have a visual dimension to them. This kind of humor may be described as humor of identity: it involves something problematic with identity, as in the case of a dog begging in front of a statue of a man who seems to be holding something to eat or a porcupine mistaking a cactus for another porcupine and saying to it, "I love you."

VISUAL PUNS.   Here we take a linguistic pun and play with it and generate visual puns to go along with it. I have, for example, taken the word *con* (as in *convict*) and drawn a number of visual puns based on the term: content, concave, and so on. These puns use the cartoon convention of the convict as a person in striped clothing and sometimes chained to a huge iron ball as a point of departure (Figure 8.11).

COMIC ILLUSTRATIONS.   With this technique, a drawing comments on or relates somehow (often quite indirectly) in a funny way to something in the text. The secret is to visualize a drawing or cartoon that people will connect with the content of the text.

HUMOROUS ALLUSIONS.   Here the artist plays on certain historical, legendary, or mythological figures or events in the public's mind for comic effect, essentially by parodying them. Heroes and heroines from films, novels, or the comics can also be used. This technique is often used in political cartoons,

∎ FIGURE 8.11
*Arthur Asa Berger,
"CONS." These drawings
are visual puns that play
with sounds and mean-
ings. What are these
"cons"? See page 220 for
answers. By Arthur Asa
Berger.*

where a politician is shown as a would-be Superman or a Greek god or
some other figure, except that the drawing pokes fun at the person (who is
also caricatured). In some cases, the cartoonists use "types" of persons or
characters, such as Huns or wimps or zanies of one sort or another. There is
an unflattering connection (or comparison) made between the figure and
the type portrayed (Figure 8.12).

The cartoon, then, by utilizing our collective consciousness and various
techniques of visual comedy, is a powerful and popular art form.

Animated Cartoons

The term *animation* has to do with giving life to something, with making
something seem alive and active. Animation can be defined as the process of

❙ FIGURE 8.12
Cartoon images permeate
contemporary art. Here
they are used in a work of
electronic art—George
Legrady's *Slippery Traces.*
Used with permission of
George Legrady.

filming two-dimensional drawings or three-dimensional objects (such as puppets or clay figures) so as to produce the illusion of motion. Animated cartoons are drawings that originally were photographed on movie film to give the illusion that the characters drawn are alive and can move and talk.

The movie cameras used for making animated films have to be fitted with a device that allows single-frame action—that is, one frame to be shot at a time. With computers, of course, this is not necessary. (Computer animation that simulates real-life figures is discussed in Chapter 9.)

With 35-mm and 70-mm movie cameras, twenty-four frames are shot each second for sound film. This means that an artist must draw twenty-four pictures, each with a minimal increment of movement, to create the illusion of motion. If fewer than twenty-four pictures are drawn for a second's worth of film, the motion seems jerky. Winsor McKay, a comic strip artist, generally is credited with producing the first successful animated film—*Gertie, the Trained Dinosaur*—in 1909. In 1928, Walt Disney produced *Steamboat Willie,* which featured synchronous sound (sound effects that were synchronized with the visual images). With the release in 1937 of Disney's first feature, *Snow White and the Seven Dwarfs,* the age of animated feature-length films was upon us.

As noted previously, other methods of animation besides drawings created by artists or generated by computers are available. Another important animation technique is *claymation,* a form of object animation in which figures sculpted in clay are changed very slowly, with each change filmed, to give the illusion of motion. Clay figures typically are changed twenty-four times for a second's worth of animated film. Objects like dolls, puppets, animal figures, and the like can also be animated and, so to speak, brought to life.

If it takes 24 drawings to do one second of a typical animated film, that means it takes 1,440 frames to do one minute (60 times 24) and 86,400 frames to do an hour-long film. Obviously, prior to the development of computer animation programs, the amount of work needed to make animated films was enormous. Whole armies of artists were needed to make the earliest feature-length animated films; *Snow White,* for example, used some 400,000 drawings.

One shortcut that was used before computers was cel animation. Using clear plastic overlays known as *cels,* artists drew not completely new images for each shot, but only the parts of the images that moved—for example, a finger or facial expression. These cels are now quite valuable and are sold as works of art, at very high prices, in many art galleries.

Animation using cartoons or drawings—technically, two-dimensional animation—should not be regarded as an art form exclusively for children. Many artists have used animation to create powerful films dealing with political and social issues, often using humor or, in countries where there was repression and censorship, indirection. In fact, numerous festivals worldwide are held to present the best animated films.

Animators distinguish between character animation, which involves drawings of people and objects, and graphic animation, which involves material such as logos, graphics, and photographic stills. Animators also work for different media: some for broadcast media or home video, and others for disk-based media, such as CDs, floppy disks, interactive media, and so on. Each of these media has different requirements.

For example, character animation involves issues such as how characters walk and move, how they use their mouths to make sounds, and how they rearrange their features to express emotions. Usually, artists draw their characters on paper and scan the drawings and then use computers to set the characters in motion, mask them, and colorize them. In some cases, animators take film footage of characters doing certain things and then animate this footage by a process known as rotoscoping. Fractal's *Painter* is one of the most commonly used software packages for this kind of work, but there are many others. In Hollywood, many animators use high-end packages like *Amazon Paint, Power-Animator, Pandemonium,* and *Liberty* that run on Silicon Graphics platforms.

In sum, animation is an important branch of the film medium. And the development of inexpensive computer animation software programs has opened up even greater possibilities for writers and artists who wish to take advantage of the unique properties of animation.

THE IMPACT OF COMICS AND CARTOONS

The elements in comic strips and cartoons may be relatively simple—line drawings and words, for the most part—but the impact of these art forms can be quite strong. We now recognize that seemingly simple phenomena can trigger powerful emotional responses in people, because these phenomena (the sound of rain, a symbol, a kind of lighting) often are connected to profoundly important experiences people have had, which are stored in their memories and called to mind, somehow, by something in the comic strip or cartoon—just as they are by verbal or visual images in "classic" literature or art.

The pictorial arts have a long history—from drawings on the walls of caves, thousands and thousands of years ago, to the latest episode of *Peanuts* or *Doonesbury* found in the morning newspaper. There is a kind of magic and power to capturing an image that we have recognized and made use of—for millennia, it would seem. Some scholars have suggested that precursors of the comic book appeared centuries ago, and we know that the political cartoon has been around for hundreds of years.

One reason the comic book and cartoon have been so popular is that they are extremely flexible and can be used for a variety of purposes. For example, the U.S. Army has found that it is helpful to use the comic book format in teaching soldiers how to use and maintain some equipment. And many people use a form of cartoon—greeting cards—to express emotions indirectly, especially emotions that they find it hard to communicate directly (Figure 8.13).

Comics and cartoons also can be used for advertising; the comic strip simulates action and has the power of the storyboard, which is used in designing commercials. From McLuhan's point of view, the storyboard, having less information than the commercial, would generate stronger involvement on the part of readers than would the commercial itself.

And we all have seen how the comic strip has evolved into the animated film, which is a remarkable medium that can generate very powerful experiences. The early animated films were simple and funny; but as animation has developed, it has led to what might be described as serious animated films that use the power of the artist to create incredible characters, scenes, and events. The animated film makes possible a style called "the fantastic" and expands our horizons immeasurably.

Finally, there is the matter of the power comic strips and cartoons have to generate humor (Figure 8.14). Humor is a great enigma; philosophers and scientists have been fascinated by it all throughout history, and many of our greatest minds, from Aristotle to Sigmund Freud, have tried to explain what humor is and what functions it has for people. Cartoons and comics usually generate a smile or two rather than laughter—but this smile is a signifier of

Figure 8.15
This is part of a comic book that a student passed in as an assignment in a popular culture course I taught many years ago. Shelley Moore. Comic book assignment.

CARTOONS ARE POWERFUL

When I published the first edition of Seeing is Believing, a reviewer commented that it seemed strange that I would include a chapter that dealt with cartoons, comics, and animated film. I don't imagine that reviewer would make the same comment after the incredible reaction of some Muslims to the cartoons of Mohammed that appeared in the Danish newspaper *Jyllands-Posten* on September 30, 2005. In that issue of the newspaper, there were twelve cartoons dealing with Mohammed, including one with him wearing a bomb that was lit in his turban. Some Danish Muslims protested the cartoons and sent copies of them to some Muslim countries, which led to an explosion of violence for several weeks in February in which Danish consulates were attacked and huge mobs of angry Muslims protested in many Muslim countries. A feature article in the February 11, 2006 issue of *The Wall Street Journal* dealt with the matter in an article with the headline "The Cartoons That Shook the World."

On the Internet, the cartoons were available on many sites and were circulated widely. Jewish groups pointed out that Muslim newspapers and publications contained numerous anti-Semitic and anti-Catholic and anti-Christian cartoons and complained that the Muslims were being hypocritical. They didn't mind publishing cartoons attacking Jews and Christians but didn't like cartoons attacking their religion. Those supporting the Danish newspaper argued that free speech was the issue and that it was important to defend free speech against the Muslim attack. By the middle of February, the number of Muslim protests diminished. Political scientists pointed out that the cartoons exposed a deep rift between modern democratic states and contemporary Muslim states. The Muslim reaction to the cartoons demonstrates, clearly, that images of all kinds have incredible power and, in certain circumstances, can "shake" the world.

---

some kind of a humorous message that has been received and understood. How this happens is still a considerable mystery. We know what techniques the cartoonists and comic strip artists and writers use, but we do not know why pictorial humor makes us laugh.

CONCLUSIONS

The fact that many comic strips and comic books are funny has led people to underestimate their significance, because people often assume that things that are funny (or not serious) do not have the same status as so-called serious works. We no longer make this mistake, and now many scholars and researchers are studying humor, in all of its manifestations, and acknowledging its great importance. We have discovered that humor has important psychological, sociological, political, and even physiological significance. Humor stimulates the heart and produces various kinds of relaxation effects.

It is worth noting, then, that some of our greatest humorists are our comic strip artists and cartoonists. And, in the same vein, some of our most significant—in terms of their impact on the general public—creative artists have been our comic strip and comic book creators and our cartoonists.

APPLICATIONS

1. Assume you have been hired by a company that creates comic books. Create a comic book superhero or superheroine and draw the cover. How will you make your character different? Interesting? Use colors and make your drawing the size of comic books (seven by ten inches).

2. Create an origin tale, two pages long, for your character. (The origin tale of *Superman* is two pages long.) Be sure to use all the conventions of the comic book: frames, dialogue, action, and so on. Do you think you have created a compelling tale? Why or why not? Did you enjoy the process?

3. Make a content analysis of the comics page of your local newspaper. Do the following: count the number of frames, count the number of words spoken by male and female (and other) characters, count the number of times you see male and female figures, classify the strips in some manner, and list the topics discussed or alluded to. What do the comics (or, at least, the ones you've studied) reflect about American society and culture? Are any groups underrepresented? Or not represented at all?

4. Try drawing caricatures of your friends. You might find profiles are easiest, but you can try full face or three-quarter face if you wish. Try to capture their likenesses and, at the same time, exaggerate their features. Does this exercise make you see them in a new light?

5. Using a mirror, try drawing full-face caricatures of yourself. Which features will you exaggerate? Does this exercise make you see yourself in a new light?

6. Using your skill as a caricaturist, try drawing a political cartoon. You can use the work of political cartoonists as models to imitate, but the idea for the cartoon should be your own. Does this exercise give you a better appreciation of these cartoonists?

7. Do you have any visual novels? If so, write a book review of one of them, explaining how a visual novel differs from a comic book. Why do you think visual novels have become popular in recent years? Why not earlier?

8. Try your hand at making a book of cartoons or a short comic book (see Figure 8.15 for an example).

ANSWERS:

"CONS"
(A) Second baseman
(B) Concave
(C) Content
(D) Condor

"Nosology"
(A) Agnosetic
(B) The Nose of Kilmanjaro
(C) Noseferatu
(D) Cyranose de Bergerac

KEY TERMS FOR CHAPTER 8

comic strip   animation
cartoon   graphic novel

COMPUTERS AND GRAPHICS:
Wonders from the Image-Maker

For capturing new images, the computer is an instrument of unparalleled reach. Entirely new worlds suddenly come into view: the thermal tides of the human body and the activity of the brain, for example; the geological and biological patterns of the earth's surface; or the radiowave signatures of objects in space. Like the historic invention of the microscope and telescope, the development of computer-image processing has expanded our vision far beyond the range of the unaided human senses.

—Joseph Deken,
Computer Images: State of the Art

COMPUTERS AND GRAPHICS

Computers have had an enormous impact on all the arts—in areas such as desktop publishing, photography, videos and filmmaking. Now, with the development of Internet print-on-demand publishing programs such as www.lulu.com, just about anyone with a computer and a modem can become a "published" writer at minimal expense. We are all aware of the way computers and the Internet have affected our lives and our societies and we find ourselves both awestruck about the power of computers and a bit fearful about how computers may be used against us by governmental agencies, hackers, terrorists, and others.

Our ambivalence toward the computer was reflected in the famous Macintosh "1984" commercial that introduced the Macintosh computer. The commercial, made in England by Ridley Scott, shows a group of people with shaved heads (skinheads were used) who are captives of some gigantic organization. They are in a huge auditorium being brainwashed by a middle-aged functionary in that organization who is babbling nonsense (Figure 9.1.) The Macintosh was introduced as a means of helping people escape from what was portrayed as enslavement.

The "1984" commercial shows a beautiful blonde woman, clutching a large sledgehammer, being pursued by helmeted guards (Figure 9.2.) She races into the large auditorium where the inmates are being brainwashed and throws her sledgehammer at the screen. It explodes. This destroys the hold the brainwasher had on his victims, who stare open-mouthed at the

❙ FIGURE 9.1
Scene from the Macintosh "1984" commercial—taken from television screen. Courtesy of Apple Computer, Inc. and Chiat/Day Advertising.

❙ FIGURE 9.2
Close-up from the Macintosh "1984" commercial. Taken from television screen. Courtesy of Apple Computer, Inc. and Chiat/Day Advertising.

events that are transpiring. It is certainly one of the more famous television commercials. But it also suggests an unconscious ambivalence toward computers, which have, it is suggested, the power to enslave us.

The words spoken by the person seen on screen are doubletalk and viewers of the commercial can see the irony that informs it.

> For today, we celebrate the first glorious anniversary of the Information Purification Directives. We have created, for the first time in all history, a garden of pure ideology. Where each worker may bloom secure from the pests of contradictory and confusing truths. Our Unification of Thought is more powerful a weapon than any fleet or army on earth. We are one people. With one will. One resolve. One cause. Our enemies shall talk themselves to death. And we will bury them with their own confusion. We shall prevail!

It is when "We shall prevail" is spoken that the sledgehammer hits the screen and it explodes. I would suggest that the speaker represents the IBM Corporation, the enslaved workers represent consumer users "imprisoned" by IBM, and the blonde woman represents Apple Corporation and the Macintosh computer.

We can analyze the image of the woman throwing the sledgehammer on four levels:

The Literal Level:	The image we see in the commercial
The Textual Level:	Where the image fits in the commercial
The Intertextual Level:	How the image calls to mind Orwell's *1984*
The Mythic Level:	The biblical story of David and Goliath

Images, we can see, are resonant and have many different levels of meaning—some of which are not apparent to us when we first see them. The Macintosh, so Apple suggests, will save us from IBM and MS-DOS, but who will save us from the Macintosh if it becomes an instrument of psychological domination?

THE NATURE OF THE COMPUTER

Computers are digital devices that can perform manipulations and calculations of data at incredible speeds, using a program or set of instructions. Though computers are capable of remarkably fast operations with numbers and other data, for our purposes it is best to think of them as devices that can be used to manipulate symbols and visual data of all kinds. The most important symbols the computer can manipulate, as far as graphics and visual communication are concerned, are *pixels* (pixel is short for "picture element" or, in essence, dots) which can be used to create lines, shapes, and other visual material.

❙ FIGURE 9.3
Notice how the astronaut is in the center of all the vectors in this scene from Stanley Kubrick's classic film, *2001: A Space Odyssey* (1968). A number of critics have argued, as the image here suggests, that the computer HAL is the real star of the film. Courtesy of Museum of Modern Art, New York, Film Stills Archive.

Peter Lunenfeld offers a useful explanation of the term digital in his book *The Digital Dialectic: New Essays on New Media* (1999:xv):

> Digital systems do not use continuously variable representational relationships. Instead, they translate all input into binary structures of 0's and 1's, which can then be stored, transferred, or manipulated at the level of numbers or "digits" (so called because etymologically, the word descends from the digits on our hands with which we count out those numbers). . . . The digital photograph, instead of being a series of tonally continuous pigmented dots, is instead composed from pixels, a grid of cells that have precise numerical attributes associated with them, a series of steps rather than a continuous slope.

It is the ability of computers and other digital devices to turn images into pixels that has been all important, for we can capture and manipulate these pixels as we wish. For Lunenfeld, the development of digital devices has led to a new digital culture—a culture in which we spend enormous amounts of time and money on cell phones, iPods and other brands of music players, video game players, and games, CDs, DVDs, and numerous other kinds of devices.

Computer images are a mosaic of pixels, arranged in rows and columns similar to the tiles in a mosaic. Each of these pixels is assigned a location and a predetermined color by the computer, which puts this information into memory and can call it up and manipulate it in innumerable ways. In addition to computers, there are now many inexpensive scanners, which can scan printed images and turn them into digital images that can be stored on computers in programs such as Picasa and used in blogs, e-mail, and on

Facebook and other programs. People who use computers to create and manipulate images now have increasingly powerful and inexpensive computers and software programs to work with. Most artists prefer Macintosh computers because they don't crash, they are easy to use, and they have sophisticated software programs.

COMPUTER GRAPHICS SOFTWARE

In recent years the price of computers has fallen dramatically. For example, in 2009 it was possible to purchase a Dell Vostro 220 Mini Tower Computer with an Intel Core 2 Duo Processor, Windows 7 Home Premium, 2 GB of memory, a 320-GB Hard Drive, a Dell 20-inch Widescreen Flat Panel Monitor, and a DVD-RW drive for $429. And every year, the price of computers goes down and their capabilities go up.

There are numerous paint programs, animation programs, morphing programs and other kinds of image manipulation programs available such as Windows MovieMaker, Adobe Photoshop CS4 (and a less powerful Adobe Photoshop Elements), CorelDRAW Graphics Suite X4, free programs such as Gimp, Photoscape, Paint.net and Google's Picasa. The Macintosh, which has about 8 percent of the personal computer market, has its iLife program that includes iPhoto, iMovie, iDVD, and iWeb. Computers now make it possible to manipulate images and edit videos and films with surprising degrees of professionalism. These capacities were only possible before with very expensive computers.

One of the most popular genres of computer programs is presentation software such as PowerPoint. It enables speakers to display images and textual material on large screens. PowerPoint is probably the most widely used presentation program and is simple to use. But it has to be used carefully, because if all speakers do is show slides full of textual material, members of audiences quickly become bored. Presentation software is very effective, however, in using images and other forms of infographics to communicate information and ideas.

SPECIAL EFFECTS

In the early days, it took very powerful computers to generate special effects, such as those shown in the Luxo Jr. images. But now, as the power of the ordinary computer has grown, it is possible to create all kinds of special effects such as:

Mirroring. The computer takes an image and creates a mirror image of it. With some programs, multiple mirror images can be created on one screen and the mirrors can be overlapped if desired.

Mosaic. The computer maps squares onto an image, simulating a mosaic.

Strobe. A freeze effect of an image is held for a short time and released as another is frozen. This stylized effect dramatizes movement within the screen.

Shattered Image. An image is fractured into slivers or other shapes.

Chroma-Key. This process removes red, blue, or green from an image and replaces it with a different color or image.

Posterization. This process involves increasing image contrast (luminance value) which produces, at the extreme, a cartoon-like quality.

Animation. Computers and new software programs make it easier to do animation, as the figure with the marching rabbits demonstrates.

These are some of the more common effects that can be created with computers and imaging software programs. In addition to being used for artistic purposes, computer imaging plays an increasingly important role in medicine and has been used to diagnose illnesses and to aid surgeons by providing them with more precise information before they start operating.

INFOGRAPHICS

The term "infographics" is a combination of two words—information and graphics—and suggests how strong the relation is between information and the ways it can shown. The more common kinds of infographics are lists, maps, tables, charts, and diagrams. It has been estimated by Edward Tufte, author of *The Visual Display of Graphic Information,* that several billion infographics are created every year. This shows the important role they play in newspapers, magazines, television programs, and other media.

What infographics does, when it is done correctly, is enable us to see trends and relationships between phenomena. *USA Today* makes extensive use of infographics, which suggests that the newspaper gives the publication of data relationships a very high priority. Seeing an image that shows relationships enables us to recognize them much better than reading about them. When reading about income distribution or testing results on children or any other topic, if the information is buried in paragraphs of text, we find it difficult to recognize relationships and trends. But once that data are shown in a chart or table or some other kind of graphic, we can see relationships and trends right away.

As Ned J. Racine writes in *Visual Communication: Understanding Maps, Charts, Diagrams, and Schematics* (2002:2):

Visual communication surrounds us. It helps us navigate the computer world or an interstate highway. It organizes information on the sports page of

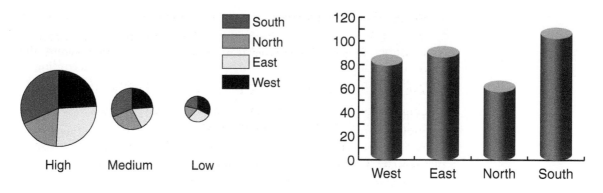

I FIGURE 9.4
Charts. These charts were generated on a micro-computer. Charts, graphs, and diagrams show relationships visually and thus are able to convey a great deal of information in an economical manner.

a newspaper or the maintenance manual of a nuclear reactor. And, as business people strive to win customers around the world, visual communication carries their message, usually more clearly than words.

That is because, he adds, visual communication is not as easily misinterpreted as words, it can show relationships very directly, it is helpful to visual and spatial learners, and to the large numbers of people in America who read below the fifth-grade level (20 percent) and who have literacy problems.

Racine offers examples of many different forms or kinds of visual communication, such as Chinese ideograms, icons, signs, diagrams, charts (pie charts, bar charts, column charts, etc.), tables, and timelines. There is a free program, www.WolframAlpha.com, that enables us to enter topics of interest and obtain information, often in graphical form, relating to a given topic. And there are many free programs that enable us to make charts and other kinds of informational graphics.

VIDEO GAMES

In the last twenty years, the **video game** industry has become an enormous industry, with sales of video game consoles or gameboxes and video game software exceeding those of the film industry. In 2009, according to an article in *The Los Angeles Times* (January 15, 2009) Americans spent more than $21 billion on video game players, games, and accessories. Some video games can be played on computers but the most dedicated game players play them on special gameboxes, which are really mini-super computers, designed for the games. There is a video game player "war" going on between Sony's Playstation 3, Microsoft's Xbox 360, and the Nintendo Wii. Since video game consoles cost $200 or $300 and video games often cost around $50, playing video games can become quite expensive.

The Appeal of Video Games

Video games are similar to animated films except that in video games, the player has an input into the events that transpire in the game. According to Janet H. Murray, who discusses video games in her book *Hamlet on the Holodeck: The Future of Narrative in Cyberspace,* video games have certain characteristics. First, they are **immersive** and enable players to project themselves into the action in a simulated world. Second, they are **interactive** in that players shape, to varying degrees, the outcome of the story. That is, players have a sense of agency. And third, they are **transformative,** in that they can have an emotional impact on players.

Murray describes the first of these three characteristics, immersion, as (1997:98):

> The experience of being transported to an elaborately simulated place is pleasurable in itself, regardless of the fantasy content. We refer to this experience as immersion. *Immersion* is a metaphorical term derived from the physical experience of being submerged in water. We seek the same feeling from a psychologically immersive experience that we do from a plunge in the ocean or swimming pool: the sensation of being surrounded by a completely other reality.

We can see that there are powerful psychological gratifications from immersion as we escape from the routines of everyday life and immerse ourselves in new worlds.

Murray defines the second of these three characteristics, agency, as (1997:126) "the satisfying power to take meaningful action and see the results of our decisions and choices." She adds that while we expect to feel agency when we work at the computer on various programs like spreadsheets but don't expect to experience it in a narrative environment, one that is "dynamically altered by our participation."

The third pleasure we get from video games is that they are transformative. Murray explains (1997:154):

> The transformative power of the computer is particularly seductive in narrative environments. It makes us eager for masquerade, eager to pick up the joystick and become a cowboy or space fighter, eager to log on to the MUD [multi-user domain] and become ElfGirl or Black Dagger. Because digital objects can have multiple instantiations, they call forth our delight in variety itself.

Murray's use of the terms "seductive" and "delight" suggest that these video games offer many pleasures and help us understand why they can become addictive.

Problems and Positive Aspects of Video Games

As the gameboxes have increased in power, the quality of the images found in video games has increased considerably, and the images are now much more realistic than they were when the gameboxes were less powerful. One of the most popular of the early games, *Pac-Man,* was, by present-day standards, very simple. It didn't have avatars (representations of human beings) but dots and simple characters who ate these dots. There is a world of difference between playing *Pac-Man* and playing contemporary video games, which have remarkable graphics and complex story lines.

In playing video games, just as viewing films, what is important is the "suspension of disbelief" that enables us to empathize and identify with various characters, and the vastly improved quality of the images in video games now makes them a very powerful and in many cases addictive experience. As video game consoles gain power, playing video games becomes increasingly like being an actor in a film. The fact that players are part of the action makes the violence found in video games a big problem, for there is a difference between being a spectator to violence and being a character who behaves in a violent way. We know that exposure to violence on television has a serious negative impact on a lot of children. We don't know what effect participating in violence, even if it is make-believe, will have on players, but there is reason to suspect the impact of this violence will be harmful to them.

There are a number of other negative aspects connected to playing video games, such as addiction, alienation, and physical problems such as repetitive stress injuries and an increased likelihood of becoming obese. But there are also a number of positive aspects of video games. Video games are used the U.S. Army to train soldiers and to help people deal with anxieties, phobias, eating disorders, addictions, and other psychological difficulties. Players who participate in "massively multiplayer online role playing games" (MMORPGs) are able to participate in an alternative reality that provides numerous gratifications that are very powerful.

The new generations of video game consoles are very powerful, but even the Xbox 360 (see Figure 9.5) still can only produce about a fifth of the 2.4 billion polygons per second that are needed to obtain true visual realism in video games—what Alvy Ray Smith of Pixar has called "the reality threshold." Nevertheless, playing games with the new video game consoles is much closer to film-like realism than previous generations of consoles (see Figure 9.6).

It is worth noting that a number of universities, such as the University of Southern California, now offer courses and degrees in making computer games. One of the most celebrated is the Media Lab at the Massachusetts Institute of Technology. Many universities also offer courses and programs that deal with the Internet and other aspects of visual communication—in broadcasting, communications, and art departments.

❙ FIGURE 9.5
This is the Microsoft XBox 360, a powerful device for generating images and sounds. Video game consoles are really mini supercomputers dedicated to playing video games, but they have other uses as well. Courtesy of Microsoft Corporation.

❙ FIGURE 9.6
Notice the incredible realism in this image. Video games now have progressed to the point where they are close to films as far as the quality of the images is concerned. This image is Joanna Dark in *Perfect Dark: Zero*™ created by Microsoft Game Studios. Courtesy of Microsoft Corporation.

E-MAIL, SOCIAL MEDIA AND THE INTERNET

The Internet has revolutionized modern life and its impact upon everything in our lives and the societies in which we live is still evolving. It affects our jobs, our social lives, and the traditional media; for instance, it has led to the decline of newspapers and magazines and has had a major impact on radio, television, and films. Pirated films, for example, are now often available on the Internet before the original films are released to the general public.

E-mail (sometimes written as email) now competes with regular or "snail" mail, and as a result of e-mail, the U.S. Post Office has had a troubling decrease in the number of first class letters being sent. There are some negative aspects of e-mail to be considered. First, there are hackers who use e-mail to gain control of computers in an attempt to find credit card numbers and other information that can be used for criminal purposes. Then there are all the spam messages we get—though e-mail providers like Yahoo mail, Hotmail, and Gmail are becoming increasingly proficient in weeding out this spam. And then there is the problem of people being overwhelmed by hundreds of e-mail messages when they turn on their computers in the morning.

The development of sites such as YouTube and Facebook, which enable people to upload images, has also been very important. People who make videos and films can now place them on YouTube and make them available to large numbers of people. There are now inexpensive video cameras, such as the Flip, that enable video makers to send their videos directly to YouTube. In addition, anyone can now have a blog where they can show photographs and other kinds of images. So the Internet has opened things up for all kinds of image-makers.

The Internet now is a major advertising site and has led to a significant change in the way people purchase goods and services. Amazon.com is now a powerful Internet merchandizing company that has played a major role in

---

EMOTICONS

Emoticons are images made from letters and punctuation marks that are meant to display feelings, attitudes, or emotions in e-mail messages. The word *emoticon* is a combination of "emotion" and "icon," an icon being something that communicates by resemblance. Some of the more common emoticons are shown below:

:-)	Smiley
:-(	Crying
]:->	Devil
:-()	Loudmouth
:-*	Kiss
:-[	Bored

There are many others, but Smiley and others using colons are probably the most commonly used emoticons. Some e-mail programs also provide pictorial emoticons that can be inserted into messages.

getting Internet users to purchase book and other products that it sells. It has only taken a little more than a decade for Google to emerge as a power-house that is revolutionizing the way people use the Internet to find information and buy things. Google's search engine, which sells advertising, is the major source of its revenue. It owns Picasa, an Internet site that allows people to store digital photographs, manipulate these images, and send them to friends or to image processing sites, where they can be developed. It also owns Blogger, which enables people to create blogs and place images in them. And it has many other programs, such as Gmail and the browser Chrome. Google is also developing new companies that will do a host of other things. It is even making cell phones.

There is now streaming video and audio and as technologies evolve, the Internet is becoming an important part of people's daily media usage. The Internet has progressed very rapidly from a means of sending e-mail text messages to becoming a powerful visual medium, and its impact has been nothing less than revolutionary in everything from merchandizing to politics.

Most newspapers and other publications have a presence on the Internet and some newspapers are trying to figure out ways of delivering newspapers electronically rather than the way they do now on paper, and making money from their Websites. Book publishers are also selling electronic copies of their books to be read on special devices that have become increasingly popular in recent years.

DEMOGRAPHICS OF INTERNET USE

Some interesting statistics about the demographics of Internet use in the United States for 2005 and for 2009 follow (adapted from www.pewinternet.org):

	2005	2009
Adult Women	69%	76%
Adult Men	75%	78%
Ages 18–29	84%	93%
Ages 30–49	85%	83%
Ages 50–64	71%	77%
Ages 65 and older	30%	43%
No high school degree	38%	37%
High school degree	62%	72%
Some college	83%	87%
College or graduate degree	92%	94%

Income less than $30,000	54%	62%
Income $30,000 to $49,999	78%	84%
Income $50,000 to $75,000	85%	93%
Income over $75,000	94%	95%
Dial-up connections	39%	37%
High-speed connection	59%	63%

These figures provide a good overview of who is using the Internet. In 1995 only about 12% of the American public used the Internet; by 2009 around 80% of Americans were on the Internet and approximately 63% of them had high-speed or broadband connections.

COMPUTER ANIMATION

Computer animation gained prominence in 1982 when Disney's *Tron* was released, a technological triumph but a box-office disappointment. Since *Tron*, there have been more than sixty full length animated films have appeared, with *Shrek 2* earning more than $440 million and a number of other animated films earning more than $300 million. A number of films have used animation for various scenes, such as *2001, The Last Starfighter, The Abyss,* and *Young Sherlock Holmes.* But it was *Terminator II: Judgment Day* that captured the public's imagination and represents a truly successful use of computer animation. It took approximately thirty-five computer animators almost a year to produce images of T-1000—images that appeared on the screen for only about five minutes.

Disney's *Toy Story,* a huge box office success, was the first fully computer animated film and helped lead to a new era of animated films. Pixar, the

I FIGURE 9.7
Luxo, Jr. These images were created using extremely powerful computers and software imaging programs. The Luxo images are from an animated film. Luxo Images.

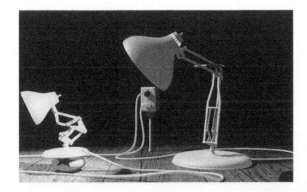 

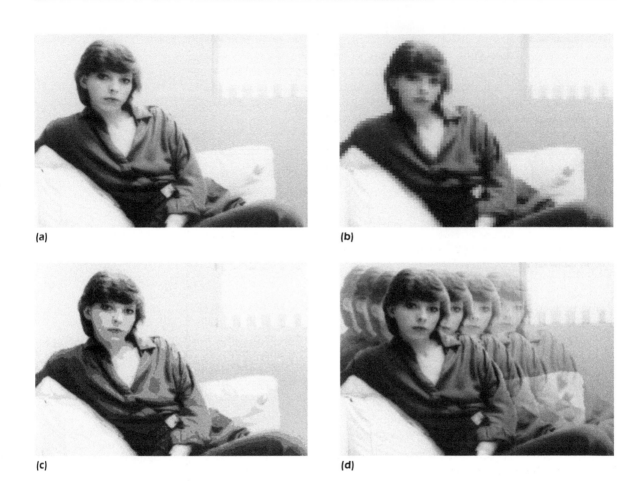

(a)   (b)

(c)   (d)

❙ FIGURE 9.8

Bob Malecki, "Special Effects." These special effects were all created by sophisticated computer imaging processes. These images are *(a)* an unmodified photo of Jan, *(b)* a mosaic, also known as a pixelated image, *(c)* a solarized or painted image, and *(d)* a frame move repeated with varying degrees of image wash. Courtesy of Island Graphics Corporation. Reproduced with permission.

company that that produced the animation, used twenty-seven animators to create the many characters in the seventy-five minute film. In December, 2009, James Cameron's *Avatar,* a 3-D film that cost more than $300 million to produce and around $150 million to market, was released.

Using computer animation, filmmakers can now create whatever images they want. Anything is possible now. But that doesn't mean that the films these filmmakers create using computer animation and other new technologies are worth watching. In the final analysis, films—like other dramatic works of art in other media—require good stories, with interesting characters and exciting plots. It is the script that is a critical factor and all the special effects in the world can't save an uninteresting story.

There may also be something in computer technology that deadens works and drains the vitality out of them; animation may fascinate filmmakers so much that they lose sight of the other elements needed to make a successful film. What computer animation does is to enlarge the possibilities open to those who make films. But when it comes to films, television shows, and other kinds of narratives, the most important computer software is not the animation software but the word-processing/script-writing software. It was the poor scripts of the last few *Star War* films that doomed them to mediocrity, not the technology that Lucas had to work with.

THE POWER OF COMPUTER-GENERATED IMAGES

Computer-generated images are now widely used for segments in films such as *Star Wars* and *Lord of the Rings*. And computer-generated images have now replaced hand-drawn images in most animated films. We find these computer-generated images in films such as *Finding Nemo*, *Shrek*, and *The Incredibles* in the United States and *Swept Away* in Japan, to name just a few of the more notable examples. Since *Toy Story*, there have been fewer than a dozen feature-length films that were made completely by animation, but in 2006 a number of computer-animated films appeared, including *Ice Age 2*, *Flushed Away*, and *Charlotte's Web*.

In an article, "From 'Toy Story' to 'Chicken Little'" that appeared in *The Economist* (December 10, 2005), Alvy Ray Smith, one of the cofounders of Pixar, discussed computer animations. He is quoted as saying "I call it magic, because they convince us that a stack of polygons has emotions and is conscious." It is computer-generated polygons that are the building blocks of computer-animated films. Some film animators maintain a cartoonlike quality in their images while others strive for realism, but it is very difficult to generate a human face that is convincing to people, since they are so used to seeing real faces and artists still can't capture the complexities of facial expressions. There is a debate among computer animators about how much realism they need to generate that "suspension of disbelief" that we get from films and other narrative texts that make us empathize with the characters.

CONCLUSIONS

Have all of the remarkable video effects that computers can generate led to an important new kind of art, or are computer effects essentially one more form of "commercial art," and not really a serious art medium? This is a subject of much debate.

Video is still a relatively new medium, so we must give it time to develop and not make any premature judgments. At the same time, a great deal of work has been done in video, so its potentialities should be discernible (Figure 9.9).

Michael Noll, who was one of the first people to write about the subject, expresses a great deal of optimism about the medium in his 1967 essay

❙ FIGURE 9.9
Detail from *Pixellage,*
1983. Choreography by
Betty Erickson. Music by
A. Corelli. This ballet,
appropriately named,
used computer-generated
images to create remark-
able effects. Photography
by Marty Sohl. Courtesy
of San Francisco Ballet.

"Computers and the Visual Arts": "In the computer, man has created not just an inanimate tool but an intellectual and active creative partner that, when fully exploited, could be used to produce wholly new art forms and possibly new aesthetic experiences." By 1982, however, Noll had serious reservations. As he writes in the art show catalogue of a SIGGRAPH (Special Interest Group on Computer Graphics):

> It is in its use as a serious artistic medium in the visual arts where the digital computer has not yet achieved its anticipated potential. Digital computers are being used to create visual imagery, but many people feel that something is missing.
>
> The images sometimes appear to be attempts to mimic other media. Many are cold and sterile and are somewhat devoid of human expression. Randomness combines with geometric structure to create designs that are frequently interesting but that are little more. One is frequently left with the impression that many patterns are simply experiments in learning the new medium.

Noll raises the question as to whether there is some kind of fundamental antithesis between technology and the arts, between machines and what might be called "the human spirit" (Figure 9.10).

(a)

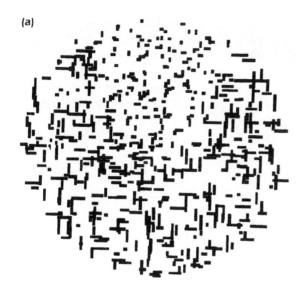

(b)

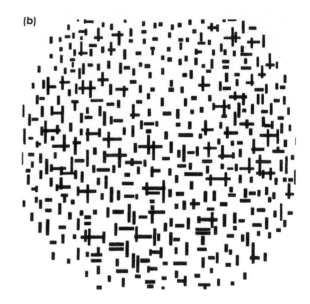

▌ FIGURE 9.10

(a) Michael Noll, *Computer Composition with Lines,* 1964. Used with permission from A. Michael Noll. *(b)* Piet Mondrian, *Composition with Lines,* 1917. Used with permission from the Kröller-Müller Foundation. The computer-generated image *(a)* was created to be very similar to *(b)*, Mondrian's work. When Noll showed audiences the two images, labeling them *(a)* and *(b)*, and asked which was the Mondrian, large percentages thought that the computer-generated image *(a)* was the Mondrian. This occurred because, it is hypothesized, the computer-generated image was more irregular or random than the Mondrian painting. Another of Mondrian's paintings, *Composition with Blue and Yellow,* is shown in Figure 0.20.

What will happen with video remains to be seen. There are serious video artists who are experimenting with video and trying to create works of significance. But how different is their work from film or television, except for the greater use of special effects?

It is worth noting that a number of universities, such as the University of Southern California, are now offering courses and degrees in making computer games and that Oxford University has begun to offer a Doctor of Philosophy (Ph.D.) in "Information, Communication and the Social Sciences" in the Oxford Internet Institute. And, of course, there is the celebrated Media Lab at the Massachusetts Institute of Technology and various other institutions in Australia and elsewhere which are involved in media, in general, and by implication, the awesome power of the Internet. Many universities also offer courses and programs that deal with the Internet and other aspects of visual communication—in broadcasting, communications, and art departments.

The future will tell us what to make of computer art and video. For the moment, computers enable people to create and manipulate images of all sorts in remarkable ways. Whether this technology will develop into a "serious" art that creates ennobling works of lasting quality remains to be seen.

APPLICATIONS

1. What impact do you think computers have had on society? (If you have a computer, what effect has it had on your life?) Be as specific as you can in answering this question.

2. In what ways have computers directly impacted your life? Make a list of particulars and briefly explain each item. You might take one day in your life and see where and how computers are involved with your activities, either directly or indirectly.

3. Newspapers often run stories about young students, known as "hackers," who use their computers to get into the computer systems of the military or other large organizations. What do you think motivates these hackers? What should be done to hackers who are caught?

4. Use a computer to create a newsletter to give to your friends. Decide on a title, a topic, and a format. (If you don't have a desktop publishing program, you can make a pasteup with printed matter from the computer and artwork you do by hand.) Did the computer facilitate the process?

5. Play some games on a computer for an hour. Write a short essay describing what the experience was like. What were the graphics like? What about the plot? Did you enjoy it? Why or why not?

6. Play sociologist. Go to a video game arcade and survey the players. What questions should you ask them? Make sure some of the questions involve obtaining quantitative data. When you are done, examine the data and write a report describing what you found and explaining what it means.

7. Watch *Tron*, which contains about twenty minutes of computer animation. Write a review of the film, focusing on its aesthetic aspects. What, if anything, worked in the film? What were its drawbacks? How would you have improved it?

8. What programs do you have on your computer that you can use for creating and manipulating visual images? How have these programs affected your visual sensibility and your ability to create images?

9. Invent some new emoticons. How can you be certain that people will interpret your emoticons correctly?

KEY TERMS FOR CHAPTER 9

infographics
desktop publishing
computer-aided design
video game

immersive
interactive
transformative
Internet

GLOSSARY

A-B axis   The axis that goes from the left side of a screen to the right side. (See *Z-axis shot.*)

Aesthetics   The branch of philosophy concerned with questions related to the nature of the beautiful: what is the relationship between truth and beauty, between form and content, and so on. Applied aesthetics, in contrast, is interested in how to obtain certain effects through the use of color, lighting, certain camera shots, editing, and so on.

Analogy   A mode of communication in which meaning is generated by making comparisons. Metaphors are based on analogies, as are similes, which are weaker forms of analogies.

Animation   The process of filming drawings or clay sculptures to generate the illusion of motion; literally means "giving life to."

Association   A mode of communication, such as metonymy and synecdoche (a weaker form of metonymy), in which meaning is generated by using associations, connections people have in their minds between two things.

Asymmetrical   See *informal balance.*

Autoeroticism   In aesthetics, sensual pleasure caused by contemplation of one's image.

Axial balance   Formal balance in which elements in a visual field are arranged symmetrically on both sides of an axis.

Balance   Balance refers to the arrangement of elements in a composition. In axial or formal balance, the elements are arranged equally on both sides of an imaginary axis. In asymmetrical balance, the elements are arranged in an assymetrical manner, generating stress, energy and visual excitement.

Bicameral brain   The two hemispheres of the brain, each of which has certain characteristics. The left hemisphere is associated with logic and is linear; the right hemisphere is associated with imagination and is holistic.

CAD (computer-aided design)   Software programs that enable users such as architects and engineers to create designs on computers and manipulate the images for various purposes. There are now CADD (computer-aided design and drafting) programs as well, for draftspersons and others.

Caricature   A form of humorous drawing that captures the likeness of a person but exaggerates and distorts various features of that person.

Cartoon   A drawing, usually in one frame, depicting some kind of humorous situation, which is generally accompanied by a caption.

Chart   A means of presenting information in visual form so that relationships can immediately be seen.

Chiaroscuro lighting   A form of lighting characterized by very strong lights and darks, as opposed to flat lighting, which diminishes the differences between lights and darks.

Chroma-key   The process of electronically removing red, blue, or green from a computer image and replacing it with a different color or image.

Close-up   A film or television camera shot that shows a person's head. There are also extreme close-ups, which show only part of a person's face. Many people suggest that because of its small screen size, television is a close-up medium.

Codes   Ways of interpreting signs and symbols and organizing behavior. There are highway codes, which are known and which people are tested on, and aesthetic codes, which often escape our awareness but also often shape our behavior.

Color   The description we use for things based on the way light is reflected or emitted from objects. Colors are differentiated in terms of hue, saturation, and brightness. We also distinguish between primary colors—red, yellow, and blue—and secondary colors—orange, green, and purple.

Colorization   The capacity of certain computers and software programs to modify the colors in images. As a result of this process, black-and-white films and television programs can be turned into color, though there is a great deal of dispute about the propriety of doing so.

Comic strip   A popular art form, generally found in newspapers, characterized by continuing characters, a number of panels, and dialogue presented in balloons. Comic strips can be either serious or humorous and often are extremely long-lived.

Communication models   Communications refers to the messages carried in the process of communication. Models have been defined by Denis McQuail and Sven Windahl in *Communication Models for the Study of Mass Communication* as (1993:2) "a consciously simplified description in graphic form of a piece of reality. A model seeks to show the main elements of any structure or process and the relationship between these elements."

Composition   The arrangement of elements in a visual field so as to please the eye or obtain an intended effect.

Computer-aided design   See *CAD*.

Condensation   The psychological process by which the mind unifies and pulls together disparate images in dreams so as to avoid the dream censor. The condensed image generally has a sexual dimension to it, though this is not apparent. We also react to the sexual content of condensed images when we are awake, though we do not create these images.

Contrast   A difference between two visual elements (such as simple and complicated, dull and bright, or dark and light) to generate emphasis.

Cool medium   One that provides relatively few data and thus generates strong involvement on the part of the viewer or listener.

Culture   A term used by anthropologists and others for the ideas, values, beliefs, patterns of behavior, and ways of living of a group passed on from generation to generation. When used in reference to the arts, culture is thought to involve the elite arts (so-called "high" culture as contrasted with "popular" culture) such as opera, classical music, and serious poetry and novels.

Cut and paste   Process whereby video artists capture sections of an image and place them elsewhere in the image while manipulating color, shape, and size.

Depth of field   The capacity of a camera to keep objects, located at different distances from it, in focus. Depth of field can vary, based on the f-stop of the camera, the focal length of the lens, and the distance from the camera to the object being photographed.

Design   The arrangement of elements in a visual field and the manner in which they relate to one another.

Desktop publishing   The use of computers, powerful software programs that enable users to manipulate textual and visual material, and laser printers to produce high-quality printed matter (such as reports, pamphlets, books, and so on).

Digital   The translation of all input into binary structures of 0s and 1s, which can then be stored, transferred, or manipulated.

Digitized image   An image put into a computer that can then be manipulated for various purposes.

Direct eye gaze   A natural response we have to return the gaze of people who are gazing at us.

Direction   The line of movement of some aspect of an image. These directions are sometimes known as vectors.

Displacement   The psychological process by which the mind invests an object or symbol with significance taken from some other object or symbol. Frequently, this significance has a sexual dimension to it, and the displaced objects often are similar (in shape or function) to the object that is displaced.

Dot   A small, round mark. Dots are made by the intersection of two lines. Computers generate dots (on monitors) that are called pixels.

Dot-matrix printer   A kind of printer, used with computers, that uses dots to form letters and other visual material. The typical dot-matrix printer generates 75 dots per inch, in contrast to the laser printer, which produces 300 dots per inch.

Drama   A narrative or story, usually involving strong emotions and conflict among or between characters and the resolution of the conflict by action.

Editing   The process in film or television that takes place after images have been taken by a camera. Editing involves putting together the various elements or components of a film or television program in a manner that produces the impact and effect desired. This often involves cutting (eliminating) some material and splicing bits and pieces together. Editing is often done manually in films, but new devices have been developed that enable the editing process to be done electronically.

Ego   In the human psyche, according to Freud, the ego is involved with the perception of reality and adaptation to it. It mediates between the demands of the id (desire) and superego (conscience). (See *id, superego*.)

E-mail   Messages sent by people with computers and modems via the Internet.

Ethics   The branch of philosophy that deals with right conduct and moral considerations. There is a great deal of debate about the role that ethical considerations should play in the media, in general, and in visual media such as film and television, in particular.

Evidence   The notion that visual images can be relied on to tell the truth about something or some event. Now that computers can manipulate images and photographs so easily, visual images no longer are seen as reliable—seeing can no longer be equated with truthfulness and accuracy.

Figure-ground   A relationship between an object and the background against which we see the object. The background affects the meaning figures have, because they often are ambiguous.

Film frame   The basic unit of a film. The frame, in essence, is a photographic negative of a static image. Film is projected at 24 frames per second, which—because of a visual phenomenon known as an afterimage—produces the illusion of movement.

Flat lighting   Lighting in which differences between lights and darks are minimized or flattened. The opposite of *chiaroscuro* lighting.

Flush left   Type lined up in a straight line on the left margin of a page. Flush right involves lining it up in a straight line on the right margin of a page. Textual matter in books and magazines is generally flush left and flush right or "justified." Ragged right, in which lines do not line up in a straight line, is held by many typographers to give a more modern or contemporary look to a page.

Focus   The clarity or sharpness of an image. Soft focus generates images that are not precise and clear and produces a dreamlike effect.

Formal balance   See *axial balance*.

Frame   A single or a discrete image. A film is a collection of frames that are run through a projector, usually at twenty-four frames per second. Also known as a still.

Freeze-frame   The capacity of computers using certain software programs to capture an image and keep it immobile, or maintained as if it has been frozen. Freeze-frame is also used in film to suggest arrested motion and to generate a feeling of surprise or shock.

Genre   Kinds of stories, programs, or films. We make a distinction between a medium (film, television, and so on) and the kind of programs or genres in a given medium. For example, the medium of television includes many genres: soap operas, quiz shows, sports shows, interview shows, news shows, documentaries, and so on.

Gestalt The psychological process by which we combine a number of disparate elements into a whole that is greater than the sum of its parts and whose properties cannot be derived from the various parts. We commonly use the term to mean "putting things together" and getting some kind of an insight.

Glamorization The process by which we invest people or objects with qualities that we find appealing and desirable. A photographer can glamorize through the use of lighting, background, camera angles, and filtering devices.

Grain The prominence of the minute dots that make up a photograph: the more dots used in a photograph, the less grainy it is.

Graph A form of visual display showing quantitative relationships, often in the form of bars or points on a field.

Grid layout A collection of crisscrossing lines that make simple forms. These grid forms are used to help people without much knowledge of design format visual material in an attractive manner and avoid mistakes. Some desktop publishing software programs come with grids in them and include advice about good layout.

Haptical The term used by art historian Alois Riegl for finding pleasure in the texture and grain of objects.

Hegemony A term from the Greek word for "rule" or "leadership," made popular by the Italian Marxist thinker Antonio Gramsci. He argues that the ideological principles of the ruling classes found in capitalist societies are all-pervasive in the culture and serve to convince people that their domination by elites is both legitimate and natural and thus not able to be changed.

Hot medium One that provides a lot of data and thus fails to generate strong involvement on the part of the viewer or listener.

Icon In semiotic analysis, something that communicates meaning by resemblance. Thus, a photograph is iconic because it resembles the person who has been photographed.

Id In Freud's theory, the id represents a person's drives and desire for immediate gratification. The id is a source of energy but it doesn't have direction and thus requires the ego and superego to channel its energy constructively. (See *ego, superego.*)

Illustration The use of drawings, paintings, or other visual material to exemplify, give focus to, or decorate textual material.

Image A visual representation of something or someone. Images can be thought of as being complex pictorial phenomena, often having symbolic significance and unconscious meanings. Image also refers to the concept we have about someone or something.

Imagination The ability of the mind to create new ideas and images or to visualize things not present. The term suggests that there is a link between images or visual phenomena and creative behavior.

Immersive Video games are held to be immersive in that players, as a result of the "suspension of disbelief," become extremely involved in, or "submerged" in, the games they are playing. One is surrounded, so to speak, by a different reality that dominates our perceptual apparatus.

Index Signs that signify by logic or causal connection, as in the case of smoke and fire.

Infographics This term refers to using visual or graphic means, such as charts, drawings, and diagrams, generally in combination with words, to convey information. Infographics facilitates the communication of complicated relationships and information in ways that are easy to grasp.

Informal balance Elements of a composition that are not arranged equally on both sides of imaginary axes.

Information overload A numbness and inability to process information caused by overexposure to it.

Interactive Interactivity involves a response to our input in some situation. Thus, in video games, we participate in shaping the outcome of the game through our play—that is, our actions and decisions. Video games are interactive because they are designed to respond to the responses of players to events in the games.

Internet The open interconnection of networks through which connected computers can transmit visual and sound data. The most popular uses of the Internet are for transmitting e-mail and for finding information on the World Wide Web.

Intertextuality   According to this theory, all texts (works of art in all media) are influenced, either directly or indirectly, consciously or unconsciously, by works that have preceded them. Sometimes, as in the case of parody, this "borrowing" is done consciously, but in many other cases, stylistic and other matters are not consciously adapted from earlier works.

Jump cut   A quick cut from one scene to another that leaves out some intermediate scenes and thus speeds the action.

Laser printer   A printer, commonly used in desktop publishing, that offers relatively high resolution—300 or more dots per square inch.

Layout   See *composition.*

Lighting   Lighting involves the amount of illumination given to objects, which shapes our perception of them. Strong lights and weak shadows is called flat lighting and strong lights and shadows is called chiaroscuro lighting.

Line   A line is a succession of dots in which the dots are not distinguishable. They are sometimes formed on their own but also formed as the edges of shapes.

Logo   A design, sometimes made of letters, used by an organization as a means of establishing its identity.

Metaphor   A figure of speech indicating an analogy or similarity between two things—for example, "My love is a rose." (See *simile.*)

Metonymy   A method of generating meaning through the use of association. For example, a mansion suggests wealth (and good taste).

Mimetic desire   Desire that imitates the desires of others.

Mirroring   In computer graphics, a method of creating mirror images of an image.

Model   An abstract representation, in graphic form, that shows how some phenomena function.

Montage   A series of images and sounds that, when combined in a certain way, generate a powerful effect.

Morphing   The process of restructuring images, in minute stages, so they turn into images of something, or in the case of individuals, someone else.

Mosaic   A form of pictorial representation in which an image is created out of small, colored pieces of stone or some other material. This effect can also be created by computers with the right imaging software.

Movement   A sense of activity or change in position. It is created in films and television by the actions of characters and in static visual fields by use of line, shape, lighting, and color.

Music television (MTV)   Videos, generally performed by music groups, that either dramatize a song or show it being performed. Many of these videos use avant-garde film techniques.

Narcotization   A sense of deadness and boredom created, for example, by watching too much television, which can prevent the alternating of left-brain and right-brain activity.

Optical   The term used by art historian Alois Riegl for scanning objects according to their outline.

Optical illusion   A visual image that confuses the viewer and is deceptive.

Painting   In computer graphics, a still image overlaid with color in many different ways.

Persistence of vision   The process that enables us to connect the frames of a film and "see" the film as continuous.

Perspective   The ability to represent objects that are three-dimensional and give a sense of depth on a two-dimensional plane.

Phallic symbol   Any object that, for one reason or another, such as resemblance in shape or similarity in function, suggests the male sex organ.

Pica   A unit of measurement in type equivalent to 12 points or approximately one-sixth of an inch.

Pixel   An abbreviation of "picture element." Essentially, a point or dot that is shown on a computer monitor and that is the building block out of which lines, shapes, and images are created.

Plotter   A printing device used to reproduce drawings, architectural renderings, and other visual phenomena using computers and graphics software programs.

Point   A unit of measurement in typography equal to approximately 1/72 inch. Twelve points make a pica.

Pose   A particular posture for a portrait or photograph that reflects feelings and attitudes and generates a desired image.

Posterization   Process by which video artists increase image contrast.

Postmodern   A term for works that use a number of different styles and that abandon a traditional linear narrative.

Proportion   A relationship between elements in a visual field in which a part is considered with respect to the whole.

Psyche   The mind in all its conscious and unconscious functions and capacities, as a center of thoughts, emotions, and behavior. Freud suggested that the psyche is made up of an id (drives), a superego (conscience), and an ego (rationality) that mediates between the two opposing forces—the id and superego. (See *id, ego, superego.*)

Psychological closure   The way the mind combines elements into wholes and completes visual phenomena that are incomplete.

Reaction shot   A television or film shot showing a person's reactions (by facial expression) to some event. These shots generate a sense of drama and excitement.

Responsive chord   A theory of communication that focuses upon utilizing information stored in people's minds, which can be triggered by the right stimuli, in contrast to other communication theories that focus on the transfer of information from one person to others.

Reverse print   White type on a black background (or some variation on that theme), instead of the usual black type on a white background.

Roman typeface   A typeface characterized by upright letters, lines of varying thicknesses, and serifs.

Saccades   The quick, intermittent movements the eye makes when it fixes on one point after another in a visual field. Each saccade lasts approximately one-twentieth of a second.

Sans serif typeface   A typeface without serifs, the little marks that finish off the main strokes of letters in certain typefaces.

Scale   A relationship of size between objects or elements in a visual field.

Scanner   A device that can input graphics or textual material directly into a computer.

Selective perception   The process by which people tend to see only certain things in a given situation. They focus on material of interest to them and neglect other things that are present.

Semiotics   The science of signs that investigates the way meaning is produced and transmitted. (See *sign.*)

Serif typeface   A typeface that uses short cross-lines at the ends of letters.

Shape   The visible configuration or outward form of something.

Shattered image   An image broken into pieces to achieve a desired aesthetic effect through the use of computers and imaging software.

Shot angle   The angle at which a photo, film, or television shot is taken; used to promote an effect or feeling in viewers.

Sign   One of the basic concepts of semiotics. A sign is anything that can be used to stand for something else. Words, images, facial expressions, clothing, hairstyles—just about everything can be seen as a sign. The way signs work and the problems connected with signs are the subject matter of semiotics.

Signifier/signified   According to Ferdinand de Saussure, the division of signs into signifiers (sounds or objects) and signifieds (the concepts generated by the signifier). The relationship between signifiers and signifieds is arbitrary or conventional.

Simile   A figure of speech, using "like" or "as," in which a weak relationship between two subjects is posited—for example, "My love is like a rose." (See *metaphor.*)

Sound effects   The use of made-up sounds or noises (generally in dramatic presentations) to simulate real sounds and noises and generate emotional responses and a sense of verisimilitude in those who hear them.

Spatiality   The sense of space, determined in large part by the amount of "white" space, in a visual field.

Stenciling In computer graphics, the process by which shapes are created to protect areas of the screen from a given effect or to dictate where the effect should go.

Stereotype A widely held but simplistic, inaccurate, and generally negative portrayal of a category of people according to such matters as profession, region, gender, race, religion, age, and ethnicity.

Strobe A special effect characterized by short, bright pulses of light turning on and off.

Superego In Freud's structural analysis of the psyche, the superego is involved with such processes as approval or disapproval and has the role of trying to constrain the id. The functions of the superego operate below our level of awareness. We need the superego to channel our energy in constructive ways, but if it is too strong, it leads to passivity and an overpowering sense of guilt. (See *id*.)

Supergraphics Use of letters and words and other visual phenomena on a very large scale.

Surrealism A twentieth-century artistic (and literary) movement that attempted to capture the working of the subconscious by using fantastic imagery and trying to approximate a dreamlike state.

Symbol A form of sign, for Peirce, in which the meaning is conventional and must be learned. In ordinary use, anything that stands for something else, often on the basis of convention or association.

Symmetrical See *axial balance*.

Synecdoche A form of metonymy in which the part stands for the whole or the whole for the part. Thus, the Pentagon is used to stand for the American military establishment and the White House for the presidency in the United States.

Table A visual means of presenting numerical relationships among data, generally in columns and rows.

Talking heads Television programs in which there is little physical action and basically nothing but conversation takes place.

Taste cultures This is the term used by sociologist Herbert Gans for his analysis of the cultural levels of the American public. He argues that there are five taste cultures in the United States and each is suited to the intellectual level and needs of its group.

Transformative A term that deals with the way video games can have very powerful emotional impacts on players and thus "transform" them in various ways. This transformation can be positive and lead to socially constructive behaviors or negative and lead to antisocial behaviors of various kinds.

Typography The art of selecting and using typefaces for maximum effect. It also involves such matters as the composition of the page and the sizing of illustrations and other graphics.

Unconscious Freudian theory (his "topographic" hypothesis) posits the existence of three levels of consciousness in the human psyche. There is consciousness, preconsciousness (which we can access), and a level of the psyche that we cannot access and of which we are unaware, the unconscious. An iceberg can be used to represent these levels. The part of the iceberg we see is consciousness; the part just below the sea, which we can dimly make out, is the preconscious level; and the greater part of the iceberg, which we cannot make out, is the unconscious.

Unity A sense of harmoniousness and wholeness created by the relationships of elements in a visual field.

Video game An interactive electronic text that enables players to experience immersion and to feel agency in that their actions affect the outcome of the game. Videogames are played on increasingly powerful consoles that are specially designed for game playing, and in some cases, on computers. There are many different genres of games, such as first-person shooters, sports, racing, strategy, puzzles, and action adventures. Some games have elements of several genres in them.

Visual literacy Literacy involves the ability to read and write, but also an understanding of how words and texts function. It involves an enhanced understanding of how images in all media communicate, the impact these images have on our psyches and our culture, and an appreciation of the role visual phenomena play in contemporary society.

WYSIWYG (What You See Is What You Get) The ability of certain software programs to provide users with an accurate picture of what a page will look like when it is printed out. This feature is of particular importance in desktop publishing.

Zapping The process of using a remote-control tuner to "flip" from one television station to another. People zapping do not watch programs, but instead, create their own programs from bits and pieces of what is on the air.

Z-axis shot A shot in which the action is vertical to the screen image and moves toward or away from viewers. This kind of shot is particularly important in television because the screen is so small. (See *A-B axis.*)

Zoom shot A shot in which the lens of a camera is used to move in on a scene for a closer view (or, in the reverse, move away from a scene). If used too frequently, zoom shots lose their impact and disturb viewers.

SELECTED ANNOTATED BIBLIOGRAPHY

The literature on visual communication is vast. There are an incredible number of books on aesthetics, art, design, graphics, film, television, and related concerns. And with good reason, for if we are "thinking creatures" (homo sapiens), we are also "seeing creatures" (homo oculans). What follows is a listing and brief description of some of the more important and interesting books in the field. A more complete listing of resources (including those cited in the text) follows in the References.

BERGER, ARTHUR ASA. *Li'l Abner: A Study in American Satire*. 1970. Twayne Publishers.
This study deals with the social, cultural, and political significance of one of America's most important comic strips, Li'l Abner. It considers such topics as comics and popular culture, satire, and graphic techniques in the comics.

BERGER, ARTHUR ASA. *The Comic-Stripped American: What Dick Tracy, Blondie, Daddy Warbucks and Charlie Brown Tell Us About Ourselves*. 1973. Walker.
This book analyzes the cultural and symbolic significance of many of America's classic comic strips.

BERGER, ARTHUR ASA. *Signs in Contemporary Culture: An Introduction to Semiotics*. 1984. Longman.
This book explains some of the basic concepts of semiotic theory and applies them to various topics, many of which involve visual matters.

BERGER, JOHN. *Ways of Seeing*. 1972. Penguin Books.
This book is based on a series of four television broadcasts that the English critic John Berger made for the BBC. It has four written essays (on images, the portrayal of women in art, politics and art, and advertising) and three pictorial ones.

BERGER, JOHN. *About Looking*. 1980. Pantheon Books.
This collection of essays previously appeared in an English magazine, New Society. The essays deal with such topics as why we look at animals, how we use photography, and what significance various artists and works of art have.

CLARK, KENNETH. *Looking at Pictures*. 1968. Beacon Press.
This book contains a number of analyses by Clark that are meant to teach us how to look at paintings in as profound and discerning a manner as possible. Clark argues that knowing about a painter's life, personality and beliefs and values, where the painting fits into a painter's total work, and what the art of the painter's time was like, are necessary to interpret a given work and understand pictures (in general) fully.

DEKEN, JOSEPH. *Computer Images: State of the Art.* 1983. Stewart, Tabori & Chang.
This book is full of remarkable four-color images generated by computers. It deals with computers and images, the way the computer affects our aesthetic sensibilities, the role of computer images and fantasy, and related topics.

DICHTER, ERNEST. *Packaging: The Sixth Sense? A Guide to Identifying Consumer Motivation.* 1975. Cahners Publishing.
Dichter, the father of motivation research, deals with the power of packaging and shows how it is involved with deep-seated psychological anxieties we all experience. The book contains much interesting material on how people interpret symbols and relate to visual phenomena, especially as these matters apply to packaging and "commercial communication."

DONDIS, DONIS A. *A Primer of Visual Literacy.* 1973. M.I.T. Press.
This early textbook on visual communication deals with visual literacy, composition, visual techniques, the way visual arts function, and similar topics. It contains numerous line drawings and other illustrations and offers a good introduction to the principles of design.

EISENSTEIN, SERGEI. *Film Form: Essays in Film Theory.* Edited and translated by Jay Leyda. 1949. Harcourt Brace Jovanovich.
This series of essays by a famous film director focuses on various aspects of film theory. Eisenstein deals with such topics as the nature of film form, film language, montage, and the structure of film. A companion book of essays, Film Sense, is available from the same publisher.

EVANS, JESSICA AND STUART HALL. (eds.). *Visual Culture: The Reader.* Sage Publications.
This is a collection of theoretically important essays on the relationship between visual phenomena and culture. It has sections with articles on topics such as photography, gender, and race, and writings by authors such as Roland Barthes, Walter Benjamin, Guy Debord, Michel Foucault, Sigmund Freud, and Laura Mulvey.

FOUCAULT, MICHEL. *This Is Not a Pipe.* 1983. University of California Press.
This fascinating little book deals with the work of the Belgian surrealist, René Magritte. One of his most famous paintings shows a pipe, and underneath it is written "this is not a pipe." Foucault attempts to explain what Magritte's visual non sequiturs mean.

GOTTSCHALL, EDWARD M. 1989. Cambridge, MA: MIT Press.
This large format (11 3 15) book offers a definitive examination of typography as it has evolved over the years. It has numerous illustrations that show, in considerable detail, the important role that typography has played in the design of various forms of visual communication.

GOWANS, ALAN. *The Unchanging Arts: New Forms for the Traditional Functions of Art in Society.* 1971. J. B. Lippincott.
Gowans deals with the functions of art in society and covers everything from the arts of antiquity to advertising and comic strips. His scope is incredible and his insights are astounding.

GOWANS, ALAN. *Learning to See: Historical Perspective on Modern Popular/Commercial Arts.* 1981. Bowling Green University Popular Press.
This book carries forward and updates the arguments of The Unchanging Arts. Gowans deals with everything from Chinese junks to soap operas and football. Provocative and fascinating.

GROTJAHN, MARTIN. *The Voice of the Symbol.* 1971. Delta Books.
This book provides a Freudian psychoanalytic interpretation of many of our most important symbols and addresses such topics as television, dreams, and the work of Hieronymus Bosch.

HALL, STUART. (ED.) *Representation: Cultural Representations and Signifying Practices.* 1997. London: Sage.
As its title suggest, this edited volume deals with various aspects of representation. The first chapter about cultural representation is by Hall, who contributed another chapter on the representation of "the other" in the media. Other chapters are on soap operas and gender, ways of exhibiting masculinity, and "Frenchness" in postwar photography.

JUNG, CARL G. (ED.). *Man and His Symbols.* 1964. Dell Books.
This book contains articles by Jung and his followers on the relationship between the symbol and the psyche, with much material on art and other forms of visual

communication. Jung elaborated a different psychology from Freud, and it is instructive to see how Jungians analyze things. Profusely illustrated.

KRIS, ERNST. *Psychoanalytic Explorations in Art.* 1964. Schocken Books.
This collection of essays by Kris (sometimes collaborating with other authors) applies psychoanalytic theory to expressive behavior. It has chapters on art and psychoanalysis, the art of the insane, caricature, and the creative process.

KURTZ, BRUCE. *Spots: The Popular Art of American Television Commercials.* 1977. Arts Communications.
This book was written to provide readers with a conceptual framework to understand television commercials. The book shows how commercials work, how they relate to (and borrow from) other works and media. It also includes interviews with some important makers of commercials and analyses of their work.

MESSARIS, PAUL. *Visual Persuasion: The Role of Images in Advertising.* 1997. Sage Publications.
Messaris offers a comprehensive analysis of the part that visual images play in advertising, but his analysis has implications for all visual communication in general. He has chapters dealing with the "Image as Simulated Reality," "Image as Evidence," and "Image as Implied Selling Proposition," and an epilogue on ethics and visual persuasion.

MIRZOEFF, NICHOLAS. *An Introduction to Visual Culture.* 1999. Routledge.
A scholarly treatment of visual phenomena covering areas such as the relation between the visual and culture, the relationship that exists between painting and photography and virtual reality and culture. The last section of the book deals with British Princess Diana's death and its role in the development of a global visual culture.

RACINE, NED. *Visual Communication: Understanding Maps, Charts, Diagrams and Schematics.* 2002. Learning Express. *Racine's book is designed to teach readers how to create effective forms of visual communication. The appendix contains lists of online and print resources.*

SONTAG, SUSAN. *On Photography.* 1973. Delta Books.
This series of philosophical essays focuses on the nature of photography, its relation to other art forms, and its social and political significance. It also discusses the work of many important photographers. The book originally was written as a series of essays in The New York Review of Books. *Provocative and illuminating.*

UDE-PESTEL, ANNELIESE. *Betty: History and Art of a Child in Therapy.* 1977. Science and Behavior Books.
This fascinating book deals with a extremely disturbed child and her paintings and drawings. The book contains twenty-six paintings by Betty that show how she changes as the result of her therapy, from a deeply disturbed child to a "normal" one.

WORTH, SOL. *Studying Visual Communication.* Edited, with an introduction, by Larry Gross. 1981. University of Pennsylvania Press.
This is a collection of scholarly essays by a filmmaker and theorist of visual communication. The essays deal with topics such as the semiotics of film, the nature and functions of symbolism, and the uses of film in education.

ZETTL, HERBERT. *Sight, Sound, Motion: Applied Media Aesthetics.* 1973. Wadsworth Publishing.
This pioneering work, encyclopedic in nature, discusses the principles of aesthetics, with particular reference to film and television. Zettl shows how important a role aesthetic matters—light, color, sound, camera work, and so on—play in the media. Lavishly illustrated.

REFERENCES

ADATTO, KIKU. 1993. *Picture Perfect: The Art and Artifice of Public Image Making.* New York: Basic Books.

ALBERS, JOSEPH. 1971. *Interaction of Color.* New Haven, Conn.: Yale University Press.

ARNHEIM, RUDOLF. 1953. *Film as Art.* Berkeley: University of California Press.

ARNHEIM, RUDOLF. 1966. *Toward a Psychology of Art.* Berkeley: University of California Press.

ARNHEIM, RUDOLF. 1969. *Visual Thinking.* London: Faber & Faber.

ASHTON, DORE. 1989. "The Elemental Fascination of Portrait Photography." *The Chronicle of Higher Education* (April 12).

AUFDERHEIDE, PAT. 1987. "The Look of the Sound." In *Watching Television,* ed. Todd Gitlin. New York: Pantheon Books.

BARNES, BROOKS. 2009. "Watching You Watching Ads." July 26, 2009. *The New York Times.*

BARNHURST, KEVIN G. 1994. *Seeing the Newspaper.* New York: St. Martin's Press.

BARTHES, ROLAND. 1957. *Mythologies.* New York: Hill & Wang.

BASSETT, RICHARD. 1969. *The Open Eye in Learning.* Cambridge, Mass.: MIT Press.

BAUDRILLARD, JEAN. 1968/1996. *The System of Objects.* London: Verso.

BECKER, HOWARD S. 1982. *Art Worlds.* Berkeley: University of California Press.

BEHRENS, ROY R. 1984. *Design in the Visual Arts.* Englewood Cliffs, N.J.: Prentice-Hall.

BERGER, ARTHUR ASA. 1976. *The Comic-Stripped American.* New York: Walker.

BERGER, ARTHUR ASA. 1982. *Media Analysis Techniques.* Beverly Hills, Calif.: Sage.

BERGER, ARTHUR ASA. 1984. *Signs in Contemporary Culture.* New York: Longman.

BERGER, JOHN. 1972. *Ways of Seeing.* New York: Penguin.

BERGER, JOHN. 1988. *About Looking.* New York: Pantheon.

BOGGS, JOSEPH M. 1978. *The Art of Watching Films.* Menlo Park, Calif.: Benjamin/Cummings.

BRENNER, CHARLES. 1974. *An Elementary Textbook of Psychoanalysis.* Garden City, NY: Doubleday.

BRONOWSKI, J. 1978. *The Visionary Eye*. Cambridge, Mass.: MIT Press.

BULLEN, J. B. 1981. *Vision & Design*. London: Oxford University Press.

CARROLL, LEWIS. 1960. *Alice's Adventures in Wonderland and Through the Looking Glass*. New York: Signet Classics.

CLARK, KENNETH. 1960. *Looking at Pictures*. Boston: Beacon Press.

COLLIER, JOHN. 1967. *Visual Anthropology*. New York: Holt, Rinehart & Winston.

CURTISS, DEBORAH. 1987. *Introduction to Visual Literary: A Guide to the Visual Arts and Communication*. Englewood Cliffs, N.J.: Prentice-Hall.

DANESI, MARCEL. 1995. *Interpreting Advertisements: A Semiotic Guide*. Toronto: Legas.

DEKEN, JOSEPH. 1983. *Computer Images: State of the Art*. New York: Stewart, Tabori & Chang.

DENZIN, NORMAN. 1991. *Images of Postmodern Society: Social Thought and Contemporary Cinema*. London: Sage.

DIMITRIUS, JO-ELLAN, and MARK MAZZARELLA. 1999. *Reading People*. New York: Ballantyne Books.

DONDIS, DONIS. 1973. *A Primer of Visual Literacy*. Cambridge, Mass.: M.I.T. Press.

EDWARDS, BETTY. 1979. *Drawing on the Right Side of the Brain*. Los Angeles: J. P. Tarcher.

EDWARDS, BETTY. 1986. *Drawing on the Artist Within*. New York: Simon & Schuster.

EISENSTEIN, SERGEI. 1942. *The Film Sense*. New York: Harvest/HBJ.

EISENSTEIN, SERGEI. 1949. *Film Form*. New York: Harvest/HBJ.

EISNER, ELLIOT W. 1972. *Educating Artistic Vision*. New York: Macmillan.

ESSLIN, MARTIN. 1982. *The Age of Television*. San Francisco: W. H. Freeman.

FELDMAN, EDMUND BURKE. 1973. *Varieties of Visual Experience*. New York: Abrams.

FRANSECKY, R. B., AND DEBES, JOHN L. 1972. *Visual Literacy*. Washington, D.C.: Association for Educational Communication.

FREUD, SIGMUND. 1960/1965. *The Interpretation of Dreams*. New York: Avon.

GANDELMAN, CLAUDE. 1991. *Reading Pictures, Viewing Texts*. Bloomington: Indiana University Press.

GATTEGNO, CALEB. 1969. *Towards a Visual Culture*. New York: Avon.

GEERTZ, CLIFFORD. 1973. *The Interpretation of Cultures*. New York: Basic Books.

GILLAM, BARBARA. *"Geometrical Illusions."* Jan. 1980. Reprinted in WOLFE, J. ED. 1986. *The Mind's Eye: Readings from Scientific American*. New York: W. H. Freeman.

GIRARD, RENÉ. 1991. *A Theatre of Envy: William Shakespeare*. Oxford: Oxford University Press.

GOMBRICH, E. H. 1960. *Art and Illusion*. New York: Pantheon.

GOTSCHALK, D. W. 1947. *Art and the Social Order*. New York: Dover.

GOTSCHALL, EDWARD M. 1989. *Typographic Communication Today*. Cambridge, MA: MIT Press.

GOWANS, ALAN. 1971. *The Unchanging Arts: New Forms for the Traditional Functions of Art in Society*. Philadelphia: Lippincott.

GOWANS, ALAN. 1981. *Learning to See*. Bowling Green, Ohio: Bowling Green University Popular Press.

HALL, EDWARD T. 1969. *The Hidden Dimension*. New York: Anchor Books.

HALL, STUART. ED. 1997. *Representation: Cultural Representations and Signifying Practices*. London: Sage.

HANKS, KURT, ET AL. 1978. *Design Yourself*. Los Altos, Calif.: Kaufmann.

HANSON, JARICE. 1987. *Understanding Video*. Newbury Park, Calif.: Sage.

HOGG, JAMES, ED. 1970. *Psychology and the Visual Arts*. Baltimore: Penguin.

HUME, DAVID. 1949. *An Enquiry Concerning Human Understanding.* LaSalle, Ill.: The Open Court Publishing Company.

HUXLEY, ALDOUS. 1942. *The Art of Seeing.* New York: Harper.

JUNG, CARL, ED. 1964. *Man and His Symbols.* New York: Doubleday.

JUNG, KARL. 1968. *Man and His Symbols.* New York: Dell.

JUSSIM, ESTELLE. 1974. *Visual Communication and the Graphic Arts.* New York: Bowker.

KANIZSA, GAETANO. April 1976. "Subjective Contours." *Scientific American.* Reprinted in *Readings from the Scientific American: The Mind's Eye* (1986). Introductions by Jeremy M. Wolfe. New York: W. H. Freeman.

KANT, IMMANUEL. 1959 (1785). *Fundamental Principles of the Metaphysics of Morals.* Trans. Lewis W. Beck. New York: Liberal Arts Press.

KELLOWAY, LUCY. 2002. "Lessons in Smiling That Have Left Me Open-Mouthed." July 20, 2002. *The Financial Times.*

KEPES, GYORGY. 1944. *Language of Vision.* Chicago: Paul Theobald.

KEPES, GYORGY. 1965. *Education of Vision.* New York: Braziller.

KRIS, ERNST. 1964. *Psychoanalytic Explorations in Art.* New York: Schocken.

LAKOFF, G., AND JOHNSON, M. 1980. *Metaphors We Live By.* Chicago: University of Chicago Press.

LESTER, PAUL MARTIN. 2003. *Visual Communication: Images with Messages.* Belmont, Ca.: Thompson Wadsworth.

LIEBERMAN, J. BEN. 1968. *Types of Typefaces.* New York: Sterling.

LINDSTROM, MIRIAM. 1962. *Children's Art.* Berkeley: University of California Press.

LOTMAN, JURI. 1977. *The Structure of the Artistic Text.* Ann Arbor: Michigan Slavic Contributions.

LUNENFELD, PETER. (ED.). 1999. *The Digital Dialectic: New Essays on New Media.* Cambridge, Mass.: MIT Press.

LUNENFELD, PETER. 2000. *Snap to Grid: A User's Guide to Digital Arts, Media and Cultures.* Cambridge, Mass.: MIT Press.

LYOTARD, JEAN-FRANCOIS. 1984. *The Postmodern Condition: A Report on Knowledge.* Minneapolis: University of Minnesota Press.

MCKEON, RICHARD. 1941. *The Basic Works of Aristotle.* New York: Random House.

MCKIM, ROBERT H. 1980. *Thinking Visually.* Belmont, Calif.: Wadsworth.

MCLUHAN, MARSHALL. 1965. *Understanding Media: The Extensions of Man.* New York: McGraw-Hill.

MEHRABIAN, ALBERT. 1971. *Silent Messages.* Belmont, Calif.: Wadsworth.

MESSARIS, PAUL. 1994. *Visual Literacy: Image, Mind & Reality.* Boulder, Colo.: Westview Press.

MIZROEFF, NICHOLAS. 1995. *An Introduction to Visual Culture.* London: Routledge.

MOHOLY-NAGY, LASZLO. 1947. *Vision in Motion.* Chicago: Paul Theobald.

MONACO, JAMES. 1977. *How to Read a Film.* New York: Oxford University Press.

MORGAN, JOHN, AND PETER WELTON. 1986. *See What I Mean: An Introduction to Visual Communication.* London: Arnold.

MORIARTY, SANDRA R. 1996. "Abduction: A Theory of Visual Interpretation." *Communication* (May).

MURRAY, JANET H. 1997. *Hamlet on the Holodeck: The Future of Narrative in Cyberspace.* Cambridge, MA: MIT Press.

NELSON, GEORGE. 1977. *How to See: A Guide to Reading Our Manmade Environment.* Boston: Little, Brown.

NOLL, A. MICHAEL. 1967. "Computers and the Visual Arts." *Design and Planning #2.* New York: Hastings House.

NOLL, A. MICHAEL. 1982. Catalogue of SIGGRAPH art show.

NOVITZ, DAVID. 1977. *Pictures and Their Use in Communication*. The Hague: Martinus Nijhoff.

ORNSTEIN, ROBERT E. 1972. *The Psychology of Consciousness*. San Francisco: W. H. Freeman.

PAIVIO, ALLAN. 1979. *Imagery and Verbal Processes*. Hillsdale, N.J.: Lawrence Erlbaum.

PEIRCE, C. S. 1931–1958. *Collected Papers*. Cambridge, Mass.: Harvard University Press.

PREBLE, DUANE AND SARAH. 1985. *Artforms*. New York: Harper & Row.

PRYLUCK, CALVIN. 1976. *Sources of Meaning in Motion Pictures & Television*. New York: Arno Press.

RACINE, NED. 2002. *Visual Communication: Understanding Maps, Charts, Diagrams and Schematics*. New York: Learning Express.

RAPAILLE, CLOTAIRE. 2006. *The Culture Code*. New York: Broadway Books.

REITBERGER, RHEINHOLD, AND FUCHS, WOLFGANG. 1972. *Comics: Anatomy of a Mass Medium*. Boston: Little, Brown.

SABIN, ROGER. 1993. *Adult Comics: An Introduction*. New York: Routledge.

SAUSSURE, FERDINAND DE. 1966. *Course in General Linguistics*. New York: McGraw-Hill.

SCHIRATO, TONY, AND JEN WEBB. 2004. *Understanding the Visual*. Thousand Oaks, Ca.: Sage Publications.

SCHWARTZ, TONY. 1974. *The Responsive Chord*. New York: Doubleday.

SEBEOK, THOMAS A. 1979. *The Sign and Its Masters*. Austin: University of Texas Press.

SOLOMON, JACK. 1990. *The Signs of Our Time: The Secret Meanings of Everyday Life*. New York: Harper & Row.

SONTAG, SUSAN. 1966. *Against Interpretation*. New York: Farrar, Straus & Giroux.

SONTAG, SUSAN. 1973. *On Photography*. New York: Farrar, Straus & Giroux.

STERN, RAPHAEL AND ESTER. 1983. *Changing Concepts of Art*. New York: Haven.

STURKEN, MARITA, AND LISA CARTRIGHT. 2001. *Practices of Looking: An Introduction to Visual Culture*. Oxford: Oxford University Press.

TAYLOR, JOSHUA C. 1975. *To See Is to Think: Looking at American Art*. Washington, D.C.: Smithsonian Institution.

UDE-PESTEL, ANNELIESE. 1977. *Betty: History and Art of a Child in Therapy*. Palo Alto, Ca.: Science and Behavior Books.

WEAVER, MARCIA. 1999. *Visual Literacy: How to Read and Use Information in the Graphic Form*. New York: LearningExpress.

WILDE, JUDITH, AND RICHARD WILDE. 2000. *Visual Literacy: A Conceptual Approach to Graphic Problem Solving*. New York: Watson-Guptill.

WILEMAN, R. E. 1980. *Exercises in Visual Thinking*. New York: Hastings House.

WINICK, CHARLES. 1995. *Desexualization in American Life*. New Brunswick, NJ: Transaction.

WOLFE, JEREMY M. 1986. "Preface" and "Introductions" in *Readings from the Scientific American's The Mind's Eye*. 1986. Introductions by Jeremy Wolfe. New York: W. H. Freeman.

WORTH, SOL. 1981. *Studying Visual Communication*. Philadelphia: University of Pennsylvania Press.

YOUNGBLOOD, GENE. 1970. *Expanded Cinema*. New York: Dutton.

ZELANSKY, GENE. 2001. *Say It with Charts: The Executive's Guide to Visual Communication*. New York: McGraw-Hill.

ZETTL, HERBERT. 1973. *Sight, Sound, Motion*. Belmont, Calif.: Wadsworth.

ILLUSTRATION CREDITS

All illustrations not otherwise credited have been provided by the author.

Introduction

0.4 Photograph by Arthur Asa Berger
0.5 Courtesy of Annaliese Ude-Pestel, author of *Betty: History and Art of a Child in Therapy.*
0.6 Courtesy of Annaliese Ude-Pestel, author of *Betty: History and Art of a Child in Therapy.*
0.7 Courtesy of Annaliese Ude-Pestel, author of *Betty: History and Art of a Child in Therapy.*
0.8 Courtesy of Apple Computer, Inc. and Chiat/Day Advertising. 1984 commercial.
0.9 Photograph by Arthur Asa Berger
0.10 Collection of Arthur Asa Berger. *Barong and his Monkey Helper*, by I. Wayan Santica.
0.11 Photograph by Arthur Asa Berger of Barong in a dance in Bali.
0.12 Photograph by Arthur Asa Berger of a painting, *Elephant.*
0.13 Courtesy of Michael Noll. Untitled.
0.14 © Pixar. All Rights Reserved.
0.15a Jason Berger
0.15b Jason Berger
0.16 Photograph by Arthur Asa Berger.
0.17 Pastiche by Arthur Asa Berger
0.18 George Legrady © 1995

0.19 Photograph by Joanna Ebenstein.
0.20 Adam by Marilyn Powers.

Chapter 1 Seeing is Believing

1.1 Ally & Gargano Advertising. Art Director, Ron Arnold. Copyright Tom Messner.
1.2 By Arthur Asa Berger
1.3 By Arthur Asa Berger
1.4 Photograph by Gerald Hill.
1.5 By Arthur Asa Berger
1.6 Foote, Cone, & Belding Advertising. Reproduced courtesy of Levi Strauss & Co.
1.7 Illustration by Lorelle Raboni in *Eye Movements and Visual Perception* by David Norton and Lawrence Stark. Reproduced courtesy of Lorelle Raboni.
1.8 Aristotle drawing by Arthur Asa Berger
1.10 Drawing of Jean Baudrillard by Arthur Asa Berger
1.11 Photograph by Arthur Asa Berger

Chapter 2 How We See

2.1 By Arthur Asa Berger
2.2 By Arthur Asa Berger
2.3 By Arthur Asa Berger
2.4 By Arthur Asa Berger
2.6 By Arthur Asa Berger
2.7 McGraw-Hill Companies

2.8 Courtesy of Landor Associates and General Motors Corporation

2.9 By Arthur Asa Berger

2.10 By Arthur Asa Berger

2.11 Courtesy of Irfan Essa. Faces showing emotions.

2.12 Reprinted with permission of Smith/Greenland, Inc.

2.13 By Arthur Asa Berger

2.14 By Arthur Asa Berger

2.15 Courtesy of the Museum of Modern Art, New York, Film Stills Archive

2.16 Courtesy of National Gallery Publications Limited.

2.17 Courtesy of Jason Berger.

Chapter 3 Elements of Visual Communication

3.1 By Arthur Asa Berger

3.2 By Arthur Asa Berger

3.3 By Arthur Asa Berger

3.4 By Arthur Asa Berger

3.5 By Arthur Asa Berger

3.6 By Arthur Asa Berger

3.7 By Arthur Asa Berger

3.8 By Arthur Asa Berger

3.9 Courtesy of Safeway Stores, Inc.

3.10 Courtesy of Gumps, Inc.

3.11 Used by permission of Hal Riney & Partners, San Francisco, California

3.14 By Arthur Asa Berger

3.15 Reprinted with permission of Smith/Greenland, Inc.

3.16 Samuel H. Kress Collection, Philbrook Museum of art, Tulsa, Oklahoma

3.17 Photo by Arthur Asa Berger.

Chapter 4 Typography and Graphic Design

4.2 Photograph by David Powers. Used with permission of San Francisco Opera.

4.3 Reprinted with permission of U&lc, International Journal of Typographics.

4.4 Reprinted with permission of U&lc, International Journal of Typographics.

4.5 American Committee for the Weitzmann Institute of Science. Used with permission.

4.6 Used by permission of Hal Riney & Partners, San Francisco, California

4.8 Reprinted with permission of U&lc, International Journal of Typographics.

4.9 By Arthur Asa Berger

4.12 Used with permission of New Management.

Chapter 5 Photography

5.1a Courtesy of Dennis McNicoll

5.1b Courtesy of Dennis McNicoll

5.1c Courtesy of Dennis McNicoll

5.2 Used by permission of Herman Krieger

5.3 By Arthur Asa Berger

5.4 By Arthur Asa Berger

5.5 Used by permission of the White House

5.6 Used by permission of the White House

5.7a By Arthur Asa Berger

5.7b By Arthur Asa Berger

5.8 Courtesy of the Museum of Modern Art, New York, Film Stills Archive

5.9 Courtesy of the Museum of Modern Art, New York, Film Stills Archive

5.10 Courtesy of the Museum of Modern Art, New York, Film Stills Archive

5.11 Courtesy of the Museum of Modern Art, New York, Film Stills Archive

5.12 Used by permission of the San Francisco Ballet

5.13 Courtesy of the Museum of Modern Art, New York, Film Stills Archive

5.14 Used by permission of the White House

5.15 Used by permission of the White House

5.16 Used by permission of the White House

5.17 Courtesy of Marilyn Powers.

Chapter 6 Film

6.1 Courtesy of the Museum of Modern Art, New York, Film Stills Archive

6.2 Courtesy of the Museum of Modern Art, New York, Film Stills Archive

6.3 By Arthur Asa Berger

6.4 Courtesy of the Museum of Modern Art, New York, Film Stills Archive

6.5 Courtesy of the Museum of Modern Art, New York, Film Stills Archive

6.6 Courtesy of the Museum of Modern Art, New York, Film Stills Archive

6.7 Used with permission of Gilbert Shelton.

6.8 Courtesy of the Museum of Modern Art, New York, Film Stills Archive

6.9 Courtesy of the Museum of Modern Art, New York, Film Stills Archive

6.10 Courtesy of the Museum of Modern Art, New York, Film Stills Archive

6.11 Courtesy of the Museum of Modern Art, New York, Film Stills Archive

Chapter 7 Television

7.4 By Arthur Asa Berger

7.5 By Arthur Asa Berger

7.6 Reproduced with permission of Levi Strauss & Company and Foote, Cone & Belding.

7.7 Reproduced by permission of Apple Computer, Inc.

7.8 Used with permission of George Legrady.

7.9 Reproduced by permission of Lynn Hershman

7.10 Reproduced by permission of Lynn Hershman

7.11 By Arthur Asa Berger

Chapter 8 Comics, Cartoons, and Animation

8.2 Streetcar Romance. Script by Donelle Merton; art by Sarah Kortum.

8.3b Used with permission of Gilbert Shelton.

8.4 Used with permission from David Yurkovich.

8.5 Courtesy of AltaMira Press, a division of Rowman & Littlefield Publishers.

8.6 Courtesy of the Museum of Modern Art, New York, Film Stills Archive

8.9 Reproduced with permission of Levi Strauss & Company and Foote, Cone & Belding.

8.11 By Arthur Asa Berger

8.12 Used with permission of George Legrady.

8.13 © The Main Line Company, Rockport, ME. Used with permission.

8.14 By Arthur Asa Berger

8.15 Shelley Moore. Comic book assignment.

Chapter 9 Computers and Graphics

9.1 Courtesy of Apple Computer, Inc. and Chiat/Day Advertising.

9.2 Courtesy of Apple Computer, Inc. and Chiat/Day Advertising.

9.3 Courtesy of Museum of Modern Art, New York, Film Stills Archive.

9.5 Courtesy of Microsoft Corporation.

9.6 Courtesy of Microsoft Corporation.

9.7 Luxo Images

9.8 Courtesy of Island Graphics Corporation. Reproduced with permission.

9.9 Photography by Marty Sohl. Courtesy of San Francisco Ballet.

9.10a Used with permission from A. Michael Noll.

9.10b Used with permission from the Kröller-Müller Foundation.

NAMES INDEX

Abelson, Robert, 39
Abrams, M. H., 35–36
Adatto, Kiku, 149–150, 191
Albers, Joseph, 99
Albertson, Alaina, 138
Allen, Woody, 169
Antonioni, 135
Aristotle, 36
Arnheim, Rudolf, 20
Arnold, Ron, 22
Ashton, Dore, 136
Aulderheide, Pat, 192

Bakhtin, M. M., 9
Barnes, Brooks, 31
Barthes, Roland, 88–89, 142
Baudrillard, Jean, 44
Benayoun, Robert, 205
Berger, Jason, 76
Berger, John, 50, 145–146
Bergman, Ingmar, 171
Boggs, Joseph M., 153
Boudreau, Diane, 24
Brenner, Charles, 29, 148–149
Breton, André, 192

Cartright, Lisa, 147
Casey, William, 57
Christie, Linford, 71

Clark, Kenneth, 1
Cleopatra, 138
Clinton, Bill, 131

Daguerre, Louis Jacques, 125
Dali, Salvador, 192
Danesi, Marcel, 9
Denzin, Norman K., 167
Dichter, Ernest, 43
Dimitrius, Jo-Ellan, 140
Disney, Walt, 31, 213, 233
Dondis, Donis, A., 19, 81
Dusen, Chris Van, 216

Eastman, George, 125
Eco, Umberto, 56–57
Eisenstein, Sergei, 9, 15, 159
Ekman, Paul, 57, 58
Essa, Irfan, 58
Esslin, Martin, 168, 180
Eyck, Jan van, 69
Ezekiel, 66

Figuegnon, Marie-Louise, 39
Freud, Sigmund, 3–4, 5, 29–30, 64, 66, 170, 172, 215

Gandelman, Claude, 73–74, 75
Gans, Herbert, 27–28

Geertz, Clifford, 55
Gillam, Barbara, 80
Gingrich, Newt, 64
Girard, René, 36, 42, 148
Gombrich, E. H., 20
Gottschall, Edward, M., 103–104
Gould, Chester, 205
Gowans, Alan, 8, 17
Gregg, L. C., 209
Gutenberg, Johannes, 105, 106

Hall, Edward T., 2, 19–20, 79
Hall, Stuart, 71–72
Hanson, Jarice, 30, 33
Hershman, Lynn, 193, 194
Hume, David, 96, 97

Jakobson, Roman, 38–39
Johnson, Ben, 71
Johnson, Mark, 62, 64
Jung, Carl G., 3, 4–6, 70

Kanitza, Gaetano, 79–80
Keaton, Buster, 137
Kekule, 3
Klapp, Orrin, 24
Kortum, Sarah, 202
Krieger, Herman, 129
Kurosawa, Akira, 30

SUBJECT INDEX